Advance Praise for *Who Governs?*

"Who governs the United States in an emergency, and with what limits and what authority? This fascinating study shows the answer is not simple but varies with time, location, type of emergency, and the party in power. With novel data and fresh wisdom, this is a pathbreaking guide to what likely will be a recurrent problem in American politics."

— JACK GOLDSTONE, Hazel Professor of Public Policy, George Mason University

"Fiorina and his co-authors fittingly ask who should shout 'Emergency!' in a crowded city—unelected public health officials, mayors, governors, legislators, or courts? By describing the crazy quilt of state and local emergency powers, their problematic definitions, and the questions of accountability and representation surrounding their use, *Who Governs?* convincingly makes the case for rethinking how and when we employ emergency powers."

— HENRY E. BRADY, Professor of Political Science and Public Policy, University of California–Berkeley

"Officials at the federal, state, and local levels have recently invoked extraordinary emergency powers that most of us did not know they even had, at the cost of democratic accountability, individual liberties, separation of powers, and administrative regularity. That is okay—it is necessary—for once-in-a-lifetime events. But this book's examination of COVID emergency powers raises the question: Will government by emergency decree become the new normal?"

— MICHAEL W. MCCONNELL, Richard and Frances Mallery Professor, Stanford Law School, and director, Stanford Constitutional Law Center

Who Governs?
Emergency Powers in the Time of COVID

Who Governs?

Emergency Powers in the Time of COVID

Edited by Morris P. Fiorina

Contributing Authors
Cameron DeHart
Emily M. Farris
John Ferejohn
Mirya R. Holman
Didi Kuo
David L. Leal
Victoria Ochoa
Miranda E. Sullivan
Yiqian Alice Wang

HOOVER INSTITUTION PRESS
Stanford University | Stanford, California

 With its eminent scholars and world-renowned library and archives, the Hoover Institution seeks to improve the human condition by advancing ideas that promote economic opportunity and prosperity, while securing and safeguarding peace for America and all mankind. The views expressed in its publications are entirely those of the authors and do not necessarily reflect the views of the staff, officers, or Board of Overseers of the Hoover Institution.

hoover.org

Hoover Institution Press Publication No. 726
Hoover Institution at Leland Stanford Junior University,
Stanford, California 94305-6003

Copyright © 2023 by the Board of Trustees of the Leland Stanford Junior University

All rights reserved. No part of this publication may be reproduced, stored in a retrieval system, or transmitted in any form or by any means, electronic, mechanical, photocopying, recording, or otherwise, without written permission of the publisher and copyright holders.

For permission to reuse material from *Who Governs? Emergency Powers in the Time of COVID*, ISBN 978-0-8179-2525-3, please access copyright.com or contact the Copyright Clearance Center Inc. (CCC), 222 Rosewood Drive, Danvers, MA 01923, 978-750-8400. CCC is a not-for-profit organization that provides licenses and registration for a variety of uses.

Efforts have been made to locate the original sources, determine the current rights holders, and, if needed, obtain reproduction permissions. On verification of any such claims to rights in the materials reproduced in this book, any required corrections or clarifications will be made in subsequent printings/editions.

First printing 2023
29 28 27 26 25 24 23   7 6 5 4 3 2 1

Manufactured in the United States of America
Printed on acid-free, archival-quality paper

Cataloging-in-Publication Data is available from the Library of Congress.

ISBN 978-0-8179-2525-3 (pbk)
ISBN 978-0-8179-2526-0 (epub)
ISBN 978-0-8179-2528-4 (PDF)

Contents

	Preface **Morris P. Fiorina**	vii

PART I: STATE EMERGENCY POWERS

1	Emergency Powers: An Introduction **John Ferejohn**	3
2	Emergency Powers in the American States **Cameron DeHart and Morris P. Fiorina**	33

PART II: EMERGENCY POWERS IN PRACTICE

3	California and Public Health Authority **Didi Kuo**	71
4	Texas and COVID-19 Emergency Orders **Miranda E. Sullivan and David L. Leal**	97
5	Using the *Emergency* in Emergency Orders: Municipal Policy Action and Federalism during the COVID-19 Crisis **Emily M. Farris, Mirya R. Holman, and Miranda E. Sullivan**	151

PART III: RESPONSE TO THE EXERCISE OF EMERGENCY POWERS

6	Public Opinion on the COVID-19 Pandemic: From Consensus to Conflict **Yiqian Alice Wang**	175

7	Court Evaluation of COVID-19 State Emergency Orders: Upholding Fundamental Rights during Times of Crisis **Victoria Ochoa**	207
8	Legislative Opposition to the Exercise of State Emergency Powers **Cameron DeHart and Morris P. Fiorina**	241
9	COVID Restrictions and Democratic Governance **Morris P. Fiorina**	257
	About the Contributors	279
	Index	282

Preface

On March 16, 2020, six San Francisco Bay Area counties and the City of Berkeley issued shelter-at-home orders, shutting down much of the regional economy and imposing restrictions on personal behavior, arguably including liberties guaranteed by the US Constitution. As a political scientist committed to democratic governance, my reaction was one of surprise and a bit of shock. California residents are regularly subjected to short-term emergency orders, generally associated with natural disasters like wildfires and floods, along with the occasional medfly infestation, but few living memories contained anything on the scale of the March orders.[1] The question was not whether the possibility of a lethal pandemic called for drastic action; certainly, it did. Rather, for some of us, the question was, Who, under the circumstances, could legitimately assume what are essentially dictatorial powers? For these sweeping orders were not issued by an elected executive such as the governor (Governor Gavin Newsom did not weigh in with a statewide order until three days later), or elected bodies like the state legislature, or even county boards of supervisors. Rather, exercising powers authorized by state constitutional provisions and statutes, *appointed* local officials suspended economic activity and dictated limitations on personal behavior. This was something outside my experience and, as I soon learned, outside the experience of most other political scientists. Thus, this volume begins with a chapter by New York University law professor John Ferejohn, which reviews the historical and philosophical basis of emergency powers in the context of today's world.

Gathering the data is usually an early step in a social science research program. I inquired of various colleagues in the legal and public policy communities where I could find a compendium of state and local emergency powers. The disappointing answer came back that no one knew of such a source, only a few partial listings. That might have been the end of the project but for a fortunate coincidence in an otherwise difficult spring. Bruce Cain, director of Stanford's Bill Lane Center for the American West noted that his center already had hired student interns for the summer, but pandemic restrictions prevented their placement in various government agencies. Here was a supply of labor that could help construct a database. Cain also offered the expert organizational assistance of Lane Center administrator Iris Hui. Cameron DeHart, then a Stanford political science PhD student, organized the data gathering and compilation and acted as overall study director. The student interns read and coded the provisions of fifty state constitutions, and of Washington, DC, and five territories, producing a database that includes nearly sixty variables. Chapter 2 summarizes this data. Those who would like to take a deep dive into the database can find the details in appendix 1.[2]

As political scientists and public administration scholars have long known, formal powers written down on parchment only begin the process of public policy making. Implementation is a critical stage between formal powers and policy outcomes. That implementation process is particularly complicated in a decentralized federal system such as that which characterizes the government of the United States. In chapter 3 Didi Kuo of Stanford's Center on Democracy, Development and the Rule of Law, reports in detail how California officials went about implementing orders issued by state and various local governments. By way of comparison, in chapter 4 Miranda Sullivan and David Leal report on the experience of Republican-governed Texas, which reacted to the pandemic with far fewer restrictions than California. Moving from the particular to the general, in chapter 5 Emily Farris, Mirya Holman, and Miranda Sullivan examine local governments' adoption of shelter-in-place orders and eviction moratoriums across the country not only as a function of objective pandemic conditions, partisanship, and ideology but also as a function of the constraints of the federal system.

Given the initial motivation of this project, it is only natural that we take a close look at the subject of the consent of the governed. A great deal of public opinion polling in 2020 revealed two trends. First, the utilization of emergency powers quickly became politicized, with Republicans showing much less support for various measures such as mask wearing, shutdowns, and travel restrictions (as well as whether the pandemic even constituted an emergency). Yiqian Alice Wang provides a description of these trends in public opinion in chapter 6. Second, when Americans feel that government is infringing on their rights, they appeal to the courts. Lawsuits regarding infringement on religious practices were filed very quickly after the issuance of executive orders restricting large gatherings, and others followed. Thus, I approached Liza Goitein, director of the Liberty & National Security Program at New York University's Brennan Center for Justice, for assistance outside the expertise of those already involved in the project. Happily, she agreed to partner with us and appointed an advanced law student to compile and analyze court cases arising from emergency power restrictions. Victoria Ochoa analyzes 156 COVID-related cases in 2020–21 in chapter 7. The database she compiled can be accessed in appendix 2.[3]

In response to public opinion, court decisions, and their own ideologies, legislatures in many states moved to amend or restrict the emergency powers on the books in their states. While partisan conflict was most apparent, legislative–executive conflicts also were evident, and by late 2021 federal and state conflicts also arose. One of the important questions that emerged in implementation is who would enforce orders issued by the various public health agencies and other government units. The task falls in some cases to employees of the health agencies and other bodies that issued the orders; in some cases to other local or state agencies such as alcohol control and other licensing boards; in some cases to police departments; and in still other cases to elected sheriffs—in about two thousand of the country's more than three thousand counties, the sheriff is the chief law enforcement officer. Early in the course of the pandemic it became apparent that there were systematic differences in enforcement activities between appointed and elected officials. In addition, in the late stages of the pandemic, state governors and local units of government became embroiled in conflicts over local exercise of emergency powers, such as the attempt by governors in Florida and Texas to prevent the imposition of vaccine mandates by local government units and private businesses. We briefly discuss these intragovernmental conflicts in chapter 8, many of which are continuing as we write.

The final chapter returns to the concern that animated this project—the implications of the COVID-19 pandemic for democratic governance. In chapter 9 I conclude by discussing some of the issues raised in 2020–21 that deserve serious attention before the next national emergency. In short, this chapter considers the classic political science question, Who governs?[4]

Having provided an overview of the topics that the chapters in this volume address, let me emphasize what they do not. First, except in passing, we make no attempt to evaluate the efficacy of the health restrictions imposed by state executive orders. There is a large and growing literature on how efficacious the various restrictions were in alleviating the worst health outcomes caused by the pandemic. The myriad studies in this literature exploit variation within individual states, within the fifty American states, and across the world. The knowledge produced by this literature will be extremely valuable when new health crises arrive in the coming years, but that is not our focus in this volume. Second, and more generally, there is another large, growing, and contentious literature on the costs and benefits of the various health orders. Even assuming widely accepted estimates of the health benefits of emergency orders in combatting COVID, how did these compare with the estimated economic, educational, mental health, and other costs they imposed? Put simply, however efficacious the restrictions were in dealing with COVID, were they worth it when situated in the larger socioeconomic context? This volume does not attempt to answer such questions. The perspective of this volume is that those are political questions, not public health questions. Who should weigh the costs and benefits and make the trade-offs raises fundamental questions of democratic governance. In this volume we aim to advance the conversation along those lines.

Funding for this project came from Stanford's Bill Lane Center for the American West, Hoover Institution, and Center on Democracy, Development and the Rule of Law; and New York University's Brennan Center for Justice. While the research foci of these organizations vary, we are united by a commitment to democratic governance.

MORRIS P. FIORINA
STANFORD, CALIFORNIA
OCTOBER 2022

Notes

1. Although there are some examples of long-standing states of emergency, these are usually associated with under-the-radar issues that do not visibly affect the general public (e.g., water policy).
2. Appendices 1 and 2 to this book are online supplements and can be viewed at https://www.hoover.org/research/who-governs-emergency-powers-time-covid.
3. See https://www.hoover.org/research/who-governs-emergency-powers-time-covid.
4. Robert A. Dahl, *Who Governs?: Democracy and Power in an American City* (New Haven: Yale University Press, 1961).

Part I

STATE EMERGENCY POWERS

Chapter 1

Emergency Powers
An Introduction

John Ferejohn

Emergency powers may be justified in three ways, or, if you prefer, emergency powers rest on three sources of authority: necessity, constitutional provisions, and legislation. In most emergencies, governments choose to exercise legislative emergency powers, claiming authority under enacted statutes, rather than asserting either necessity or direct constitutional authority. This is because most "emergencies" do not appear to be so urgent and threatening as to warrant reaching past the legislature either to basic law in the constitution, or to existential necessity. Enacted laws are usually sufficient for the job or, if they are not, the legislature can be convinced to enact new laws if necessary. While legislative emergency powers may be adequate in most cases, they raise the danger that emergency laws become part of the regular legal system. In effect, the executive is given a reservoir of special powers that may be used at his or her discretion. This raises the specter of creeping executive unilateralism and plebiscitarian rule, in which the executive accrues more and more delegated authority as successive emergencies come and go.[1]

Major wars, economic depressions, and plagues can test any government, especially constitutional governments with separation of powers and the rule of law. When it first appeared in early 2020, COVID-19 posed such a test. It had the hallmarks of plague: geometric rates of spread, uncertainty as to where and whom it would strike, and lethal consequences. Moreover, there were no effective measures in public or private health for defending against it. Because medical treatments for the disease were inadequate to deal with the illness, many countries (including the United States) rapidly began turning to public health measures with the aim of "flattening the curve," allowing hospitals a chance to catch up to the disease. Countries closed borders and restricted domestic travel as well, essentially shutting down the hospitality, entertainment, and travel industries. Schools and universities suspended in-person learning, and businesses started to allow those who could to work remotely. States and localities experimented with more direct controls on individual behavior (e.g., requiring masks, social distancing, mandatory testing, quarantines). Taking measures of this sort risked interfering with various constitutionally protected rights. Coercive public health measures are inherently threatening in a liberal society accustomed to personal freedoms, especially when those orders remain in place for a long time and target such an invisible "enemy."

It appeared to many officials, at all levels of government, that under the circumstances they faced in early 2020, they had sufficient "emergency" powers to take these actions. But there was really no surefire way to gauge in advance which of their measures were actually legal. Executive officials could find authority in previous laws, but any particular order might or might not be legally permissible if challenged in court. Normally, government orders that trespass on protected rights are subject to strict scrutiny, a kind of proportionality test: the community must have a compelling interest in imposing the measure, and the measure must be narrowly targeted to avoid overburdening constitutional rights. In the early 2020 environment, it may have seemed clear that the first prong (compelling state interest) was probably satisfied for many coercive measures, but there really was no timely way to determine whether measures were overbroad (or underbroad for that matter). In any case, courts were reluctant to intervene, at least at first.

Emergency Powers in the Pandemic

The pandemic was rapidly and widely recognized in every country as an "emergency" both because of the severity and geometric contagion of the disease and because hospitals and other critical health resources were unable to deal with it. Still, it was not clear that the pandemic—however extreme its outcomes—represented an *existential* threat to the capacity of governments to govern, or that it required the delegation of special powers to executive officials and the short-circuiting of the judicial and legislative processes. Perhaps certain rights would need to be suspended for a time to permit governments to take actions limiting movement and freedom of association. And perhaps governments needed to take actions that threatened the capacity of hospitals to manage a deluge of urgent cases. But the overall structure of government did not seem to need immediate suspension or reformation. Or did it?

What may have seemed like ordinary governmental responses to emergencies—which I call the *legislative* model, which relies on authority delegated by the legislature—risks creating permanent new government authority that would last beyond the current emergency, and apply to new and unforeseen circumstances in the future. Such authority might permanently impair rights and even transform the regime itself. This worry about creeping regime transformation has been expressed from the beginning of the republic. Early on it was stated as a worry about permanent or standing armies. James Madison, writing as "Publius," worried that wartime can lead to *permanent* changes that undermine liberty and undermine republican government:

> Of all the enemies to public liberty war is, perhaps, the most to be dreaded, because it comprises and develops the germ of every other. War is the parent of armies; from these proceed debts and taxes; and armies, and debts, and taxes are the known instruments for bringing the many under the domination of the few. In war, too, the discretionary power

of the Executive is extended; its influence in dealing out offices, honors, and emoluments is multiplied; and all the means of seducing the minds, are added to those of subduing the force, of the people. The same malignant aspect in republicanism may be traced in the inequality of fortunes, and the opportunities of fraud, growing out of a state of war, and in the degeneracy of manners and of morals, engendered by both. No nation could preserve its freedom in the midst of continual warfare.[2]

The worry that emergency rule could corrupt the regime—transforming a liberal or constitutional democracy into an authoritarian system—may be a reason to separate emergency rule from the normal political/legal system.[3]

Many classical political scientists (Polybius, Machiavelli, Locke, Rousseau, to name a few) have argued that *constitutional* emergency powers—the temporary concentration of decision-making authority in an executive—are necessary if a constitutional government, a government with limited powers, is to sustain itself. The idea endorsed by these political thinkers is that the emergency regime should be created in a kind of bubble that is insulated from the workings of the ordinary political/legal system: the regular rights-protecting constitutional government. The emergency regime is to be created and empowered to take necessary but extreme measures in order to resolve the emergency; but the legal effect of those measures should cease once the emergency ends and constitutional government (and public liberty) is restored. Montesquieu, for example, suggested that "the practice of the freest nation that ever existed induces me to think that there are cases in which a veil should be drawn for a while over liberty, as it was customary to cover the statues of the gods."[4]

Unless there are constitutional provisions for an emergency regime of this kind, so the theory goes, regular executive authority will likely be permanently altered in ways that permit the regular government to interfere with constitutional liberties. Thus, the refusal to provide for constitutional emergency powers will lead to the creation of a permanent discretionary (or prerogative) power in the executive to deal with whatever emergencies come along. That may or may not be a good idea. John Locke argued for a prerogative power of this kind on the ground that law—laws enacted by the legislature—could not anticipate all eventualities and therefore discretion must exist in its application or execution. Locke thought that gaps in law and emergencies, what Carl Schmitt called the "exception," were sufficiently common that executive prerogative power was needed. Unlike Schmitt, Locke did not conclude that the executive was (on that account) sovereign.[5] Indeed, Locke insisted that if the executive abused the prerogative the "people" (as sovereign) might make an appeal to "heaven"—that is to say, the people reserve an inalienable right to revolution.

The classical example of a *constitutional* emergency regime was found in the early years of the Roman Republic. The standard account is that institutions such as the *tribunate*, which protected the plebes from despotic treatment by magistrates and also provided a plebeian role in legislation, were created as settlements of class conflicts that limited the powers of magistrates. Each tribune, for example, could force a magistrate to provide "due process" (a trial) to a detained individual and could veto any action of the Senate or other magistrates. The tribunes also substantially controlled lawmaking. In that respect the institution of the tribunate provided the plebes, as a class, and any Roman citizen, with protection against arbitrary acts of the government. The tribunes could also veto each other's actions. The Senate and magistrates held vetoes as well. While this constitutional scheme protected Romans from arbitrary actions by their leaders, the elaborate system of vetoes in Rome hobbled the republic in dealing with internal tumult and invasions. Thus, at a very early stage, Rome adopted the institution of the dictator, who was given the authority to exercise special powers including the power to suspend due process rights during emergencies. In other words, a dictator could execute a person without trial if he thought it necessary to resolve the crisis.

The dictator was used ninety-five times during the first three hundred years of the republic and was, in that respect, a regular institutional safety valve that could be employed when the Republic was threatened.

Normally, Roman citizens enjoyed procedural rights protected by the tribunes, but when circumstances threatened the city, those rights could be suspended during the course of the emergency. It is important to emphasize that, though the republican constitution was not written down, the dictatorship was a *constitutional* institution. Its practices were guided by widely accepted norms among the Roman elites. Dictators were chosen by a regular (legal) procedure: the Senate declared an emergency by asking the consuls to appoint a dictator, and, once a dictator was appointed, the authority of the consuls, Senate, and other institutions was suspended for its duration. Dictators were, however, term-limited, either to accomplish a specified and limited objective, or to six months of service, whichever came first. After that their mandate was finished and constitutional order was restored. Also, dictators were chosen in a way that tended to pick out trustworthy, experienced, and competent men for the job. In fact dictators were normally trustworthy old men who had held high office previously, and who had no further ambition for higher office or longer service. The model was, of course, Cincinnatus, George Washington's hero, who put aside his plow to serve the republic as dictator to resolve a crisis, returning to his plow afterward.

As noted earlier, there are essentially three kinds of (or justifications for) emergency powers: *necessary* or existential powers, constitutional emergency powers, and legislative emergency powers.[6] Niccolò Machiavelli, John Locke, Carl Schmitt, and many others argued, using different terms, that emergency powers are an existential *necessity* for a constitutional regime: if some official has the capacity to save the regime or constitution, he or she has the moral *authority* and the *duty* to take all actions *necessary* to achieve that goal. Machiavelli argued from Livy's histories of the Roman Republic. He praised the dictatorship as never doing any harm to the republic.[7] Locke argued for the necessity of the (royal) prerogative for dealing with things that law could not anticipate, such as emergencies. Schmitt argued, similarly, that laws are inherently incomplete and unable to handle what he called the *exception* and so the executive must have powers to deal with such things (including especially existential emergencies).[8] Without that power, a constitutional government would not exist in a world of hostile powers, both internal and external.

These were not mere abstract sentiments of political theorists. When Abraham Lincoln imposed emergency powers in 1861 by illegally suspending the writ of habeas corpus, he recognized and admitted its illegality later by asking Congress to approve his actions retrospectively. He stated the matter when addressing Congress in 1863: "Are all the laws but one to go unexecuted, and the Government itself go to pieces lest that one be violated? Even in such a case, would not the official oath be broken if the Government should be overthrown when it was believed that disregarding the single law would tend to preserve it?" Lincoln offered a further justification for his actions afterward:

> I did understand however, that my oath to preserve the Constitution to the best of my ability, imposed upon me the duty of preserving, by every indispensable means, that government—that nation—of which that constitution was the organic law. Was it possible to lose the nation, and yet preserve the constitution? By general law, life *and* limb must be protected; yet often a limb must be amputated to save a life; but a life is never wisely given to save a limb. I felt that measures, otherwise unconstitutional, might become lawful, by becoming indispensable to the preservation of the constitution, through the preservation of the nation.[9]

Alexander Hamilton in *Federalist*, no. 23, argued that emergency powers are not only necessary but cannot be confined ex ante: "The circumstances that endanger the safety of nations are infinite, and for this reason no constitutional shackles can wisely be imposed on the power to which the care of it is committed. This power ought to be coextensive with all the possible combinations of such circumstances." The extent of these powers was defined by necessity: "The authorities essential to the common defense are these: to raise armies; to build and equip fleets; to prescribe rules for the government of both; to direct their operations; to provide for their support. These powers ought to exist without limitation." These powers, he continued, "ought to be under the direction of the same councils which are appointed to preside over the common defense."[10] Evidently this argument fits with his advocacy (in *Federalist*, no. 70) of a single responsible and energetic executive who would have the authority to enforce the laws. Such an executive would also be responsible to wield emergency powers for whatever duration he thought necessary. Hamilton's argument might be seen as a special case of Locke's argument for the necessity of the *prerogative* power "in any government in which the executive and legislative powers are separated—laws cannot anticipate all circumstances of their proper application ... and therefore there must exist someone who has the authority to use discretion to exercise authority to preserve the government and people, in the absence or even against the laws."[11]

One question for the necessity theory advanced by Hamilton is how to define its limits. The notion of necessity cannot be restricted to any test of logical necessity; its scope must be defined by its holder in light of the actual event. That is, if the executive asserts that necessity requires that he or she take some act, this assertion cannot be subjected to a review or test without losing its essential value in protecting the republic. This idea is closely related to Madison's metaconstitutional defense of the necessary and proper clause:

> The power to make all laws which shall be necessary and proper for carrying into execution the foregoing powers, and all other powers vested by this Constitution in the government of the United States, or in any department or officer thereof. . . . Without the SUBSTANCE of this power, the whole Constitution would be a dead letter. . . .
>
> No axiom is more clearly established in law, or in reason, than that wherever the end is required, the means are authorized; wherever a general power to do a thing is given, every particular power necessary for doing it is included. (*Federalist*, no. 44, Madison)

The same argument—that without the power to deal with emergencies the republic would collapse—leads to the conclusion that emergency powers exist whether or not they are found in the Constitution and are necessarily unconfinable by previously adopted constitutional or ordinary law. These arguments have the effect of showing the only way that necessity-based emergency powers may be limited is by the virtue or character of the executive. He or she is trusted to judge correctly whether there is an emergency and which actions may be taken to deal with it. This is why Cincinnatus, and George Washington, are seen as exemplary. Both men decided what actions they could take and resigned their commission when the emergency each faced was resolved. Washington, it is said, shocked Europe by stepping away from his army after the revolution and returning, like Cincinnatus, to his farm to make (I believe) whiskey. He repeated the same self-denial in refusing to stand for a third presidential term though I doubt that he faced any sort of emergency then.

An alternative theory is that, as with the Roman Republic, emergency rule must be established legally by *constitutional* procedures (whether written or unwritten). In Rome, the Senate had to judge whether there was an emergency of sufficient danger to warrant asking the Consuls to appoint a dictator. For another example, the Weimar Constitution had a provision—Article 48—that conferred emergency powers on the president, allowing him to rule through decrees rather than through laws. The constitution of France's Fifth Republic contains Article 16, outlining emergency powers. Such provisions are found in many modern constitutions, and most of them (like Articles 48 and 16) impose legal restrictions on emergency powers, limiting which rights can be suspended and often requiring some real-time review by courts or legislatures.[12] The key feature of constitutional emergency powers is that the constitution itself confers emergency powers directly on an executive to take actions to resolve emergencies.

The US Constitution has no explicit recognition of emergency powers. Arguably, however, specific emergency powers are conferred in parts of the Constitution: Article I, Section 9, confers (apparently on Congress) the authority to suspend habeas corpus in certain kinds of emergencies; Article II vests (undefined) executive powers in the president;[13] the commander in chief clause makes the president the head of the armed forces; the take care clause gives the president the authority (and duty) to see that laws (including treaties and the Constitution) are enforced. While legal thinkers may disagree, each of these constitutional sources confer quite open-ended powers and duties on the president to uphold or protect the Constitution and the republic. Or, perhaps, such powers could be found elsewhere—in Article I's militia clause, or in its general welfare clause—both of these are, like the suspension clause, inconveniently located in Article I and may seem to empower Congress rather than the president. Or (god forbid) we might locate special presidential duties in the preamble: "We the People of the United States, in Order to form a more perfect Union, establish Justice, insure domestic Tranquility, provide for the common defence, promote the general Welfare, and secure the Blessings of Liberty to ourselves and our Posterity, do ordain and establish this Constitution for the United States of America." Insofar as this lays out the purposes and justifications of the Constitution, and insofar as the president is the one official elected by the whole people, the preamble might be seen as empowering him constitutionally to act in emergencies. Pretty dangerous path, it seems to me.

In 1863 Lincoln asked Congress retrospectively to authorize his suspension of the writ of habeas corpus in 1861 (Congress was not in session at the time), which was seen by many (including Chief Justice Roger Taney) as a congressional rather than a presidential prerogative. This was not the president's view of the Constitution; rather, Lincoln endorsed Hamilton's "necessity" theory but he gave it a constitutional foundation. Lincoln insisted that his authority to suspend the Great Writ could be rooted in the "original meaning" of the Constitution: "Now it is insisted that Congress, and not the Executive, is vested with this power; but the Constitution itself is silent as to which or who is to exercise the power; and as the provision was plainly made for a dangerous emergency, it cannot be believed the framers of the instrument intended that in every case the danger should run its course until

Congress could be called together, the very assembling of which might be prevented, as was intended in this case, by the rebellion."[14]

A problem with requiring constitutional procedures to establish emergency powers is that there may be a genuine emergency in which the required constitutional procedures fail to establish emergency rule. A president with constitutional emergency powers may fail to exercise them or may find it politically advantageous to refuse. Or perhaps constitutional processes may themselves interfere with the effective operation of emergency rule. A key feature of constitutional emergency powers in the United States, for example, is that the courts—whose duty it is to say what the law is—are given the role of regulating emergency powers, before, during, or after the fact. The president always has the Jackson-Lincoln option of ignoring a Supreme Court's order if he thinks it impairs his ability to deal with the emergency, but there is no guarantee that an emergency will not occur under a James Buchanan rather than an Abraham Lincoln. In view of that political possibility and the idea that the executive is presumed to have the knowledge and capacity to deal with emergencies, courts can usually be expected to be deferential to executive assumption of power during emergencies. And if the *Korematsu* case is still a guide, judicial deference may extend well beyond the emergency itself.

Legislative Emergency Powers

The third type of emergency regime is *legislative*. Legislative emergency powers also derive from the constitution in the sense that the legislature is exercising powers conferred on it by the Constitution. But emergency powers are not delegated directly to the executive. Rather, the legislature delegates emergency powers to the executive by enacting ordinary statutes. An important feature of legislative emergency powers is that, like constitutional emergency powers, they usually (always?) contain procedural restrictions and regulations that limit what the executive can do legally. As with ordinary law, emergency laws may also fail to provide the authority to deal with a new and urgent crisis. Thus, legislative emergency powers may be inadequate to deal with an emergency, and the executive may be forced to rule on another basis, tempting him to take emergency measures on his own by claiming either direct constitutional authority or necessity. However, while legislative emergency powers may be enacted during a specific emergency, the authorizing statutes often are not repealed or amended once the specific emergency has passed. As a result, it is common for the executive to justify his assumption of emergency powers by referring to authority contained in old statutes that have remained on the statute books.[15] Even if the new emergency seems to be different from older ones, the president's lawyers can deploy techniques of statutory interpretation to bend old laws to new uses. By finding authority in old statutes, he may even be able to assert bipartisan "support" for his measures. The Brennan Center has usefully identified 123 statutory powers that the president can currently use upon his declaration of an emergency.[16] Of course, the legislature can, and sometimes does, amend or repeal delegated authority. This seems to happen only during politically exceptional circumstances.

The most famous instance of repeal and revision is the National Emergencies Act (NEA), which was enacted by post-Watergate Democratic congressional majorities and signed by President Ford in 1976. The act terminated all then-current declared emergencies, placed a term limit on new declarations,[17] asserted that Congress may (by concurrent resolution) terminate a declared emergency, and required specific congressional authorization for an emergency after six months.[18] These provisions have mostly proven to be toothless, especially after *INS v. Chadha* eliminated the legislative veto.[19] After *Chadha*, any congressional "action" under the NEA must be subject to Article I, Section 7, requirements. Concurrent resolutions, unless signed by the president or passed by veto override, have no legal effect, and the president is free to ignore them. In any case, Congress has been reluctant to interfere in presidentially declared emergencies (by refusing to use its expenditure powers, for example) for more mundane political reasons as well. This is especially so when the president's party controls at least one house of Congress. The Brennan Center has counted seventy-one national emergencies that have been declared after the National Emergencies Act was passed, allowing the use of numerous previous laws.[20] Thus, the US president can usually justify an emergency measure by locating the authority to apply it in some legislative statute.

Executives may have other political reasons to rely on legislative authority in emergencies. Unilateral rule forces the president to bear the whole blame if things go wrong. If, however, Congress "buys into" the president's assertion of emergency powers, he can argue that Congress has a continuing obligation to support the president's actions. Buy-in usually requires new congressional action, but in the heat of the moment, Congress has sometimes been willing to enact such laws. In any case, Congress has rarely been able or willing to restrain the president's use of legislative emergency powers during declared emergencies. This is not to say that congressional opponents have not criticized the presidents' use of delegated (as well as asserted) powers, nor to deny that this criticism has sometimes been effective when the opposition party controls one or both congressional houses and can make use of investigatory weapons. The National Emergencies Act serves as both an example and a counterexample.

The fact that the president's army of lawyers can interpret old statutes to confer new powers comes with the prospect that the courts can and usually will review these interpretations. Eventually. But whether courts will actually choose to intervene *during* a declared emergency, as Chief Justice Taney attempted to do, remains constantly in question. The Supreme Court is normally reluctant to second-guess presidential actions during emergencies and, even when it seems to do so, as in the Guantanamo cases, it rarely orders the president to do something that he can simply refuse to do. Alexander Hamilton may not have been wrong in this instance to say that, in this respect, when facing an executive who claims to be guarding the republic in extreme circumstances, the judiciary is the "least dangerous branch" (*Federalist*, no. 78).

Hamilton meant that the court was not dangerous to liberty; in the context of an asserted emergency, however, the court is not dangerous to executive power (even if that threatens liberty). Alas.

State Emergency Powers

As discussed in chapter 2, the American states have assumed special powers to deal with emergencies. These powers typically allow for waiving procedural requirements and suspending certain rights. The use of emergency powers has generally been increasing over time in response to fires, floods, earthquakes, internal disorder, and man-made disasters. But the situation in the states is different from that of the federal government. States and localities do not have foreign policy authority, and although invasion or war may cause local problems, most of the responsibility for managing threats from abroad falls on the federal government. The states possess residual powers under the Constitution and are responsible for maintaining domestic law and order through the exercise of what have been called the *police powers*. These powers generally provide ample legal means to deal with these crises. Writing in 1965, David Trickey notes that "[t]he primary source of executive emergency power is the state constitution, although statutes often codify the constitutional executive emergency authority and occasionally delegate additional legislative police powers to the governor. . . . The provisions of state constitutions from which executive emergency powers are derived display a marked uniformity." For example, he continues, "Every state constitution confers the executive power upon a governor, or designates the governor as the chief executive officer of the state. Every state constitution also designates the governor as commander-in-chief of the state military forces. . . . In addition, thirty-five constitutions explicitly authorize the governor to call out the state national guard to enforce the laws, suppress insurrection, and repel invasion."[21] These powers constitute part of the *police powers*, reserved to the states in Article I and in the Tenth Amendment. Courts have generally agreed that states have especially broad powers to take coercive measures to protect public health: the classical cases include *Jacobson v. Massachusetts* (1905), which upheld the state's authority to require vaccinations. This authority has been reaffirmed many times against various competing constitutional claims (free exercise, right to education, equal protections, etc.), though it must be said that it is not clear how the current Supreme Court may rule on exemptions of this kind.

Much has changed with respect to state legislation since the early twentieth century, even where the state constitutions themselves have not changed. Legislatures have increasingly enacted legislation aimed at restricting the scope, duration, and procedures involved in emergencies. Over the last century, moreover, the scope of the state police powers has been substantially reduced, with the incorporation of most of the Bill of Rights against the states and with the enactment of civil rights laws. Governors who exercise emergency powers are increasingly held to strict constitutional tests if they seek to suspend rights guaranteed under the US Constitution. State courts are required to enforce these constitutional limitations. The same thing applies to ordinary state legislation insofar as state laws may trespass on constitutional protections. Recent court cases concerning emergency orders infringing on religious liberties exemplify these changes, and more will surely appear in the future.

Although the state constitutions usually provide for emergency powers, governors have wanted to draw more often on legislative authorization, even though legislative statutes often contain more restrictions on the use of emergency powers than does the constitution. While the motivations for relying on laws rather than constitutional authority are similar to such motivations at the federal level, there are additional incentives at the state and local levels. Governors are, for one thing, comparatively more powerful in a political and practical sense than the president in several respects.[22] State governments are, for example, more likely to be under unified partisan control rather than divided between parties as the federal government often is. Thus checks and balances, which may restrict presidential powers, tend to be less effective in those states with unified governments.[23] In many states, moreover, the legislature meets for short terms and is often out of session. In addition, many state legislatures are poorly staffed and lack expertise and professionalism and are effectively unable to oppose gubernatorial actions. For these reasons the state legislature is unlikely to oppose gubernatorial assumption of emergency powers under unified government. And even if the state government is divided, the legislature will usually lack the resources to effectively oppose the governor's authority.

Moreover, governors are often given additional powers to manage emergencies. If the governor declares an emergency due to fires or floods or earthquakes, this often triggers federal assistance or international aid, drawing new resources into the state.[24] This permits the governor photo ops and speeches to claim credit for declaring the emergency, to draw on federal money, and, at the same time, to complain if outside assistance is inadequate or too slow in arriving. Governors sometimes enjoy additional legal advantages as well. Some have "directive" authority over their agencies, which allows the governor to substitute his or her judgment for agency determinations and findings. This is extremely hard to do under federal laws. The Administrative Procedure Act and other statutes generally require agency policies to be made under formal requirements of notice and comment rulemaking.

The role of the states in "cooperative" federalism also confers additional advantages on the governor. States are often the locus of administration of federal programs that cannot be operated successfully without state cooperation. Many federal programs explicitly confer powers to cooperate or refuse to cooperate on the governor: the FEMA statute, for example, gives the governor management authority over the administration of federal relief. As seen recently in the health area, where many state governors refused to cooperate with the implementation of the Affordable Care Act and new Medicaid regulations, a governor's refusal to cooperate can be politically advantageous.

Moreover, the governor's authority during emergencies goes in more than one direction: constitutionally, cities and counties are creatures of the state government. The governor can use this fact to criticize or to prohibit local authorities from taking emergency actions and, in many cases, there is little recourse for mayors and local administrators. Power, of course, can be accompanied by blame, and so in many recent cases, rather than issuing coercive orders, the governor produces guidelines or schemes that aim at advising local governments, which may effectively impose regulations and restrictions on local officials. While governors have great authority in the US federal system, and many other sources of political power, these powers are usually used in ways that aim at taking popular actions, avoiding unpopular actions (shutdowns and other coercive requirements imposed on people and businesses), and taking credit if things go well or, at least, if new resources are drawn into the state.

Controlling Emergency Powers

Emergency powers are supposed to be exceptional, in the sense that ordinary legal procedures and rights must be suspended in order to deal with existential or disabling threats to the regime or the nation that the ordinary laws cannot manage. And, as soon as the threat passes, the situation is supposed to return to the status quo ante—constitutional democracy. Obviously, someone who holds such powers might be reluctant to give them back, or at least not expeditiously, and so there is a danger that emergency powers will be prolonged and abused. This danger is especially great if the only justification for emergency rule is necessity. That justification leaves little room for legislatures or courts.

Constitutional emergency powers seem less dangerous than necessity-based powers, as they are controlled by laws. Constitutionally based executive orders are subject to challenge in courts, at least in principle. Justice Robert Jackson, in his famous *Korematsu* dissent, articulated this idea in stating that, under the Constitution, the state of emergency is "controlled" by law in the sense that the law remained in effect even during emergencies. He conceded that "[d]efense measures will not, and often should not, be held within the limits that bind civil authority in peace. . . . a commander in temporarily focusing the life of a community on defense is carrying out a military program." However that may be, Jackson continued, the commander "is not making law in the sense the courts know the term. He issues orders, and they may have a certain authority as military commands, although they may be very bad as constitutional law. ... if we cannot confine military expedients by the Constitution, *neither would I distort the Constitution* [emphasis added] to approve all that the military may deem expedient. This is what the Court appears to be doing, whether consciously or not."[25] There can be no clearer defense of the principle that the ordinary laws should be strictly shielded from measures taken during emergencies. He basically told the president, "Your duty may be to save the country as best you can, but that will not make your orders the law of the land." Jackson's view seems to be that the ordinary legal system is all the law there is: outside of that system there is only necessity. In other words he seems, in his *Korematsu* dissent, to imply that legality may not be effectively applied during emergencies but it still exists even if it is not enforced. If the president undertakes unconstitutional acts (or his generals do), the acts remain unconstitutional during the emergency as well as thereafter. Under Hamilton's necessity theory, by contrast, necessity makes right (legal). Under Jackson's dissent, necessity has no legal consequence at all.

An alternative view, which Pasquale Pasquino and I have called *dualism*, insists that some law remains in place during emergencies, although perhaps it is not enforceable or enforceable immediately. We can see a trace of the dualist doctrine in Justice Jackson's concurrence in *Youngstown Sheet*, where the Supreme Court denied President Truman the authority to nationalize steel companies. In *Youngstown*, Jackson provided a kind of sliding scale for presidential powers, arguing that the president's powers are at their weakest where he takes "measures incompatible with the expressed or implied will of Congress." This seems to imply that the president is, to varying degrees, bound by congressional statutes. This was of course merely a concurring opinion and so, implicitly, Jackson agreed with Justice Hugo Black's opinion for the court that "there is no statute that expressly authorizes the President to take possession of property as he did here."[26] Unlike Justice Jackson, Justice Black had supported FDR's actions in *Korematsu*, which certainly took property as effectively as Truman's steel seizure did, so it may be hard to see why the court overturned Truman's order. My guess is that the fact that Congress did not actually declare war in Korea implies that the president was not seen as having been given authority to suspend constitutional rights, as FDR claimed to have in World War II. In any case, during the Korean "war" the power that President Truman exercised was seen by Black and Jackson as essentially legislative rather than constitutional, and therefore controllable under the Constitution. And in that circumstance, Jackson endorsed a version of dualism—saying that law applied during the emergency, even if that law may have been weaker or less complete than law outside of emergencies. Of course, we cannot know what Jackson might have said had the Korean conflict been deemed a real war in the constitutional sense.

Dualism is the view that the president is authorized to suspend only *certain specified* constitutionally protected rights during emergencies, which means the set of applicable laws is smaller than the ordinary laws. This is what Weimar's Article 48 and France's Article 16 explicitly state: each lists the powers and procedures that must remain in place during an emergency. These powers and procedures are, in principle, enforceable in courts. As long as there are some legal norms that apply during emergencies, we can see the emergency rule as a legal system and, in principle, courts have a role (which they may assert perhaps only after the event) in interpreting the laws regulating executive action. An example might be laws restricting the use of "torture." While there are hard definitional problems in this area, it seems plausible that there are legal/constitutional restrictions against the use of torture that cannot be suspended in emergencies, no matter how threatening that emergency might be. Obviously, necessity theorists like Hamilton or Carl Schmitt would disagree.

The legislature may also have a role in revising or repealing laws conferring legislative emergency authority (either prior to or after the event). Some emergency power provisions in other countries in fact provide that the legislature and courts must remain open during formally declared emergencies, assigning to them specific judicial functions in emergencies. For example, the president may be required to submit emergency decrees to a constitutional court, which might have some powers to reject or revise the decree. Thus, dualism represents the legal system as having (at least) two parts: the regular constitution and laws and, during a formal emergency, a special emergency legal system with fewer legal restraints.

Federalism

It could be argued that federalism itself provides regulatory limits to the exercise of federal emergency powers. For one thing, the federal government is generally prohibited from commandeering state officials to execute federal laws. Some argue that "it is largely clear that the US federal government lacks the power found in other constitutions to intervene in the structure or functions of state government during an emergency. There appears to be no crisis exception to the anti-commandeering doctrine."[27] In principle, this means that even during federal emergencies state laws will continue to operate and state courts continue to function. People can complain to these courts if their rights under state law are infringed. It is not clear to me that this view is correct. The anticommandeering doctrine originated only recently (in 1992) and has not really been tested in emergency conditions. In the Civil War and Reconstruction period, for example, those state courts that were located in war zones were not open, and military courts (emergency courts!) took over their business. Moreover, Lincoln's Emancipation Proclamation freed slaves in those states under Union Army control. After that a number of congressional statutes were enacted that constrained the southern states from trespassing on the rights of the former slaves. These seem counterexamples to the claim that the anti-commandeering principle applies during emergencies.

The position of state courts vis-à-vis commandeering, moreover, seems unclear, as state courts are ordinarily required to enforce applicable federal laws. The authors concede, in any case, that federalism-based limits, to the extent that they exist, may produce a serious loss in state–federal and interstate coordination during emergencies. This implies that, if coordination issues are significant, we might expect the anti-commandeering doctrine to come under attack during emergencies.

Still, the authors claim that the fact "that the US president and Congress very likely cannot interfere with state structure even during emergency is an important protection against the risks of democratic erosion. Indeed, the rules . . . providing for separate state structures in key areas like courts, elections, and executive bureaucracies would mean very little if those rules could be breached during states of emergency."[28] My guess is that these authors may be correct for "minor" emergencies—emergencies that do not represent existential threats to the regime. COVID, from this point of view, may be not threatening enough to erode federalism restrictions on national emergency powers. I wonder, too, how the authors would treat the events of the Civil War and Reconstruction. The secession was illegal under the understanding of the national government, and where Confederate territory was occupied, and during Reconstruction as well, the federal government effectively commandeered state governments or parts of them.

State constitutions with emergency provisions, and state emergency statutes generally, contain limits on emergency powers. States of emergency are nearly all subject to term limits and require eventual consultation with the legislature. And, of course, neither state constitutions nor state statutes can suspend rights or procedures protected by the US Constitution. They may suspend state law and legal processes, but even these suspensions might be challenged under federal constitutional law. So, on the face of things, state emergency powers seem legally weaker than federal laws. As a matter of political fact, however, this conclusion should not be overdrawn. Because of the political circumstances of the state governments (discussed above), states may actually have more political capacity and incentive to declare emergencies than the federal government. And given the likely duration of state emergencies, constitutional challenges may be hard to bring in a timely fashion and may not be a serious limitation on state emergency rule.

American Exceptionalism

Was the American response to the COVID pandemic unusually poor when compared with other advanced democracies? Even allowing for different ways of allocating deaths, currently (January 2022) the United States, which has a bit more than 4 percent of the world's population, has experienced more than 14 percent of the confirmed COVID-related deaths.[29] While it is possible to quibble over the numbers a bit, the percentages do not seem to vary much over time. The answer to this question probably depends on when, in the course of the pandemic, it is posed. In any case, countries varied greatly in their responses. Every country shut borders, but some countries (China, New Zealand, South Korea, Taiwan, Vietnam) imposed severe restrictions on internal travel with enforced quarantines and testing and tracing requirements and kept these measures in place for long periods. As is evident, such severe responses were not limited to authoritarian systems: some democratic countries (Australia, Germany, New Zealand, South Korea, Taiwan) seemed successful in using strict controls to slow the initial rise in cases, while some authoritarian countries, Russia and Iran, for example, were unable or unwilling to impose strict controls.

The US federal government exhibited very different responses even when compared to other advanced democracies.[30] Border restrictions were imposed quickly but were very inconsistently applied. Some parts of the federal government issued guidance that recommended restrictive measures, but the administration spoke with many voices as to the desirability of public health orders. During the Trump administration, the loudest voice—the president's—usually prevailed both in the refusal to issue orders and in forcing federal agencies to alter their messages to fit the president's theme. The national government, however, did some important things in attacking the disease itself—promoting and speeding the development of vaccines, maintaining a loose fiscal and monetary regime, and keeping restrictions on foreign travel. Still, the federal government refrained from issuing orders to individuals or businesses, and it refused to coordinate the production or distribution of health care resources to the states as many state governors asked. Effective vaccines were made available within a year of the onset of the disease. But many people still refuse to take the vaccines, partly as a result of political messaging from the former president and his followers. Probably the most effective thing the Trump administration did was to politicize the question of public health, making compliance with state or federal guidelines (such as they were) a kind of ideological litmus test for Republicans.

During the Trump administration, measures imposed directly on individuals and businesses were mostly relegated to the states or localities. The Biden government has attempted to employ mandates more frequently, but courts have slowed this effort, and there is certainly widespread popular resistance to such measures. Perhaps this is to be expected, as the US Constitution allocates "plenary" police powers to the states, leaving it to those governments to manage public health and safety. The federal government is limited in other ways too, as to its capacity to regulate individual behavior. For example, the Posse Comitatus Act (1878) generally forbids the federal government from using the armed forces for local law enforcement.[31] Moreover, since the 1990s the Supreme Court has generally prohibited the federal government from "commandeering" state officials to enforce federal programs.[32] Moreover, the Constitution protects various liberties against the states as well as the federal government and these protections limit what states and localities can do to enforce public health measures.

At lower federal levels, some severe restrictions were adopted; often these restrictions were mostly imposed by localities rather than states. Schools, universities, and public offices were closed. Businesses too were forced to close, sometimes for long periods. Retailers and churches were required to separate people in their establishments and limit attendance. However, the willingness to impose these strong public measures soon came to depend on which party was in power in the specific government. President Trump used the bully pulpit to ridicule state and local officials who imposed restrictive measures. This made it politically difficult for Republican governors or mayors to require masks, close schools, or impose restrictions on economic or religious activities. As a result, many Republican governors followed the party line in opposing mandates. Republican state legislatures often prohibited local coercive measures too—whether pushed by a Democratic governor or propounded by Democratic cities in Republican states. Partly for these reasons, blue states were more willing to apply strong measures than red states. Further, and obviously this is connected, the populations of blue states also seemed more willing to comply voluntarily with tougher restrictions than those who lived in red states. This remained the case even as the incidence of severe disease moved from the coastal states to the middle of the country and to the South, where more state and local governments were under Republican control.[33]

There is much to be said in favor of a decentralized response to the effects of the pandemic, if not to the pandemic itself. Decentralizing restrictive regulations has the virtue of permitting narrow targeting to local hotspots in space and time. However, decentralized responses present some problems. First, people often move across boundaries in ways that are hard to trace. Second, they can adjust their behavior in ways that can defeat or diminish the effectiveness of public health orders. Third, the political responsiveness of local governments may limit officials' willingness to impose restrictions and may induce them to prematurely remove those that they do impose. Many people remain unconvinced that they (or those they care about) are at risk of serious illness or believe that the costs of government restrictions to the economy, or to children, or to social life generally are unacceptably high. In some jurisdictions those views will prevail, and even if they don't, these people may refuse to comply with orders. There is a limit to what states and localities can do.

In any case, the virus is not yet finished. The recent Delta and Omicron variants have produced more recent surges in the US as elsewhere but the response in death rates is much higher than in other advanced democracies. While the Omicron variant seems less lethal than its predecessors, the American response has lagged: "Two years into the pandemic, the coronavirus is killing Americans at far higher rates than people in other wealthy nations, a sobering distinction to bear as the country charts a course through the next stages of the pandemic."[34] In each case, death rates have tended to decrease eventually, as was the case earlier. Whether the differences are due to differences in public health measures, caution by individuals, or improved treatments is not really clear. Still, US death rates have generally remained high compared to other advanced democracies.

The economy as a whole, it is important to say, never completely shut down—the current estimate is that the COVID-induced recession lasted only two months (the shortest recession in US history), bottoming out in April 2020. And the recovery has been fast by historical standards. No doubt the brevity and rapid recovery was aided by the Federal Reserve Board's easy money policies and the large income transfers enacted under both the Trump and Biden administrations. The effects of the disease, however, have been felt very unevenly. A substantial part of the workforce found it possible to remain employed and work productively from home. But tourism, hotels, travel, entertainment, and restaurants remain depressed and have barely begun to recover. People defined as essential workers—including frontline health and logistics workers—were exposed to more risk than others (even if many were young enough to bear that risk reasonably well). The federal income transfers, which were broadly targeted, have certainly helped out many people in these impacted industries. The recovery in the economy opens up jobs for people willing to switch to jobs in the fast-growing parts of the economy, and broadly targeted transfers have allowed people throughout the economy to build up savings, allowing them (again) more flexibility in job or career choice.

Explaining US Emergency Exceptionalism

I will take it for granted that the American policy pattern was unusual—exceptional—in some respects. Whether that ends up being a good or a bad thing is something we cannot know for a long time. The pressure on hospitals has mostly relented (though with the Delta and Omicron variants it is not clear for how long), but vaccine reluctance means that herd immunity remains far away. The exceptional aspect is the refusal of American governments at all levels (national, state, and local) to exercise powers that they have and could have used to impose more severe restrictions on movement and activity than they did. Specifically, American governments were reluctant to invoke all the *emergency* powers that were available. This is not to say that "emergencies" were not *declared* either officially or otherwise. Governments at all levels—federal, state, and local—did at times make use of emergency authorities of various kinds. But, often, the powers that were used were employed inconsistently, politically, and often too briefly to be effective in actually controlling the virus. Is this a bug or a feature? Federalism permits diverse policy responses and may result in policies well tailored to local conditions or at least to local policy preferences. But US federalism privileges the state governments rather than localities, and where partisan divisions exist, federalism may actually hamper responsiveness to local conditions. Moreover, insofar as policy diversity prevents the effective control of the virus, such responsiveness may be counterproductive in the larger scale.

Perhaps there are other, political, accounts of American exceptionalism that are more enlightening. No elected politician likes to issue coercive orders. It is better to let those lower down the political food chain impose orders so that higher-level politicians can take credit for the outcome while blaming locals for coercive actions. Federalism permits this response at the national level and may, in many cases, even require it. At the state level the federalism argument is not generally available—though perhaps it is in "home rule" states—but we observe the same phenomenon: governors passing the buck down, and claiming credit up.

Another political explanation points to ideological differences between the parties: Republicans are more resistant to regulation than are Democrats and, as it happened, Republicans held the presidency and many state governments at the outset of the pandemic. Republican executives therefore could have been expected to take quite different policies than their Democratic counterparts, leaving it to localities or to businesses and individuals to take difficult protective actions. Still, the fact remained that the political payoffs for opposing mandates of any kind remained attractive to Republican political leaders even during the Trump presidency.

The last option, perhaps most attractive to journalists and commentators, is that Americans are simply resistant to top-down coercion, so a regulatory response to the crisis could not work because people would not comply with orders. Strict regulations would not work for long, especially as many people found it possible to avoid risks in their own lives. If a state government did persist in imposing a strict regulatory response, the frequency of elections would soon produce a powerful political rejection. This rejection might be uneven and have a partisan aspect. But the suspicion would be that even in places accustomed to regulatory responses—blue states like California, New Jersey, or New York—political and cultural resistance would prevent the sustained application of regulatory policies.

Notes

1. Eric A. Posner and Adrian Vermeule have argued that executive unilateralism is both inevitable and, all things considered, a good thing because the Madisonian system of checks and balances has failed. *The Executive Unbound: After the Madisonian Republic* (New York: Oxford University Press, 2010). They argue that executive rule is adequately monitored and regulated by elections and public opinion (what I call plebiscitarian mechanisms).

2. James Madison, "Political Observations. April 20, 1795," in *Letters and Other Writings of James Madison* (Whitefish, MT: Kessinger, 2010), 4:491.

3. There are many ways this might be done. Emergency statutes might be required to have "sunset" provisions, for example.

4. Charles de Montesquieu, *The Spirit of the Laws* (Guildford, UK: Prometheus, 1900), bk. 12, chap. 19.

5. Carl Schmitt, *Political Theology: Four Chapters on the Concept of Sovereignty* (Chicago: University of Chicago Press, 2005).

6. Pasquale Pasquino and I have produced a typology of emergency powers that I draw on here. The focus of that article is the notion of the *exception*: the idea that there are unavoidable gaps in any legal system, eventualities that law does not provide for and which in some cases can threaten the legal/political system itself. That article does not explicitly focus on the necessity justification I discuss here. The "monist" theory that we attributed to Thomas Hobbes may be an example of necessity theory insofar as a sovereign who fails to protect the lives of his subjects—in any circumstance—will forfeit his authority to rule. John Ferejohn and Pasquale Pasquino, "The Law of the Exception: A Typology of Emergency Powers," *International Journal of Constitutional Law* 2, no. 2 (April 2004): 210–39.

7. Niccolò Machiavelli, *Discourses on Livy* (Oxford: Oxford University Press, 1997).

8. Carl Schmitt, *Dictatorship* (Cambridge: Polity Press, 2013).

9. Lincoln to Albert Hodges, April 4, 1864, in *Collected Works of Abraham Lincoln*, ed. Roy P. Basler et al., vol. 7 (New Brunswick, NJ: Rutgers University Press, 1953), 281.

10. *The Federalist Papers* (Vancouver, BC: Engage Classics, 2020).

11. John Locke, *Second Treatise of Government*, ed. Crawford Brough Macpherson (Cambridge: Hackett, 1980).

12. In the appendix to the English edition of *The Dictator*, Carl Schmitt argues that none of these restrictions should be understood to bind the dictator.

13. Julian Davis Mortenson argues that the vesting clause does not confer prerogative powers but only the power to execute the laws. He argues that this is a substantial source of authority. It is not clear to me, however, how to think of executive where law may not exist—as in foreign affairs, wars, and emergencies—or when the laws conflict or lead to absurdities or collapse of the republic. Mortenson is concerned, however, with finding and reconstructing the original meanings and does not seem to fully confront these issues. Julian Davis Mortenson, "The Executive Power Clause," *University of Pennsylvania Law Review* 168, no. 5 (2020): 1269–1367.

14. As I argued above, Lincoln was certainly willing to go beyond the Constitution if his constitutional interpretation failed to persuade.

15. The case of statutes enacted specifically for a crisis might include the Gulf of Tonkin Resolution (1964), the Authorization for Use of Military Force (2001), or the Authorization for Use of Military Force Against Iraq Resolution (2002). The paradigmatic and notorious examples were the various "enabling acts" passed

during the Weimar period, culminating in the Enabling Act of 1933 that conferred plenary powers on Hitler for four years.

16. "A Guide to Emergency Powers and Their Use: The 136 Statutory Powers That May Become Available to the President upon Declaration of a National Emergency," Brennan Center for Justice, last updated April 24, 2020, https://www.brennancenter.org/our-work/research-reports/guide-emergency-powers-and-their-use.

17. Title I asserts that "all powers and authorities conferred by law upon the President, any other officer or employee of the Federal Government, or any department, agency, independent establishment, or any other body of the Federal Government, and all powers and authorities conferred by any Executive Order pursuant to law as a result of the existence of any declaration of national emergency in effect on the date of enactment of this Act are terminated two years from the date of such enactment."

18. Pub. L. 94–412, title II, §202, Sept. 14, 1976, 90 Stat. 1255.

19. Immigration and Naturalization Service v. Chadha, 462 U.S. 919 (1983).

20. "Declared National Emergencies under the National Emergencies Act: A Running List of Presidential Emergency Declarations under the National Emergencies Act of 1976," Brennan Center for Justice, last updated November 18, 2021, https://www.brennancenter.org/our-work/research-reports/declared-national-emergencies-under-national-emergencies-act.

21. F. David Trickey, "Constitutional and Statutory Bases of Governors' Emergency Powers," *Michigan Law Review* 64, no. 2 (December 1965): 290–307.

22. Miriam Seifter, "Gubernatorial Administration," *Harvard Law Review* 131, no. 2 (December 2017): 483–542.

23. Daryl Levinson and Richard Pildes, "Separation of Parties, not Powers," *Harvard Law Review* 119, no. 8 (June 2006): 2312–86.

24. Disaster Relief and Emergency Assistance Act, 42 U.S.C. §§ 5121-5206. Here is a description of the resources available to the state if the governor successfully requests an emergency declaration: https://www.fema.gov/pdf/rrr/dec_proc.pdf.

25. "I cannot say, from any evidence before me, that the orders of General DeWitt were not reasonably expedient military precautions, nor could I say that they were. But even if they were permissible military procedures, I deny that it follows that they are constitutional. If, as the Court holds, it does follow, then we may as well say that any military order will be constitutional and have done with it," *Toyosaburo Korematsu v. United States* (1944). Justice Jackson may not have been satisfied with dualism either—at least not unless he was willing to find it in the Constitution. Following Hamilton's reasoning in *Federalist*, no. 70, where he argues that the energetic and unified executive was already embodied in the proposed Constitution, it seems to me that such a project may be feasible. But not today.

26. Youngstown Sheet & Tube Co. v. Sawyer, 343 U.S. 579 (1952).

27. David Landau, Hannah J. Wiseman, and Samuel R. Wiseman, "Federalism for the Worst Case," *Iowa Law Review* 105, no. 3 (March 2020): 1187, at 1238.

28. Landau, Wiseman, and Wiseman, "Federalism for the Worst Case," 1240.

29. "United States Coronavirus Cases," Worldometer, https://www.worldometers.info/coronavirus/country/us.

30. David E. Pozen and Kim Lane Scheppele, "Executive Underreach, in Pandemics and Otherwise," American Journal of International Law 114, no. 4 (October 2020): 608–17 (mostly focusing on the United States, Brazil, and Viktor Orbán).

31. 18 U.S.C., § 1385. "Whoever, except in cases and under circumstances expressly authorized by the Constitution or Act of Congress, willfully uses any part of the Army or the Air Force as a posse comitatus or otherwise to execute the laws shall be fined not more than $10,000 or imprisoned not more than two years, or both." There are various exceptions to the act, the most important of which excepts the National Guard from its provisions when acting under state authority. Another exception is when there is need to quash a rebellion or insurrection.

32. The anticommandeering rule appeared first in *New York v. United States*, 488 U.S. 1041 (1992) but was employed also in *Printz v. United States*, 521 U.S. 898 (1997), and in *Murphy v. National Collegiate Athletic Association*, No. 16-476, 584 U.S. (2018).

33. The transition took place at the same time that treatments were improving, equipment was becoming more widely available, and mortality rates were declining. Until January 2021, when vaccines became available, increased local incidences often strained hospital resources and often led to bad outcomes.

34. Benjamin Mueller and Eleanor Lutz, "US Has Far Higher Covid Death Rate Than Other Wealthy Countries," *New York Times*, February 1, 2022.

Chapter 2

Emergency Powers in the American States

Cameron DeHart and Morris P. Fiorina

This chapter provides a summary description of the emergency powers (henceforth EP) laws that were in effect as of mid-2020 in the fifty states, Washington DC, and the five US territories. First, we summarize the constitutional and statutory basis for emergency declarations and the exercise of EP. A case study of California provides a helpful illustration of the gubernatorial power to declare emergencies and take action within the parameters established by the state constitution and general statutes. Next, we provide a summary of the powers that can be exercised in the states and territories once an emergency is declared. As we discuss in chapter 8, by 2021 legislatures in most states had begun attempting to limit some of the existing provisions in effect when the pandemic began, and in a few cases they succeeded.

As with comparisons in many other areas, the federal system allows for considerable variation. We begin with a survey of the powers set forth in state constitutions, then turn to the statutes that specify how EP are to be exercised. Approximately 80 percent (forty-one) of the state constitutions contain provisions for the exercise of EP, as does the Commonwealth of the Northern Mariana Islands (CNMI hereinafter).[1] There does not seem to be much by way of a discernible pattern other than that all the northeastern states have such constitutional provisions.[2] Although about a quarter of the states do not have *constitutional* provisions regarding EP, all fifty states, five territories, and Washington, DC, have *statutory* provisions for the exercise of emergency powers.

The Constitutional and Statutory Basis for Emergency Declarations

Compared to the US Constitution, amended fewer than thirty times since its ratification, the various state constitutions have been amended or replaced outright numerous times over the last two centuries. Especially over the course of the twentieth century, states began to add clauses to their constitutions related to emergency preparedness and response. In the dawning decades of the Cold War, for example, many states amended constitutions to clarify the gubernatorial line of succession in the event that the state executive was incapacitated or died. This trend predated the assassination of President Kennedy and the passage of the Twenty-Fifth Amendment to the US Constitution, but such state-level reforms were no doubt legitimized by the national reform and concerns about civil defense in the nuclear age.

Constitutional Provisions

Only a handful of the state constitutions specify the officials responsible for declaring states of emergency (New Mexico, Oregon, and Texas, plus CNMI). In the remaining states, territories, and the District of Columbia the provision for emergency declarations is statutory.

The scope of constitutional provisions that provide for the exercise of EP varies from state to state. A typical provision authorizes the state legislature to pass laws related to emergency response, including provisions for the continuity of government during a disaster or foreign attack. Arizona's state constitution, using language typical of other states, grants to the state legislature the "power and immediate duty to provide for prompt and temporary succession to the powers and duties of public offices" and to "adopt such other measures as may be necessary and proper for ensuring the continuity of governmental operations."[3] As we discuss below, other constitutional provisions relate to expediting emergency legislation, such as by waiving rules about public readings or committee hearings and shielding emergency laws from referendum challenges, as well as regulations about government spending, taxation, and debt financing during emergencies.

State constitutional provisions typically do not include a comprehensive list of grounds for emergency declarations. Rather, state constitutions commonly refer to emergencies, disasters, and periods in which there is a threat to continuity of governmental operations. For example, South Carolina's constitution refers to "periods of emergency resulting from disasters caused by enemy attack."[4] Other state constitutions, such as that of Arkansas, include broader references to "the preservation of the public peace, health, and safety."[5] A provision in Delaware's state constitution to allow the General Assembly to meet in an alternate location is among the most exhaustive, specifying that emergencies may result from "enemy attack, terrorism, disease, accident, or other natural or man-made disaster."[6]

The most common EP clauses in state constitutions outline the procedures for (a) ensuring the continuity of the state government, (b) expediting emergency legislation, and (c) authorizing emergency spending. State constitutions typically do not expand the governor's executive power during an emergency. One exception is Maryland, where the governor can appoint officers on a temporary basis during an emergency, subject to removal by the next governor.

In the forty-one states with constitutional provisions for EP, thirty-two feature clauses for the continuity of the state government. These clauses allow the state legislature to convene in an alternate location during an emergency. The alternate location may be specified by law or on an ad hoc basis by the governor, the legislature, or some combination thereof.

The Brennan Center for Justice issued a report in mid-2020 with recommendations for "maintaining legislative continuity" during the coronavirus pandemic based on preexisting constitutional and statutory provisions. The National Conference of State Legislatures (NCSL) provides a helpful summary of how state constitutions and laws ensure that state legislatures can continue to exercise their duties during an emergency.[7] Common provisions related to the continuity of government include the process and authority for authorizing such provisions, convening special sessions of the state legislature, designating interim officials during an emergency, establishing lines of succession for major state government leaders, and outlining the rules for alternate locations as well as "remote participation" by state policy makers.[8] State constitutions may also include provisions for the continuity of operations for the governor, state courts, state agencies, and local governments.

From state to state, the constitutional provisions for the continuity of government may specify different conditions under which the state legislature (or other officials) can modify their operations in an emergency. The NCSL finds that many states adopted continuity provisions in the late 1950s and early 1960s as concerns mounted about the Cold War, coincident with the federal push to amend the presidential line of succession following the assassination of President Kennedy in 1963.

Constitutional amendments may expand the conditions under which continuity of government provisions can be invoked. Prior to 2019, the Washington State Constitution listed warfare as the sole condition under which certain powers, such as appointing interim officials to vacancies and establishing the line of succession for major state officers, could be used. Washington voters had approved a 1962 ballot measure, House Joint Resolution 9, that empowered the state legislature to designate a line of succession if state officials were killed or otherwise rendered unable to serve due to a war or attack in the Evergreen State. Concern about the Soviet Union and nuclear war was no doubt a strong motivator for voters in 1962, but the constitutional amendment left the legislature unable to devise similar plans in the event of *other* emergencies. Sitting along the Cascadia Subduction Zone, Washington State is vulnerable to earthquakes, and legislators and voters began to worry about the impact a massive earthquake, "The Big One," might have on the state legislature and local governments.[9] In 2019, state senator Dean Takko introduced a constitutional amendment that expanded the provisions to include "catastrophic incidents" that fall short of warfare and could pose a risk to the continuity of government.[10]

Eighteen state constitutions do not discuss the continuity of government during an emergency, although such provisions might exist in state law. During the 2020 coronavirus pandemic, legislators in California proposed a bundle of reforms that included remote participation in legislative hearings, proxy voting on bills, and other changes to transparency requirements.

The second most common constitutional clause allows the legislature to expedite the passage or enactment of emergency legislation (seventeen states). For example, constitutional provisions that require legislatures to wait a minimum number of days to vote, after introducing or debating a bill, are typically waived. Two state constitutions include clauses to allow citizens to vote on emergency legislation by referendum (Arkansas and Maine). Four state constitutions explicitly prohibit referenda on emergency laws (Alaska, Arizona, Nebraska, and Ohio).

The conditions under which expedited legislation clauses can be invoked vary from state to state, but the typical provision establishes some process by which a bill is deemed a piece of "emergency legislation" and is thus eligible for expedited hearing, passage, or enactment, as well as certain protections from voters. Even in the forty-six states without a constitutional prohibition on referenda on emergency laws, the legislature might allow certain bills to receive privileged status. In Oregon, for example, legislators can attach "emergency clauses" that allow bills to be enacted immediately. In 2015, the state legislature and governor faced scrutiny for abusing the "emergency legislation" provision to pass their legislative priorities without the threat of a citizens' referendum.[11]

Another common clause in state constitutions expands the government's ability to spend and borrow money in an emergency by incurring debt (five states: Connecticut, Illinois, Missouri, North Carolina, and Rhode Island) or accessing or amending an emergency fund in the state budget (three states: Florida, Maryland, and Oregon).

A handful of state constitutions include idiosyncratic provisions. For example, Wisconsin's constitution allows state legislators to serve as active-duty members of the armed forces during an emergency. South Carolina's constitution allows the lieutenant governor to assume executive power if the governor is missing during an emergency. Florida's constitution allows the chief judge of a circuit court to empower county judges to order emergency hospitalizations. The legislature in the Sunshine State can also pass a law to suspend or delay general elections "due to a state of emergency or impending emergency."[12]

New Mexico, Oregon, and Texas stand out for the length and specificity of their constitutional provisions related to EP. Whereas most constitutions feature only one or two clauses related to the continuity of government or emergency spending, these three state constitutions go into greater detail about these topics. For example, New Mexico and Texas are unique among the states for specifying which officers can declare and terminate emergencies. In New Mexico, the governor can make and terminate emergency declarations, but the legislature is also constitutionally empowered to end gubernatorial declarations.

Oregon's constitution is similarly specific about who can declare and end emergencies (the governor or legislature, in both cases) but is also unique for listing the "catastrophic disaster" conditions that may lead to an emergency declaration. Oregon's constitution also prohibits the legislature from declaring an emergency for the purposes of expediting a tax bill, and it extends the governor's line-item veto power to emergency legislation. Unique among the states, Oregon's constitution also allows for the creation of a joint legislative committee with the power to authorize emergency spending.

The Texas Constitution includes many details about the function of state government, including rules about when and where the legislature can convene, the percentage of legislators needed for a quorum, and mandatory wait times during the legislative process. As such, the clause related to continuity of government (Article III, Section 62) outlines the process for suspending these constitutional provisions during an emergency: the governor must issue an emergency proclamation with the concurrence of both houses, which shall last for no more than two years.

Of the three territories that are governed by a constitution, only CNMI features a constitutional provision for EP that allows the governor to declare emergencies and mobilize resources in response. American Samoa and Puerto Rico have constitutions, but their emergency powers are defined by statute.

Statutory Provisions

Most of the specific actions state governments undertake under conditions of emergency are authorized by statute. All the states, territories, and the District of Columbia have statutory provisions that specify which officials can declare emergencies, alone or in concert with other officials, as well as the grounds for such a declaration.

Who Can Declare a State of Emergency?

Generally (forty-eight states) the governor is the state official empowered to declare an emergency. In five states (Alabama, New Hampshire, North Carolina, Oregon, West Virginia) the legislature can declare an emergency on its own, and in two states (Georgia, Oklahoma) both the governor and legislature must act. In five states other officials are involved with public health emergencies: the governors in New Jersey and Utah issue such declarations in consultation with the state health officer; and state health officers can act on their own to declare a public health emergency in Florida, South Dakota, and Texas.

Grounds for Emergency Declarations

State statutes also specify *types* of emergencies arising from a set of underlying conditions. The emergency types are not consistent across states. Vermont law, for example, allows the governor to declare an emergency on nine grounds, but only specifies an "all-hazards event" as a distinct type of emergency.[13] In contrast, Minnesota law allows the governor to declare an emergency on thirteen grounds and specifies nine types of emergencies: an unspecified "emergency," major disaster, and emergencies related to public health, nuclear power plants, energy supply, national security, peacetime, air pollution, and local events.[14]

The large majority of state EP laws allow state officers to interpret the law broadly in the course of responding to an emergency. These clauses allow the state to take action that is not otherwise authorized by statute, provided they are not prohibited by the state constitution. These provisions typically allow a liberal interpretation of the EP law and leave the door open for officials to declare an emergency under conditions that are not explicitly mentioned in the statute. The former, sometimes referred to as a *construction clause*, allows state officers to broadly interpret or construe the EP laws to take any action deemed necessary in an emergency. "Catchall" emergency clauses, on the other hand, make it clear that the list of conditions under which an emergency declaration can be made is not exhaustive.

Forty states include a provision in their EP statutes that allows for broad or "liberally construed" interpretation. Alaska's EP law, for example, features a final provision entitled "Liberality of Construction": "This chapter shall be construed liberally in order to carry out its purposes" (Alaska Sec. 26.20.190). In the same chapter of Alaska law, the section on the governor's exercise of EP suggests a broad interpretation: "the Governor has and may exercise the additional emergency power . . . to perform and exercise other functions, powers, and duties that are considered necessary to promote and secure the safety and protection of the civilian population."[15]

Thirty-eight states contain a catchall emergency clause that allows state officers to declare emergencies under conditions that are not listed in the EP law. Statutory lists of emergency conditions tend to include language like "including, but not limited to" that can be construed to cover conditions and events that the legislature failed to mention in the law.

Renewal of Emergency Proclamations

Although all states and territories have constitutional or statutory authority to declare emergencies, fewer (thirty-three plus the District of Columbia and four territories) allow for the renewal of EP once they are invoked. Even in states where declarations may not be renewed, however, there are provisions for a new declaration to be issued such that de facto renewal is permitted (California, Hawaii, and West Virginia).

The governor may unilaterally renew emergency declarations in twenty-three states, in seventeen of which the governor has the sole authority to renew.[16] Four of those states allow the legislature to renew a declaration independent of the governor (Alabama, Ohio, Pennsylvania, and Rhode Island), and Texas allows the public health commissioner to independently renew public health emergencies. In Illinois and Mississippi the question of renewal seems to be uncertain.

Terminating Emergency Proclamations

Responsibility for ending states of emergency is spread more broadly. In twenty-three states the governor *or* the legislature can do so, and in nine states the legislature alone can terminate emergencies. In two states an emergency declaration can be automatically terminated after an initial renewal period (South Dakota) or if the legislature is not in session (Montana). Two other states (Connecticut and Iowa) allow a joint legislative council to terminate a governor's declaration. Ohio permits the director of the state's emergency management to terminate an emergency declaration in consultation with the governor.

As of mid-2021, some states have already terminated their emergency declarations associated with the COVID-19 pandemic. In some cases the governor self-terminated the declaration, and in other cases the legislature did so (Idaho, for example).

Illustration: Emergency Declarations in California

This section outlines the constitutional and statutory provisions that govern emergency powers in California, the first state to declare an emergency when the COVID pandemic began in the US. The Golden State has a long history of managing emergencies, from natural disasters like wildfires and earthquakes to public health crises like HIV/AIDS and the Mediterranean fruit fly infestations. The laws discussed below were in place at the start of the 2020 coronavirus pandemic.

California's emergency powers are primarily detailed in statutes, although the state constitution does allow for the legislature to expedite the process for passing emergency bills. Article IV of the state constitution requires the legislature to post the final version of any bill online for at least seventy-two hours before a final vote can be taken. The governor may waive the so-called notice period by submitting a letter to the legislature stating the bill is necessary to address an emergency for which the governor has already made a declaration. That is to say, the notice period cannot be waived unless the governor has previously declared an emergency. *Emergency* is defined in a separate section of the state constitution, Article XIII:

> As used in this paragraph, "emergency" means the existence, as declared by the Governor, of conditions of disaster or of extreme peril to the safety of persons and property within the State, or parts thereof, caused by such conditions as attack or probable or imminent attack by an enemy of the United States, fire, flood, drought, storm, civil disorder, earthquake, or volcanic eruption" (California Constitution, Article XIII B, Section 3).

A governor's waiver alone, however, is insufficient to suspend the seventy-two-hour notice period in the California legislature. Two-thirds of the membership, in whichever house the notice will be waived, must concur with the governor's waiver in a recorded roll call vote (California Constitution, Article IV, Section 8(2)).

Article IV of California's constitution includes a provision for the governor to declare a *fiscal emergency* in the event that state revenues are expected to be substantially higher or lower than the estimates upon which the most recent budget was based. Upon declaring a fiscal emergency, the governor convenes a special session of the legislature and tasks them with passing a bill to address the emergency. The governor is obligated to submit the emergency proclamation to the legislature along with proposed legislation to solve the problem. If the legislature fails to pass a bill to send to the governor "to address the fiscal emergency" within forty-five days of the proclamation, the constitution prohibits the legislature from (a) considering other bills or (b) adjourning to recess until such a bill is passed (California Constitution, Article IV, Section 10f).

Aside from the seventy-two-hour waiver and procedures for a fiscal emergency, the majority of California's emergency powers are governed by statutes and rules. Chapter 7 of the California Government Code, referred to as the California Emergency Services Act, outlines the powers available to the state government in an emergency event. Article XIII, Sections 8625–8629, lays out the governor's powers specifically. The governor of California is solely responsible for declaring an emergency; we could find no provision for the legislature to make such a declaration. The legislature may, however, terminate an emergency declaration by passing a concurrent resolution. The governor may also terminate an emergency at any point after the initial declaration.

In addition to the emergency conditions listed in the state constitution, Article II of the California Emergency Services Act specifies three broad types of emergencies: state of war emergency, state of emergency, and local emergency. The list of conditions is extensive and worth quoting at length. The conditions for a "state of emergency" and "local emergency" are identical except for the geographic scope:

"State of emergency" means the duly proclaimed existence of conditions of disaster or of extreme peril to the safety of persons and property within the state caused by conditions such as air pollution, fire, flood, storm, epidemic, riot, drought, cyberterrorism, sudden and severe energy shortage, plant or animal infestation or disease, the Governor's warning of an earthquake or volcanic prediction, or an earthquake, or other conditions, other than conditions resulting from a labor controversy or conditions causing a "state of war emergency," which, by reason of their magnitude, are or are likely to be beyond the control of the services, personnel, equipment, and facilities of any single county, city and county, or city and require the combined forces of a mutual aid region or regions to combat, or with respect to regulated energy utilities, a sudden and severe energy shortage requires extraordinary measures beyond the authority vested in the California Public Utilities Commission (Article II, Section 8558).

An emergency declaration made by the governor expires after sixty days and cannot be renewed per se, although the governor may issue an identical order to continue the state of emergency if conditions persist. Governor Newsom initially declared a state of emergency for the coronavirus pandemic in March 2020 and has issued subsequent declarations every sixty days or so to continue the state's public health measures. The emergency powers themselves are broadly construed in the first article of the statute. The California Emergency Services Act was passed, according to the statute, in order to "authorize the establishment of such organizations and the taking of such actions as are necessary and proper to carry out the provisions of this chapter" (Section 8550).

Emergency Powers Available to State Governments before 2020

In this section, we discuss the powers that are available to state governments during a declared emergency. As previously mentioned, these powers are largely defined by statutes and not by the state constitutions. Nearly all states have "emergency management" laws that enumerate the powers available to the governor and other executive branch officers during an emergency, the mission and leadership structure of the state's emergency management agency, and the laws, rules, and regulations that are automatically invoked or triggered by an emergency declaration. Next, we describe several common features that are found in EP laws across the country, with an emphasis on powers that accrue to the governor, state emergency management agencies, public health officials, and (to a lesser degree) local governments.

Emergency Powers in the State Executive Branches

Each state assigns EP to the governor's office. Each state also features an emergency management (EM) agency that shares power with the governor and other entities in the executive branch. Typically the governor appoints the leader of the EM agency, and the governor might delegate the responsibility for developing a plan or assessing needs to the EM agency. In the case of a pandemic or other public health emergency, the governor might delegate authority to the state health agency.

About three-quarters of the states (thirty-five states, three territories, and the District of Columbia) feature a statutory requirement for the governor and/or the state emergency management agency (forty-six states, all territories, and the District of Columbia) to develop a plan for responding to emergencies.[17] State laws do not offer many specifics about the plan in question, but in a general sense they entrust to the executive branch the responsibility for devising a strategy for any future emergency events. Later, we summarize a few specific aspects of the planning process, such as creating evacuation plans.

The statute that created Missouri's emergency response agency is typical of other states: "There is hereby created within the department of public safety, the 'State Emergency Management Agency', for the general purpose of assisting in coordination of national, state and local activities related to emergency functions by coordinating response, recovery, planning and mitigation."[18] Another provision allows the Missouri governor to "[e]nforce and put into operation all plans, rules and regulations relating to disasters and emergency management of resources adopted under this law and to assume direct operational control of all emergency forces and volunteers in the state."[19]

Executive branch officials are also required to assess the needs of the area(s) affected by an emergency, or to develop a plan for assessing the risks and potential needs of such areas prior to an emergency, in thirty-eight states as well as the District of Columbia and four of five territories.[20]

Although the federal district is led by a mayor, not a governor, District of Columbia law gives us a typical example of how state and territorial agencies are tasked with emergency preparedness and readiness:

> The Director shall develop a Homeland Security Program to identify and mitigate threats, risks, and vulnerabilities within the District of Columbia. The program shall include, but not be limited to: (1) Identifying public infrastructure and other public assets in the District that need protection, assessing vulnerability, and addressing priority needs; (2) Establishing measurable readiness priorities and targets that balance the potential threat and magnitude of terrorist attacks, major disasters, and other emergencies with the resources required to prevent, respond to, and recover from them; (3) Establishing readiness metrics and performance measures for preparedness in the areas of prevention, protection, response, and recovery; (4) Assisting residents and public and private entities in emergency preparedness; (5) Coordinating with federal, state, and regional authorities, and with private entities; and (6) Developing a budget to implement the Program.[21]

Suspending and Amending State Laws and Rules

Perhaps one of the most wide-ranging, and therefore controversial, powers that accrue to governors in an emergency is the ability to suspend, amend, or otherwise modify laws and rules that existed in the state before the emergency.[22] State officials can suspend many different laws during an emergency when compliance with the law would be onerous, expensive, or dangerous. Examples include enacting special rules about personal liability in a disaster zone, waiving licensing requirements for out-of-state first responders, and empowering state agents to coerce individuals to evacuate or perform certain actions (e.g., immunizations). Forty-two of the states allow governors to suspend laws during an emergency (as well as all territories but Puerto Rico).[23]

The language in Alabama law is typical of clauses that legitimize the governor's emergency actions and allows for existing laws to be suspended in the course of responding to an emergency: "All orders, rules, and regulations promulgated by the Governor as authorized by this article shall have the full force and effect of law when a copy thereof is filed in the office of the Secretary of State. All existing laws, ordinances, rules, and regulations or parts thereof inconsistent with the provisions of this article or of any order, rule, or regulation issued under the authority of this article, shall be suspended during the period of time and to the extent that such inconsistency exists."[24]

Arizona law goes into greater detail about the types of laws and rules that are eligible for gubernatorial suspension: "During a state of war emergency, the governor may . . . suspend the provisions of any statute prescribing the procedure for conduct of state business, or the orders or rules of any state agency, if the governor determines and declares that strict compliance with the provisions of any such statute, order or rule would in any way prevent, hinder or delay mitigation of the effects of the emergency."[25]

Apart from suspending state laws, forty-two states allow governors to suspend orders, regulations, and/or rules (as do all territories but American Samoa and the District of Columbia).[26] Delaware law says, "In performing the duties of the Governor under this chapter, the Governor may issue, amend and rescind all necessary executive orders, emergency orders, proclamations and regulations, which shall have the force and effect of law."[27]

The law in the Northern Mariana Islands echoes similar provisions stateside:

> During a state of major disaster or a state significant emergency, the Governor may: (1) Suspend the provision of any administrative regulation prescribing procedures for conducting Commonwealth business or the other order, rules and administrative regulations of any other Commonwealth agency if strict compliance would prevent, hinder, or delay necessary actions, including the making of emergency purchases, by the CNMI Homeland Security and Emergency Management authority to respond to the major disaster or a state significant emergency, or if strict compliance would increase the threat to the community, environment, critical infrastructures and/ or key resources.[28]

One provision that is commonly mentioned as being eligible for emergency suspension relates to hiring during an emergency. Half of all the states (plus the District of Columbia) allow the government to waive civil service or merit-based requirements for emergency hires.[29] In Florida, local subdivisions have "power and authority to waive the procedures and formalities otherwise required of the political subdivision by law pertaining to . . . employment of permanent and temporary workers."[30]

Illinois law goes into greater detail, and illustrates the types of requirements many of these states have in mind for waivers:

> If a disaster occurs, each political subdivision may exercise the powers vested under this Section in the light of the exigencies of the disaster and, excepting mandatory constitutional requirements, without regard to the procedures and formalities normally prescribed by law pertaining to the performance of public work, entering into contracts, the incurring of obligations, the employment of temporary workers, the rental of equipment, the purchase of supplies and materials, and the appropriation, expenditure, and disposition of public funds and property.[31]

Although the majority of states empower governors to suspend existing laws that may hinder emergency response, fewer states empower the governor to amend laws (four states) or to create new laws during an emergency (three states).[32]

Commanding Police and State Military Forces

In all states and territories, the governor plays a direct or indirect role in commanding the state police forces (e.g., highway patrol, state police department), the state's National Guard unit, and (where applicable) the state's defense forces, commonly referred to as SDFs or state militias. All of the states have a National Guard unit, all of which were activated to respond to the coronavirus pandemic in some way, and the governor assumes commander-in-chief status when an emergency is declared.[33] State defense forces date back to World War I, when many states sought to create a reserve of volunteer personnel who might respond to civil unrest or foreign attacks while the military was deployed to Europe. As of 2020, twenty-one states and Puerto Rico had an active SDF and twenty-three states plus Guam had inactive units.[34]

The governor is the commander-in-chief of the state military forces—the National Guard and State Defense Forces (where applicable)—according to the state constitution in all states except Massachusetts, where the adjutant general holds that position.[35] The Bay State, however, features a statute that designates the governor as commander-in-chief of the state military forces during an emergency. Thirty-seven states also have statutes that reinforce the governor's constitutional authority.[36] Governors in forty-seven states and the District of Columbia are also allowed to commandeer local police during an emergency.[37]

Minnesota law is illustrative of state provisions that empower the governor to redirect state and local resources in response to an emergency: "When the public interest requires it because of an imminent emergency, the governor may authorize and direct the police, firefighting, health, or other force of a political subdivision, called the sending political subdivision, to go to the assistance of another political subdivision, called the receiving political subdivision, and to take and use the personnel, equipment, and supplies of the sending political subdivision as the governor may direct."[38]

Although governors have broad powers to direct police resources, they are prevented in many states from making permanent changes to jurisdiction of local police forces (fifteen states and three territories).[39] Idaho's limitation on this power is typical of other states: "Nothing in this act shall be construed to . . . affect the jurisdiction or responsibilities of police forces, fire fighting forces, local emergency medical service (EMS) agencies licensed by the state department of health and welfare EMS bureau, units of the armed forces of the United States, or of any personnel thereof, when on active duty; but state, local, and intergovernmental disaster emergency plans shall place reliance upon the forces available for performance of functions related to disaster emergencies."[40]

Confiscating Private Property

State laws empower the governor and state agents to confiscate private property to a wide-ranging degree during an emergency. State officials are explicitly permitted to confiscate land and buildings (e.g., medical facilities) in forty states as well as Guam, the Northern Mariana Islands, Puerto Rico, and the US Virgin Islands.[41] A similar clause allows the government to confiscate any private property that might be deemed necessary for emergency response in forty-one states, the District of Columbia, and all five US territories.[42] In fifteen states, public officials are specifically allowed to confiscate medical supplies in the course of responding to an emergency.[43]

Restricting Sales and Regulating Prices

In addition to granting broad powers to confiscate private property, laws in six states also empower state officials to enact general price freezes in areas under an emergency declaration and to control the prices of various goods.[44] The governor is empowered to enact price controls on food in seventeen states (plus the District of Columbia and three territories) and controls on energy and fuel prices in fifteen states (plus two territories).[45] States can also enact rules to ration goods during an emergency (e.g., food, water, fuel) in nine states (plus the District of Columbia and three territories).[46] Especially relevant at the onset of the COVID pandemic, some officials were empowered to enact price controls (six states and two territories) or rationing (four states plus two territories)[47] for medical supplies such as pharmaceuticals, first aid materials, and personal protective equipment (PPE). Nineteen states, the District of Columbia, and two territories explicitly prohibit price gouging, or price increases above a certain amount, during an emergency.[48]

Many states feature laws that limit the sale of certain items during an emergency, or empower state officials to enact such limits under the right conditions. Pennsylvania law is typical: "The governor may . . . suspend or limit the sale, dispensing or transportation of alcoholic beverages, firearms, explosives and combustibles."[49] Commonly restricted items include alcohol (thirty states plus the District of Columbia and the US Virgin Islands [USVI]), firearms (twenty-eight states plus the District of Columbia and USVI), and combustibles (twenty-eight states plus USVI).[50]

In addition to these items deemed too dangerous for sale during an emergency, some states also allow for emergency restrictions on medical procedures (nineteen states and no territories).[51] No states had a law prior to 2020 that explicitly prohibited abortion procedures during an emergency, although some states attempted to create such restrictions during the coronavirus pandemic.[52]

Regulating Movement, Transportation, and Evacuations

In the course of an emergency, states might find it appropriate to evacuate residents from an area that is impacted or threatened by emergency conditions. Examples that readily come to mind include evacuations from coastal zones in the path of a hurricane, communities in the shadow of an erupting volcano, or homeowners living in a forest threatened by wildfire. Forty-six states feature a law that explicitly allows the government to enact compulsory evacuations.[53] Many states empower the governor in particular to order evacuations and to prepare plans for such events. Montana law is typical: "[The governor may] direct and compel the evacuation of all or part of the population from an emergency or disaster area within the state if the governor considers this action necessary for the preservation of life or other disaster mitigation, response, or recovery."[54] Even when residents are not required to evacuate a space, the government may also enact mandatory curfews to limit travel or business for a time period (forty-six states plus the District of Columbia and five territories).[55]

Iowa law empowers the governor to enact a curfew that prevents individuals from gathering in public spaces: "The governor may, during the existence of a state of public disorder emergency, prohibit . . . [a]ny person being in a public place during the hours declared by the governor to be a period of curfew if this period does not exceed twelve hours in any one day and if its area of its application is specifically designated."[56] Iowa, like a majority of states, also empowers the governor to limit the size of public gatherings.

Many jurisdictions empower the state health agency to evacuate people from an area or facility that is linked to a public health emergency. In the territory of Guam, for example, the public health authority can "close, direct and compel the evacuation of, or to decontaminate or cause to be decontaminated any facility of which there is reasonable cause to believe that it may endanger the public health."[57]

In addition to ordering a mandatory evacuation, state officials may also be empowered to restrict travel by individuals (forty-one states and four territories).[58] In Virginia the governor is entrusted to make these decisions: "[The governor] may direct and compel evacuation of all or part of the populace from any stricken or threatened area if this action is deemed necessary for the preservation of life, implement emergency mitigation, preparedness, response or recovery actions; prescribe routes, modes of transportation and destination in connection with evacuation; and control ingress and egress at an emergency area, including the movement of persons within the area and the occupancy of premises therein."[59]

Apart from general restrictions on travel, state officials can restrict automobile traffic and other motorized travel on public roads (forty-five states and four territories).[60] The law in the Northern Mariana Islands grants the territory's executive branch control over the roads: "[State officials are empowered] to prescribe routes, modes of transportation, and destinations in consultation with public safety authorities or the provision of emergency services. (ii) To control or limit ingress and egress to and from any stricken or threatened public area, the movement of persons within the area, and the occupancy of premises therein, if such action is reasonable and necessary to respond to the major disaster or a state."[61]

In two states, Alaska and Utah, the state law explicitly allows the state emergency management agency to create checkpoints in order to control travel in the state. In the Last Frontier State, the Division of Homeland Security and Civil Defense is permitted to "establish and operate checkpoints along private or public roadways serving critical property or facilities in the state, at the direction of the governor when the governor determines that a sufficiently high threat of enemy or terrorist attack exists to warrant the action."[62]

Mandating Vaccination and Other Public Health Powers

All states and territories had laws prior to 2020 that allowed for mandatory quarantines during an emergency. Only Minnesota and Puerto Rico did not explicitly define the penalty for violating a mandatory quarantine; most states impose a monetary penalty such as a civil fine, short-term imprisonment, or a criminal charge such as a misdemeanor or contempt.

Other states allow government officials to coerce individuals into quarantine. In New York, for example, a public health law relates to the "control of dangerous and careless patients" who refuse to quarantine after being diagnosed with a communicable disease. Local health officials can work in concert with local courts to "commit the said person to any hospital or institution established for the care of persons suffering from any such communicable disease or maintaining a room, ward or wards for such persons."[63]

Twenty-six states and four territories have laws that explicitly allowed the government to require vaccinations.[64] Massachusetts, for example, empowers local health authorities to require vaccinations: "Boards of health, if in their opinion it is necessary for public health or safety, shall require and enforce the vaccination and revaccination of all the inhabitants of their towns, and shall provide them with the means of free vaccination. Whoever refuses or neglects to comply with such requirement shall forfeit five dollars."[65]

Puerto Rico's compulsory vaccination law, dating back to 1912 (updated in 1945), empowers the island's health authority to require immunizations: "The inoculation of vaccine virus is hereby declared obligatory and binding upon all the inhabitants of the Commonwealth during such period and under such form and interval of time as the Secretary of Health may determine; the inoculation of any other organic, prophylactic, or therapeutic product in cases of epidemic being also obligatory."[66]

Other states list the conditions under which an individual can refuse a mandatory vaccine, such as in Wisconsin: "the [state health] department, as the public health authority, may do all of the following as necessary to address a public health emergency: (a) Order any individual to receive a vaccination unless the vaccination is reasonably likely to lead to serious harm to the individual or unless the individual, for reasons of religion or conscience, refuses to obtain the vaccination."[67]

Even if the law does not explicitly allow compulsory vaccinations, states typically have rules or regulations that include immunization recommendations or contingency plans for quarantining individuals who refuse a mandatory vaccine. Similarly, twelve states explicitly call for the state health agency to conduct contact tracing during a public health crisis, although other states may allow contact tracing under other public health rules.[68] In New York, for example, the public health code requires physicians and institutions such as hospitals to report cases of "communicable disease" to local public health officials.[69]

Restrictions on Emergency Powers

Many state EP laws include a chapter that lists limitations placed on the state government in the course of exercising the aforementioned powers. A majority of states feature such a general provision that limits EP (twenty-nine states plus three territories).[70] A typical limitations chapter starts with the clause, "Nothing in this Act shall be construed to," followed by a list of prohibitions. Common clauses found across the states include protections for the press, limits on firearms confiscation, and prohibitions against emergency agencies intervening in political activity and labor disputes. We provide a few examples of such provisions below.

Several states include a carve-out clause that protects members of the press from state interference during an emergency (twenty-two states plus two territories).[71] As the law in Rhode Island illustrates, however, some of these laws also open the door for the government to co-opt private resources to transmit public information: "Nothing in this chapter shall be construed . . . to interfere with dissemination of news or comment on public affairs; but any communications facility or organization (including but not limited to radio or television stations, wire services, and newspapers) may be required to transmit or print public service messages furnishing information or instructions in connection with a disaster emergency."[72]

Nine states go a step further and include protections for "first informer broadcasters" such as local television and radio stations.[73] Such clauses allow broadcast employees to enter otherwise restricted areas during an emergency to repair important infrastructure. Arizona's law is typical: "To the extent practicable and consistent with not endangering public safety or inhibiting recovery efforts, state and local government agencies shall allow a first informer broadcaster to access an area affected by an emergency or disaster to restore, repair or resupply any facility or equipment critical to the ability of a broadcaster to acquire, produce and transmit essential emergency or disaster related public information programming, including repairing and maintaining transmitters and generators and transporting fuel for generators."[74]

State laws regarding "first informer" status were superseded by a new federal law, signed by President Donald Trump, that extended first informer broadcast protections to local television and radio operators across the country. An omnibus bill incorporated an industry-backed bill, the Securing Access to Networks in Disasters Act, to grant local broadcasters the ability to access infrastructure, including towers and studios, during an emergency.[75]

Second Amendment protections are a common feature across the country. They appear to transcend region and political leaning (thirty-five states).[76] These clauses provide a carve-out for private firearms owners against government confiscation during an emergency. A typical clause prohibits the government from using EP to confiscate firearms from an otherwise law-abiding resident. Tennessee's law, for example, states: "During any state of emergency, major disaster or natural disaster, the state, a political subdivision or a public official shall not prohibit nor impose additional restrictions on the lawful possession, transfer, sale, transport, carrying, storage, display or use of firearms and ammunition or firearm and ammunition components."[77]

Utah law goes into greater detail about the limits placed on state agents when it comes to confiscating firearms:

> During a declared state of emergency or local emergency under this part: (a) neither the governor nor an agency of a governmental entity or political subdivision of the state may impose restrictions, which were not in force before the declared state of emergency, on the lawful possession, transfer, sale, transport, storage, display, or use of a firearm or

ammunition; and (b) an individual, while acting or purporting to act on behalf of the state or a political subdivision of the state, may not confiscate a privately owned firearm of another individual.[78]

The law goes further to stipulate that individuals can pursue civil action against an officer who confiscates a firearm and that law enforcement officers are empowered to refuse an order to confiscate firearms if given by a superior officer.

While prohibitions on gun restrictions are not surprising in southern and rural states, the differences between red states and blue states are less pronounced than one might expect, given the polarization of the gun control issue in American politics. In blue Oregon, for example, the law specifies: "A unit of government may not seize a firearm from an individual who lawfully possesses the firearm during a state of emergency declared under [the emergency powers law]. If a unit of government seizes a firearm from an individual during a state of emergency in violation of this section, the individual may recover from the unit of government that seized the firearm all costs incurred in the recovery of the firearm, including attorney fees, court costs and any other costs incurred in the recovery of the firearm."[79]

Hawaii law also protects gun owners during emergencies: "No person or government entity shall seize or confiscate, under any emergency or disaster relief powers or functions conferred, or during any emergency period . . . or during any time of national emergency or crisis . . . any firearm or ammunition from any individual who is lawfully permitted to carry or possess the firearm or ammunition . . . who carries, possesses, or uses the firearm or ammunition in a lawful manner and in accordance with the criminal laws of this State."[80]

A law in blue but libertarian-leaning New Hampshire empowers the governor to confiscate a wide range of real and personal property during an emergency, conditional on the advice and consent of the New Hampshire executive council. The governor has the power to seize, among other items, high explosives, motor vehicles, aircraft, ships and boats, railroad cars, buses, horses, cattle, poultry, clothing, medical supplies, "provisions for man or beast," and fuel, including gasoline.[81] Emergency powers in the Granite State cannot, however, infringe upon private gun ownership: "Under no circumstances shall this section be construed to authorize the taking, confiscation, or seizure of firearms, ammunition, or ammunition components."[82]

In addition to the First and Second Amendment carve-outs found in many state EP laws, there are also a handful of common restrictions placed on the use of EP and the conduct of the state emergency management agency. Dating back to the early Cold War period, when many states were creating civil defense agencies for the first time, state law prohibits officials from using their emergency powers to intervene in political activity (twenty-three states and Guam).[83] A Connecticut law dating back to 1951, for example, says that "[n]o organization for civil preparedness established under the authority of [the emergency management law] shall be used directly or indirectly for political purposes."[84] Wyoming law contains a similar provision: "No homeland security program established under the authority of this act shall participate in any form of political activity or be employed directly or indirectly for political purposes."[85] The key phrases in these clauses, "political purposes" and "political activity," are undefined.

A provision similar to the prohibition on political activity also prevents the state's emergency powers in general, and the emergency management agency in particular, from intervening in labor disputes (eighteen states plus American Samoa and CNMI).[86] In theory, such clauses prevent a governor from deploying state forces to resolve a strike, although such laws frequently contain language that might allow for intervention when health or safety is at risk. North Dakota's prohibition against labor interventions is typical: "Nothing in this chapter may [allow state agents to] interfere with the course or conduct of a labor dispute, except that actions otherwise authorized by this chapter or other laws may be taken when necessary to forestall or mitigate imminent or existing danger to public health or safety."[87]

Emergency Preparedness and State Executive Agencies

In addition to placing limits on the exercise of emergency powers, nearly all states feature laws that delineate who has the authority to enforce the emergency laws (forty-five states plus the District of Columbia and five territories).[88] The particular official that is empowered varies from state to state, although always located in the executive branch. In Ohio, "[t]he director of public safety . . . shall adopt, may amend or rescind, and shall enforce rules with respect to the emergency management of the state for the purpose of providing protection for its people against any hazard."[89] Other states disperse the power to local agencies, as in West Virginia:

> It shall be the duty of every organization for emergency services established pursuant to this article and of the officers thereof to execute and enforce such orders, rules and regulations as may be made by the Governor under this article. Each such organization shall have at its office available for public inspection all such orders, rules and regulations of the Governor.[90]

Penalties for Violating EP Laws

A majority of states also specify what penalties can be levied against individuals who violate the state's EP (thirty-three states plus the District of Columbia and four territories).[91] Mississippi law, for example, says, "Any person violating any provision of this article or any rule, order, or regulation made pursuant to this article shall, upon conviction thereof, be punishable by a fine not exceeding five hundred dollars ($500.00) or imprisonment for not exceeding six (6) months or both."[92]

The penalties for violating the state's emergency law(s) varies considerably. Whereas Mississippi assesses a fine not to exceed $500, states like Michigan limit fines to $100 while others, like Kansas, allow fines up to $2,500. Kentucky law increases the penalty after the first offense, with a $100 fine for the first violation of the state's emergency laws, and a fine up to $250 for each subsequent offense.[93] Some states threaten jail time for violating the state emergency law(s). In New Jersey, for example, the courts are given the discretion to subject an offender to "imprisonment for a term not to exceed 6 months or shall pay a fine not to exceed $1,000.00 or to both a fine and imprisonment."[94]

Liability Immunity for the State and First Responders

While a majority of states specify the penalties for violating EP laws, many states also offer protection to state workers, shelter providers, and the state itself, in the course of responding to an emergency. These laws grant immunity from liability in the event that someone is injured or suffers materially from actions taken during an emergency. Just seven states do not have liability immunity for the state government during an emergency.[95] Colorado is typical of the majority of states that offer immunity to the state and its agents: "Neither the state nor the members of the expert emergency epidemic response committee designated or appointed pursuant to [the emergency management law] are liable for any claim based upon the committee's advice to the governor or the alleged negligent exercise or performance of, or failure to exercise or perform an act relating to an emergency epidemic."[96]

All states except Maryland offer liability immunity to first responders. Arkansas law states:

> All functions under this chapter and all other activities relating to emergency management are declared to be governmental functions. No emergency responder, except in cases of willful misconduct, gross negligence, or bad faith, when complying with or reasonably attempting to comply with this chapter, or any other rule or regulation promulgated pursuant to the provisions of this section or pursuant to any ordinance relating to blackout or other precautionary measures enacted by any

political subdivision of the state, shall be liable for the death of or injury to persons, or for damage to property, as a result of any such activity. The immunity . . . shall extend to both emergency responders who are employees and to qualified emergency responders who are volunteers.[97]

Finally, a majority of states extend liability immunity to individuals and entities that provide shelter during an emergency, such as the owner of a large facility that is being used to house evacuees. Just ten states do not provide liability immunity for private individuals who provide shelter in an emergency on their land or property.[98]

Georgia's law is typical of other immunity clauses for shelter providers:

> When any person, firm, or corporation owning or controlling any real estate or other premises authorizes and permits any emergency management agency, board, or other authority of this state or of any political subdivision of this state to use the premises without charge therefor for the purpose of sheltering persons during an actual or practice emergency or disaster . . . the person, firm, or corporation, at such times and for such periods during which the premises are occupied and actually employed for purpose of emergency management, shall be clothed with the sovereign immunity of the state. No civil action shall be brought or maintained against any such person, firm, or corporation to recover damages for personal injuries or death of any person while on the premises during an actual or practice emergency, disaster, or enemy attack, or for the loss or destruction of personal property brought upon the premises by any person seeking shelter thereon during an actual or practice emergency or disaster.[99]

Conclusion

This chapter has summarized the EP available to the American states and territories at the beginning of the COVID-19 pandemic in 2020.

As these powers were employed during 2020–21, however, their operation provoked legislatures and citizens to attempt to modify them, mostly in the direction of restricting their use. Such ongoing attempts are the subject of chapter 8.

Notes

Appendix 1, which contains the database compiled for this chapter, may be found at https://www.hoover.org/research/who-governs-emergency-powers-time-covid.

1. The states that lack a constitutional provision for emergency powers are Alabama, Hawaii, Idaho, Illinois, Mississippi, Tennessee, Utah, Vermont, and Virginia, as well as American Samoa and Puerto Rico. The District of Columbia, Guam, and the US Virgin Islands do not have constitutions.

2. The median state constitution was adopted in 1890, but the states that lack constitutional provisions for EP are older on average (1892 vs. 1987 in states with constitutional emergency powers provisions).

3. Ariz. Const. art. IV, part 2, § 25, "Continuity of governmental operations in emergency."

4. S.C. Const. art. XVII, § 12.

5. Ark. Const. art. V, § 1.

6. Del. Const. art. XVII, § 1.

7. National Conference of State Legislatures, "Continuity of Legislature during Emergency," April 26, 2021, https://www.ncsl.org/research/about-state-legislatures/continuity-of-legislature-during-emergency.aspx.

8. See also the NCSL tracker of how state governments adapted their legislative practices to the coronavirus pandemic: National Conference of State Legislatures, "COVID-19: State Actions Related to Legislative Operations," August 4, 2021, https://www.ncsl.org/research/about-state-legislatures/covid-19-state-actions-related-to-legislative-operations.aspx.

9. Jim Camden, "'It's about The Big One': Amendment Would Give State Legislature Broad Powers in Case of Catastrophe," *Spokesman-Review*, October 24, 2019, https://www.spokesman.com/stories/2019/oct/04/its-about-the-big-one-amendment-would-give-state-l.

10. Dean Takko, "Guest Column: State Constitutional Amendment Would Prepare State for Natural Catastrophes," *Chinook Observer*, October 28, 2019, https://www.chinookobserver.com/opinion/columns/guest-column-state-constitutional-amendment-would-prepare-state-for-natural-catastrophes/article_61368d8e-f9b2-11e9-a0bb-930f9d5c6707.html.

11. "How Lawmakers Thwart Voters with Bogus Emergencies: Editorial," *The Oregonian*, August 17, 2015.

12. Fla. Const. art. VI, § 5(a).

13. Vermont law allows the governor to declare an emergency on the following grounds: natural disaster; health or disease-related emergency; accident; civil insurrection; use of weapons of mass destruction; terrorist or criminal incident; radiological incident; significant event; designated special event. (Vt. Stat. Ann. tit. 20, § 2.)

14. Minn. Stat. § 12.31. Minnesota law allows the governor to declare an emergency on the following grounds: public health emergency (bioterrorism or a new, novel, or previously controlled or eradicated airborne infectious agent or airborne biological toxin); major disaster/national security emergency (enemy sabotage or other hostile action); peacetime emergency (an act of nature, a technological failure or malfunction, a terrorist incident, an industrial accident, a hazardous materials accident, or a civil disturbance).

15. Alaska Stat. § 26.20.040 (1995).

16. The seventeen states that grant the governor sole authority to renew an emergency declaration are: Arkansas, Colorado, Delaware, Florida, Georgia, Idaho, Indiana, Iowa, Louisiana, Maine, Maryland, New Hampshire, New Mexico, New York, Oklahoma, South Dakota, Tennessee. The five additional states that grant both the governor and legislature unilateral power to renew declarations are Alabama, Ohio, Oregon, Pennsylvania, and Rhode Island. Texas grants both the governor and state health commissioner unilateral power to renew declarations.

17. The states without a statute requirement for the governor to develop a plan are Alaska, Arkansas, Kansas, Kentucky, Michigan, New Hampshire, New Jersey, Ohio, Oregon, Pennsylvania, South Dakota, Tennessee, Texas, Utah, and Washington, as well as Guam and Puerto Rico. The states that do not require the EM agency to develop a plan are Massachusetts, New Mexico, New York, and West Virginia. The governor directly appoints the head of these agencies in most cases (thirty-six states, the District of Columbia, and all territories except Puerto Rico).

18. Mo. Rev. Stat. § 44.020.

19. Mo. Rev. Stat. § 44.100 (3a).

20. The states without a law requiring assessing the needs of area(s) affected by an emergency are Connecticut, Florida, Hawaii, Idaho, Maryland, Massachusetts, New Hampshire, New Jersey, New Mexico, Oklahoma, Wisconsin, and Wyoming, as well as American Samoa.

21. D.C. Code § 7-2231.03.

22. Kelly Thompson and Nicholas Anderson, "Emergency Suspension Powers," The Policy Surveillance Program, June 21, 2017, https://www.lawatlas.org/datasets/emergency-powers.

23. The states that do not allow governors to suspend laws during an emergency are Kentucky, Massachusetts, Nevada, New Mexico, Ohio, Vermont, Virginia, and Wyoming, as well as Puerto Rico.

24. Ala. Code § 31-9-13 (2016).

25. Ariz. Rev. Stat § 26-303 (A1).

26. The states that do not allow governors to suspend orders, regulations, and/or rules are Kentucky, Massachusetts, Nevada, New Mexico, Ohio, Vermont, Virginia, and Wyoming, plus the District of Columbia and American Samoa.

27. Del. Code tit. 20, § 3115b (2018).

28. 1 CMC § 20144 (c)(1).

29. The states that allow for the waiver of hiring requirements during an emergency are Alabama, Arizona, California, Delaware, District of Columbia, Florida, Hawaii, Idaho, Illinois, Indiana, Kansas, Maine, Massachusetts, Michigan, Minnesota, Mississippi, New Jersey, New York, North Dakota, Oklahoma, Pennsylvania, Rhode Island, Texas, Washington, West Virginia, and Wisconsin.

30. Fla. Stat. § 252.38 (5d).

31. 20 Ill. Comp. Stat. § 3305/10 (j).

32. The states that empower the governor to amend laws during an emergency are Connecticut, Iowa, New Hampshire, and North Carolina. The states that empower the governor to create new laws during an emergency are Minnesota, New Hampshire, and North Carolina.

33. National Guard units were activated in the states to perform various tasks, including transporting medical supplies, transporting patients, contact tracing, COVID testing, and administering vaccinations.

34. The six states without a state defense force are Arizona, Montana, Nevada, North Dakota, West Virginia, and Wyoming.

35. Puerto Rico is the only territory that enshrines the governor's commander in chief status in the constitution or governing document. Guam and the US Virgin Islands have statutes that designate the governor as commander in chief during an emergency.

36. The states that do not have statutes reinforcing the governor's constitutional authority as commander in chief are Alabama, California, Connecticut, Delaware, Hawaii, Iowa, Michigan, Minnesota, Missouri, New Hampshire, New Jersey, New Mexico, and Wisconsin, as well as American Samoa, the District of Columbia, and the Northern Mariana Islands.

37. Governors are not allowed to commandeer local police during an emergency in Iowa, Nevada, and New Mexico, plus the five territories.

38. Minn. Stat. § 12.33.

39. The states that do not allow emergency changes to local police jurisdictions are Alaska, Colorado, Florida, Idaho, Illinois, Indiana, Kansas, Michigan, Montana, Nebraska, North Dakota, Rhode Island, Tennessee, Texas, and Virginia, as well as American Samoa, CNMI, and the US Virgin Islands.

40. Idaho Code § 46-1007(3).

41. The states in which state officials are not explicitly permitted to confiscate land and buildings are Colorado, Montana, New Hampshire, New Jersey,

New Mexico, Ohio, Oklahoma, Rhode Island, South Carolina, and Wyoming, as well as American Samoa.

42. The states in which the government may not confiscate private property that might be deemed necessary for emergency response are Alabama, Kentucky, Montana, New Hampshire, New Mexico, Ohio, Oklahoma, South Carolina, and Wyoming.

43. The fifteen states that allow confiscation of medical supplies are Delaware, Georgia, Hawaii, Indiana, Louisiana, Michigan, Minnesota, Missouri, New Hampshire, New Mexico, New York, Oregon, South Carolina, South Dakota, and West Virginia, as well as American Samoa, CNMI, and Guam.

44. The states that empower state officials to enact general price freezes and to control the prices of various goods are Illinois, Mississippi, Missouri, Montana, North Carolina, and Oregon.

45. The states with laws allowing food price controls during an emergency are Illinois, Massachusetts, Mississippi, Missouri, Montana, New Jersey, North Carolina, Oklahoma, Oregon, Rhode Island, South Carolina, Tennessee, Texas, Utah, Virginia, West Virginia, and Wisconsin, as well as American Samoa, the District of Columbia, Guam, and the US Virgin Islands. The states with laws allowing energy price controls during an emergency are Illinois, Indiana, Maine, Mississippi, Missouri, Montana, New Jersey, North Carolina, Oregon, Rhode Island, Tennessee, Texas, Vermont, Virginia, and West Virginia, as well as American Samoa and the US Virgin Islands.

46. The states that can enact rules to ration goods during an emergency are Alaska, Illinois, Indiana, Mississippi, Missouri, Montana, North Carolina, Oregon, and Utah, as well as American Samoa, CNMI, the District of Columbia, and Guam.

47. The states with laws allowing medicine price controls are New Jersey, South Carolina, Tennessee, Texas, Virginia, West Virginia, plus American Samoa and the US Virgin Islands. The states with laws allowing rationing of medical supplies are Alaska, Indiana, New Mexico, and South Carolina, as well as CNMI and Guam.

48. The states and territories that explicitly prohibit price gouging are Hawaii, Illinois, Louisiana, Montana, New Jersey, New York, North Carolina, Oklahoma, Oregon, Pennsylvania, Rhode Island, South Carolina, Tennessee, Texas, Utah, Vermont, Virginia, West Virginia, and Wisconsin, as well as American Samoa, the District of Columbia, and the US Virgin Islands.

49. 35 Pa. Stat. and Cons. Stat. Ann. § 7301 (f)(8).

50. The states that do not explicitly limit alcohol sales during an emergency are Alabama, Arizona, California, Connecticut, Hawaii, Kentucky, Maryland, Massachusetts, Minnesota, Missouri, Montana, Nevada, New Hampshire, New Jersey, Ohio, South Carolina, South Dakota, Vermont, Wisconsin, and Wyoming, as well as American Samoa, CNMI, Guam, and Puerto Rico. The

states that do not explicitly allow limits on firearms sales during an emergency are Alaska, Arkansas, Colorado, Delaware, Florida, Georgia, Idaho, Illinois, Indiana, Louisiana, Mississippi, Nebraska, New Jersey, New Mexico, New York, North Carolina, North Dakota, Pennsylvania, Rhode Island, Tennessee, Texas, and Washington, as well as American Samoa, CNMI, Guam, and Puerto Rico. The twenty-two states that do not explicitly limit the sale of combustibles and explosives during an emergency are Alabama, Arizona, California, Connecticut, Hawaii, Kentucky, Maryland, Massachusetts, Minnesota, Missouri, Montana, Nevada, New Hampshire, New Jersey, Ohio, Oklahoma, Oregon, South Carolina, South Dakota, Vermont, Wisconsin, and Wyoming, as well as American Samoa, CNMI, the District of Columbia, Guam, and Puerto Rico.

51. The states that allow for limits on medical procedures during an emergency are Alabama, Alaska, Arkansas, Colorado, Florida, Illinois, Indiana, Iowa, Kentucky, Louisiana, Maryland, Michigan, Mississippi, New Jersey, New York, Ohio, Pennsylvania, Texas, and Washington.

52. Laurie Sobel, Amrutha Ramaswamy, Brittni Frederiksen, and Alina Salganicoff, "State Action to Limit Abortion Access during the COVID-19 Pandemic," Kaiser Family Foundation, August 10, 2020, https://www.kff.org/coronavirus-covid-19/issue-brief/state-action-to-limit-abortion-access-during-the-covid-19-pandemic.

53. The states without a law that explicitly allows government-enacted evacuation are Arizona, Massachusetts, Missouri, and New Mexico.

54. Mont. Code Ann. § 10-3-104 (2.b).

55. The states without a curfew law are Arizona, Massachusetts, Missouri, and New Mexico.

56. Iowa Code § 29C.3.

57. 10 Guam Code § 19502 (d)(1).

58. The states without a law restricting travel are Arizona, Nevada, New Hampshire, New Mexico, Oklahoma, South Carolina, South Dakota, Washington, and Wisconsin, as well as Puerto Rico.

59. Va. Code Ann. § 44-146.17.

60. The states without laws restricting motorized travel are Arizona, New Hampshire, South Dakota, Washington, and Wyoming, as well as Puerto Rico.

61. 1 CMC § 20144 (h)(4).

62. Alaska Stat. § 26.20.100(2) (2016).

63. N.Y. Pub. Health Law § 2120 (2019).

64. The states that did not feature a law that explicitly permits mandatory vaccinations prior to 2020 are Alabama, Alaska, Arizona, Arkansas, California, Connecticut, Idaho, Indiana, Kansas, Kentucky, Maine, Maryland, Michigan, Minnesota, Missouri, Montana, New York, Ohio, Oklahoma, Pennsylvania, South Dakota, Tennessee, Utah, and Vermont, as well as the District of Columbia and the US Virgin Islands.

65. Mass. Gen. Laws ch. 111 § 181.

66. P.R. Laws tit. 24, § 353.

67. Wis. Stat. § 252.041.

68. The states that explicitly call for contact tracing during a public health crisis involving a communicable disease are Alaska, Delaware, Georgia, Hawaii, Louisiana, Mississippi, New York, Oregon, Rhode Island, South Dakota, Utah, and Virginia, as well as American Samoa, CNMI, the District of Columbia, Guam, and Puerto Rico.

69. N.Y. Pub. Health Law § 2101 (2019).

70. The twenty-one states without a general provision limiting EP are Alabama, Arizona, Connecticut, Delaware, Hawaii, Kentucky, Louisiana, Maine, Maryland, Massachusetts, Mississippi, Missouri, New Hampshire, New Jersey, New Mexico, Ohio, Oregon, Pennsylvania, Utah, Vermont, and Wisconsin, as well as the District of Columbia, Guam, and Puerto Rico.

71. William Powell, Jordan Murov-Goodman, and Lyndsey Wajert, "Special Analysis: Explicit Press Protections in State and Territorial Emergency Laws," *Reporters Committee for Freedom of the Press*, April 16, 2020, https://www.rcfp.org/emergency-laws-press-protections. The states with a press protection carve-out in the emergency powers law are Alaska, Arkansas, California, Colorado, Florida, Hawaii, Idaho, Illinois, Indiana, Kansas, Michigan, Mississippi, Montana, Nebraska, Nevada, North Carolina, North Dakota, Rhode Island, Tennessee, Texas, Vermont, and Virginia, as well as American Samoa and the US Virgin Islands.

72. 30 R.I. Gen. Laws § 30-15-4(2) (2012).

73. The states with first informer broadcast laws are Arizona, Georgia, Illinois, Missouri, Nevada, Oklahoma, Oregon, Virginia, and Washington.

74. Ariz. Rev. Stat. § 26-320 (c) (2018).

75. Randy J. Stine, "Broadcasters Now Guaranteed Access to Disaster Areas," *TV Tech*, March 27, 2018, https://www.tvtechnology.com/news/broadcasters-now-guaranteed-access-to-disaster-areas.

76. The states that do not have an explicit firearms carve-out in EP laws are Arkansas, Colorado, Connecticut, Illinois, Maryland, Massachusetts, Nebraska, New Jersey, New Mexico, New York, Ohio, Rhode Island, Vermont, and Washington, as well as the District of Columbia and the five US territories. Louisiana added such a law in 2020 during the coronavirus pandemic.

77. Tenn. Code § 58-2-107 (m).

78. Utah Code § 53-2a-214.

79. Or. Rev. Stat. § 401.198.

80. Haw. Rev. Stat. §§ 134-7.2.

81. N.H. Rev. Stat. § 4:46.I(c)(1-5) (2014).

82. N.H. Rev. Stat. § 4:46.I-a (2014).

83. The states that prohibit their emergency management agencies from being used for "political activity" are Alabama, Arizona, Arkansas, California,

Connecticut, Delaware, Hawaii, Illinois, Iowa, Maine, Massachusetts, Minnesota, Mississippi, Missouri, Montana, Nebraska, Ohio, Oklahoma, South Dakota, Washington, West Virginia, Wisconsin, and Wyoming, as well as Guam.

84. CT General Assembly Sec. 28-3.

85. Wyo. Stat. § 19-13-112.

86. The states that do not allow emergency powers to be used to intervene in labor disputes are Alaska, Arkansas, California, Colorado, Florida, Idaho, Illinois, Indiana, Kansas, Michigan, Montana, Nebraska, North Dakota, Rhode Island, Tennessee, Texas, Virginia, and Wisconsin, as well as American Samoa and CNMI.

87. N.D. Cent. Code § 37-17.1-03.

88. The states that do not delineate who has the authority to enforce the emergency laws are Alaska, Colorado, Missouri, Montana, and New York, as well as the US Virgin Islands.

89. Ohio Rev. Code § 5502.25 (2020).

90. W. Va. Code § 15-5-17.

91. The states that do not explicitly list a penalty for violating the emergency law(s) are Alaska, Arkansas, Colorado, Idaho, Illinois, Indiana, Iowa, Montana, Nebraska, Nevada, New Hampshire, New York, Ohio, Pennsylvania, South Carolina, South Dakota, and Wyoming, as well as the US Virgin Islands.

92. Miss. Code § 33-15-43.

93. Ky. Rev. Stat. § 39A.990.

94. N.J. Rev. Stat. § App.A:9-49 (2013).

95. The states that do not provide immunity for the state government during an emergency are Arkansas, Florida, Iowa, Maryland, Minnesota, Missouri, and Tennessee, as well as the US Virgin Islands.

96. Colo. Rev. Stat. § 24-33.5-711.5 (2016).

97. Ark. Code § 12-75-128 (2018).

98. The states that do not provide liability immunity for shelter providers are Arizona, Iowa, Maryland, Minnesota, Missouri, New Hampshire, New York, Oregon, Pennsylvania, and Utah, as well as American Samoa, CNMI, the District of Columbia, and the US Virgin Islands. Guam and Puerto Rico do provide liability immunity.

99. Ga. Code § 38-3-32 (2010).

Part II
EMERGENCY POWERS IN PRACTICE

Chapter 3

California and Public Health Authority

Didi Kuo

On March 17, 2020, six counties in the Bay Area of Northern California jointly issued the nation's first shelter-in-place orders to reduce the spread of the virus known as SARS-CoV-2. These orders, which were similar to "lockdown orders" in European countries like Italy, Spain, Britain, and France, mandated closures of businesses, workplaces, and social gatherings. Within weeks, governors and mayors across the country had issued similar restrictions. By April, these restrictions were being reversed. As President Trump decried public health guidance around sheltering in place, face coverings, and COVID testing, state and local governments were left to make their own decisions about public health measures.

Although the politicization of the pandemic in the United States made elected officials (such as governors) the face of pandemic policies, many critical decisions—not only those related to preventive measures, but also those relating to employment, housing, and education—were made by local public health officials. These were individuals serving in unelected roles, with varying degrees of autonomy to formulate and implement policies. They became the target of praise, ire, and litigation. In 2021, many state legislatures—at least fifteen—introduced legislation to limit the authority of public health officers.[1]

Public health authorities are not particularly visible bureaucrats or decision makers. Before March 2020, the nation's top health officials, including the director of the Centers for Disease Control and Prevention, the director of the National Institute of Allergy and Infectious Diseases, and the United States surgeon general, were rarely household names. While overseeing public health is one of the foremost duties of government, most Americans take for granted the health officials who ask them to stop smoking or to exercise more. Further, like many policy areas, public health is fragmented across national, state, and local lines. At the local level, public health departments are often subsets of state health departments. In addition to slowing the spread of infectious diseases, their responsibilities may also include restaurant sanitation and sewage cleanup. While we are aware that governments possess public health authority, we are far less aware of how and when that authority is exercised.

During the COVID-19 pandemic, the role and power of public health departments has become central to Americans' everyday lives. Decisions by public health officers have, in many cases, life-or-death consequences.[2] Public health officers have made decisions under tight time constraints, with little information or guidance about the new virus. Public health authority produced conflicts with elected officials at every level of government, and raised thorny questions about democratic accountability. In some states and counties, public health officers were given extraordinary powers; in other places, they have had only advisory roles, or had their decisions preempted or overturned by politicians. At worst, public health officers have faced vitriolic, even violent, public backlash.

State and local governments have had to rely on an extraordinary set of tools, including behavioral and nonpharmaceutical interventions (NPIs) such as lockdowns, physical distancing, and face coverings. These go far beyond the typical scope of state action. Local departments have also needed to shore up their capacity to test, trace, and isolate individuals, which requires an infrastructure for surveillance. State and local governments varied greatly in the extent to which they could formulate clear policies in response to COVID.

Debates about public health authority are a subset of broader concerns about American governance. The first relates to democratic accountability. Who makes decisions, and how do they make them? To whom are unelected decision makers held accountable? These questions are heightened in an emergency. Further, democratic accountability exists at multiple levels of government. What are the consequences of delegation to lower administrative units? Delegating decision making may help tailor local responses or help political officials dodge blame for unpopular policies. But delegation also creates patchwork administration and conflict.[3]

Second, debates about public health authority require us to assess whether the state is achieving its goals. Does the United States have robust public health infrastructure? In 2019, the Johns Hopkins Global Health Security Index rated the United States the country best prepared to withstand a pandemic, given high levels of state capacity. However, the Trump administration lacked a coherent or centralized approach to managing the pandemic. State and local governments, which already varied in preexisting levels of public health capacity, were left scrambling—and sometimes outright competing—for resources and guidance. Much of the nation's capacity was squandered, and the pandemic response became reliant on localities that varied in both the levels and types of capacity that they possessed.

This pandemic has made clear how important robust public health infrastructure is in emergencies, and public health officials are unsurprisingly taking this opportunity to advocate for greater resources. Are there lessons from the administration of public health in this pandemic that political officials can use to support public health moving forward? This chapter examines the relationship of emergency powers, public health, and governance through a study of public health authority in California. It uses the history of public health authority to understand why the administration of public health is fragmented, and then discusses the administrative and political role of health officers. It then focuses on the actions of Bay Area public health officials in the early days of the pandemic to map out the factors that contribute to public health capacity.

Local Public Health Authority in California

California is the nation's largest state by population. With thirty-nine million residents, it has nearly ten million more people than the second-most-populous state, Texas. It is also the wealthiest state, home to the world's fifth-largest global economy. California has been a bellwether for the pandemic's progression through the country. While its management of the pandemic has been quite conservative, with regulations in place since March 2020, it has also seen surges and hotspots. As of this writing (September 2021), there have been 4.3 million confirmed cases of COVID-19, and 67,358 confirmed deaths.[4] California ranks thirty-fourth in the country for deaths and cases per one hundred thousand residents.[5]

California was one of the first states to formulate a pandemic response, owing to its location on the West Coast and its many ties to China. California's governor, Gavin Newsom, declared a state of emergency on March 2, 2020, and issued statewide stay-at-home orders on March 19, only days after the Bay Area counties had issued theirs. Over the course of the first eighteen months of the pandemic, California at times did relatively well in its management of the pandemic. California—and the Bay Area in particular—was praised as a success story, given its combination of evidenced-based policy formulation and trust in science.[6] But there has also been political pushback from businesses and citizens. Governor Gavin Newsom was subject to a recall election in September 2021, an effort motivated by anger toward California's extended shutdowns of businesses and schools.

But Governor Newsom was not the sole authority deciding COVID policies. In fact, compared to many governors, Newsom—as well as California's mayors and many of its county boards of supervisors—deferred extensively to unelected public health officials to formulate a

COVID response. This elevated a set of previously unknown bureaucrats to sudden prominence. Public health officers made their decisions unilaterally, and their decisions, at least on paper, were not subject to any kind of review or input. The power vested in these officials existed long before the pandemic, but it is likely that they will be reconsidered as the pandemic abates.

Historical and Contemporary Perspectives on Public Health Authority

Monitoring and protecting the health of populations is one of the foremost responsibilities of government. In the United States, local governments routinely dealt with outbreaks of smallpox, cholera, and yellow fever in the eighteenth century; in 1799, the first municipal board of health was established in Boston. New York gave its local boards of health the power to quarantine and isolate individuals, and to "issue all such other regulations as they shall think necessary and proper for the preservation of public health."[7] Protecting public health is a broad mandate, and as a result, states fulfill this responsibility in myriad ways. They build hospitals and clinics, provide medical care, and develop campaigns (e.g., around tobacco cessation or prevention of chronic diseases).

In the introductory chapter to this volume, John Ferejohn described the tensions between emergency powers and democratic governance. Governments need greater discretion to act in response to emergencies such as natural disasters, wars, and pandemics. Elected officials and bureaucrats may circumvent typical democratic processes around decision making when emergency powers are granted. In the COVID pandemic, local public health departments became critical actors making binding policy decisions. This was by design: public health authorities have access to expertise and data that politicians don't, and in an emergency, they need to respond quickly without fear of political reprisal.

The pandemic pitted public health authorities against elected officials. In many states, legislatures are cracking down on the power of public health departments. At least seven states have shifted authority over public health decisions to local elected officials, or have established legislative authority over public health decisions. At least eight other states are considering similar legislation. Many of the bills originated as "model bills" from the American Legislative Exchange Council (ALEC), an arm of the Koch brothers' political organization that advocates free-market policies at the state level. ALEC's Emergency Power Limitation Act, one such model bill, limits the scope of what bureaucrats can do with emergency orders, and gives the courts and legislature the ability to review and terminate such orders. Other states are banning the use of masks, the use of quarantines, or the closure of businesses.[8]

Building Public Health Administration in California

California became a state in 1850; that same year, the state government appropriated $50,000 for the State Marine Hospital—the state's first public hospital—in San Francisco.[9] In 1855, the Pauper Act was integrated into the Welfare and Institutions Code, with counties appropriating part of their tax base to health care.[10] Counties then assumed responsibility over the health and welfare of the indigent, and built public hospitals to care for the poor. California was the second state to establish a board of health, which it did in 1870. Together, the state and counties responded to disease outbreaks, including bubonic plague in 1900 and the aftermath of the 1906 San Francisco earthquake. By 1914, almost each county had a hospital to help contain and manage disease outbreaks and care for the ill.

In 1995, California reorganized its health and safety code. The legislature passed SB 1360, which streamlined public health administration by delineating the responsibilities of the state and local health departments. The bill was the result of a yearlong review of public health, including a collaboration with health officials in the public and private sectors. This reorganization received support from the County Health Executives Association of California, the California Coalition of Local

Health Department Nursing Directors, the Western Consortium for Public Health, the California Public Health Foundation, the Office of Statewide Health Planning and Development, and the California Conference of Local Health Officers.[11]

SB 1360 created California's State Department of Health Services to oversee public health and health policy. The California Department of Public Health (CDPH) sits under the California Health and Human Services Agency. It has an annual budget of $3.5 billion, and runs six centers of health operations, including the Center for Infectious Diseases. A director of health services is appointed by the governor and confirmed by the California Senate to oversee the agency. The governor also appoints the director of the California Department of Public Health, who serves as the state public health officer.

Local public health authority is vested in fifty-eight county and three city health departments, totaling sixty-one local public health departments. Each county board of supervisors is responsible for appointing its own health officer. Health officers must be physicians, and they have 171 enumerated duties—one of which includes "broad authority to take action to prevent disease."[12] They can issue isolation and quarantine orders and can declare local health emergencies. The Health Officers Association of California, in a guide to cities on appointing health officers, recommends appointing physicians with expertise in preventive medicine or public health.

On matters related to public health, the statute stipulates that the board of supervisors of each county "shall take measures as may be necessary to preserve and protect the public health."[13] The mandate for public health is broad; the responsibilities of the health officer include managing leaks from gas pipelines, ensuring sanitation of prisons, and designating nonprofit food agencies to coordinate food donation efforts.[14]

The main duties vested in the health officers are to give orders related to public health and sanitation. Further, the county health officer "may take any preventative measure that may be necessary to protect public health" during any state of emergency or local emergency. While these preventive measures are not directly specified by the statute, they include "abatement, correction, removal or any other protective step."[15] The county-level health departments in California are all designed to be autonomous; health officers "have immense power to act independently in the interest of public health," since their "legally binding directives" do not require consent from political officials.[16]

While local health officers operate independently of one another, they are all part of the California Conference of Local Health Officers. They meet with the state-level California Department of Public Health on a monthly basis, and have two continuing medical education sessions per year that focus on public health.[17]

Public Health Authority after 9/11

After September 11, 2001, there was renewed attention on public health due to the threat of bioterrorism. The federal government and state governments alike devoted new time, attention, and resources to public health preparedness. Congress passed the Public Health Security and Bioterrorism Preparedness and Response Act in 2002, which provided federal funds to states and localities. Federal grants from the CDC and Health Resources and Services Administration (HRSA) were also administered to the states. Public health experts emphasized the need for public health police power—that is, authority to enforce civil self-protection—in order to effectively combat a bioterrorism attack.[18] Granting more power to public health officers was also seen as necessary to enforce isolation, quarantine, and health and inspection laws in an emergency.

In 2005, the California legislature passed SB 104, an amendment to the Health and Safety Code. SB 104 allowed sheriffs and local law enforcement to enforce public health orders, particularly in response to bioterrorism. The bill was cosponsored by the Health Officers Association of California (HOAC), which represented the sixty-one physician health officers. The bill clarified the authority granted to local peace officers in a health emergency, allowing law enforcement to "proactively enforce orders" intended to prevent the spread of contagious, infectious, or communicable disease. The HOAC stipulated specifically that "for emergency situations requiring actions such as quarantines, proactive enforcement is necessary to ensure public safety."[19]

The Los Angeles County sheriff also sent a letter to the California Senate Committee on Public Safety in support of the bill:

> Current law makes it a misdemeanor for an individual to violate a quarantine or isolation order issued by a health officer . . . [enforcement] is complex and problematic at best. . . . Senate Bill 104 will allow local law enforcement and health officers to work together to rapidly contain a potentially serious situation by giving the appropriate and necessary authority to rapidly enforce quarantine and isolation orders.[20]

The bill was funded through money appropriated for bioterrorism preparedness in a time when many states were investing resources in public health for similar reasons.

In emergencies, defined as "state of war emergencies," "states of emergency," or "local emergencies," public health officers "may take any preventive measure" to preserve public health. Emergency declarations often follow natural disasters (mudslides, wildfires, earthquakes, etc.), which then create public health hazards. Michael Lewis recently spotlighted the role that public health officials play during emergencies in his best seller, *The Premonition*, arguing that local officials have the flexibility (and more importantly, the power) to act decisively when other health agencies or political officials are failing to do so.

Public Health in California Today

Do California's administrative institutions effectively protect public health? I collected data on California's sixty-one public health departments to better understand how they vary in their formal and informal capacities. All the appointed health officers at the time of the pandemic were medical doctors, and thirty-two also held a master's in public health. Four had completed Epidemic Intelligence Service (EIS) training with the CDC. While it was difficult to get data on the number of staff at each department, the numbers seemed to range from the twenties (in the less populated rural counties) to the thousands (in large cities and counties like Los Angeles and San Francisco).

Funding for public health in California comes from the federal government, state government, and local taxes. Since the 2008 financial crisis, the state has cut funding for public health. Per capita spending on public health declined 18 percent between 2008 and 2019, from $97 to $79 per person; the budgets of the county departments vary. Figure 3.1 shows the amount each county spends on public health per capita. Per capita public health spending ranges from a low of around $40 to a high of $951 in low-population Alpine and Sierra Counties. The median is $98 per person per county, with a mean of $150. Figure 3.2 shows the amount of expenditures on public health as a percentage of a county's total budget. These range from a minimum of 1.8 percent to a high of 11 percent, with an average of 3.9 percent of a county's budget going to public health.

Financing, Public Health, and COVID Response

Public health departments have statutory authority to act in emergencies, and they are also staffed by expert health officers. But different budgets may impact the provision of public health, particularly during a pandemic. Although there is no easy way to assess whether or not a department's budget helped guide the pandemic response, I compared county budgets to the number of COVID cases a county experienced in the first year of the pandemic. Figure 3.3 shows the relationship of public health spending and COVID cases, as of spring 2021. There is a negative relationship between per capita public health spending and the number of COVID cases in a county. There is also little relationship between a county's public health expenditures as a proportion of its budget and its COVID cases.

This data indicates that California local public health departments vary in their levels of funding, and that the amount of money a county spends on public health does not correlate to the number of COVID

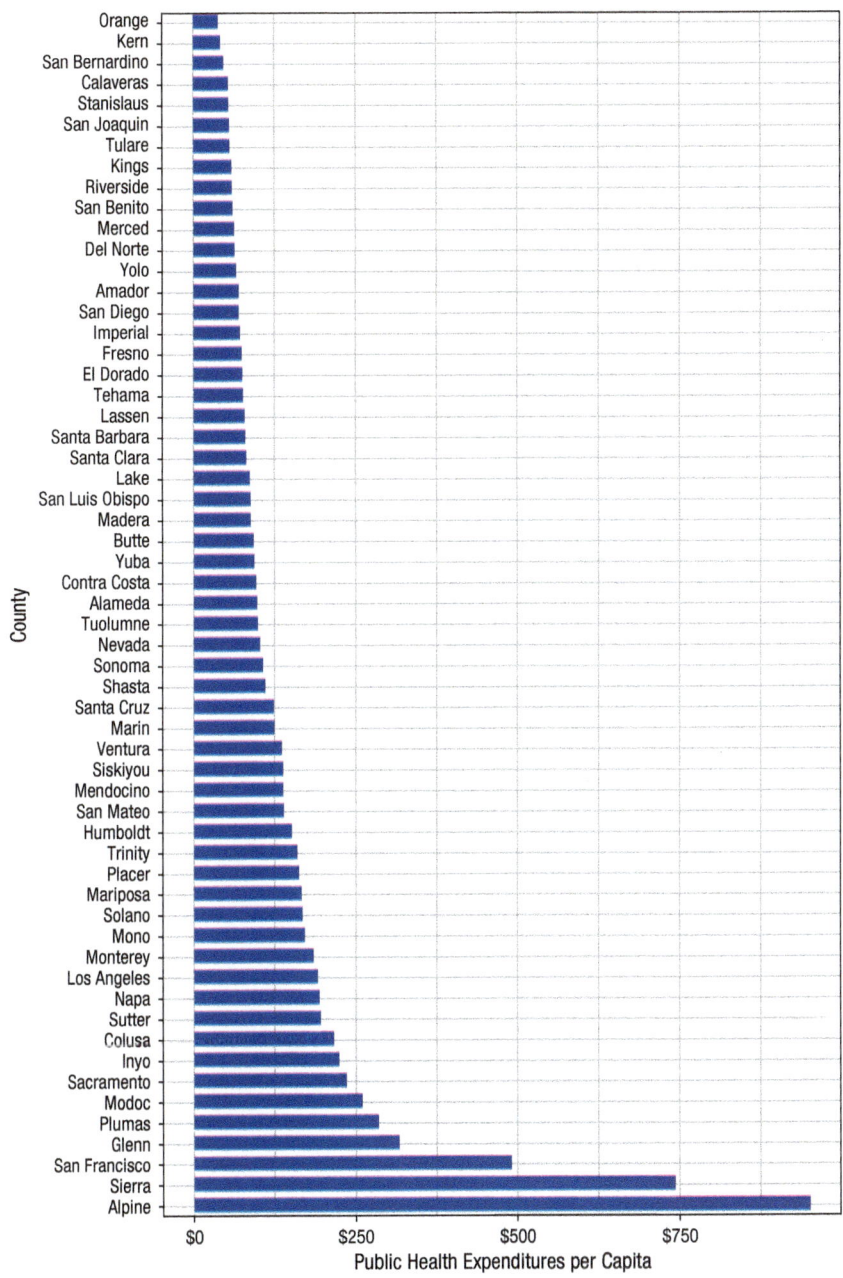

Figure 3.1. County-level public health expenditures per capita, 2019
Source: Data from the California State Controller's Office.

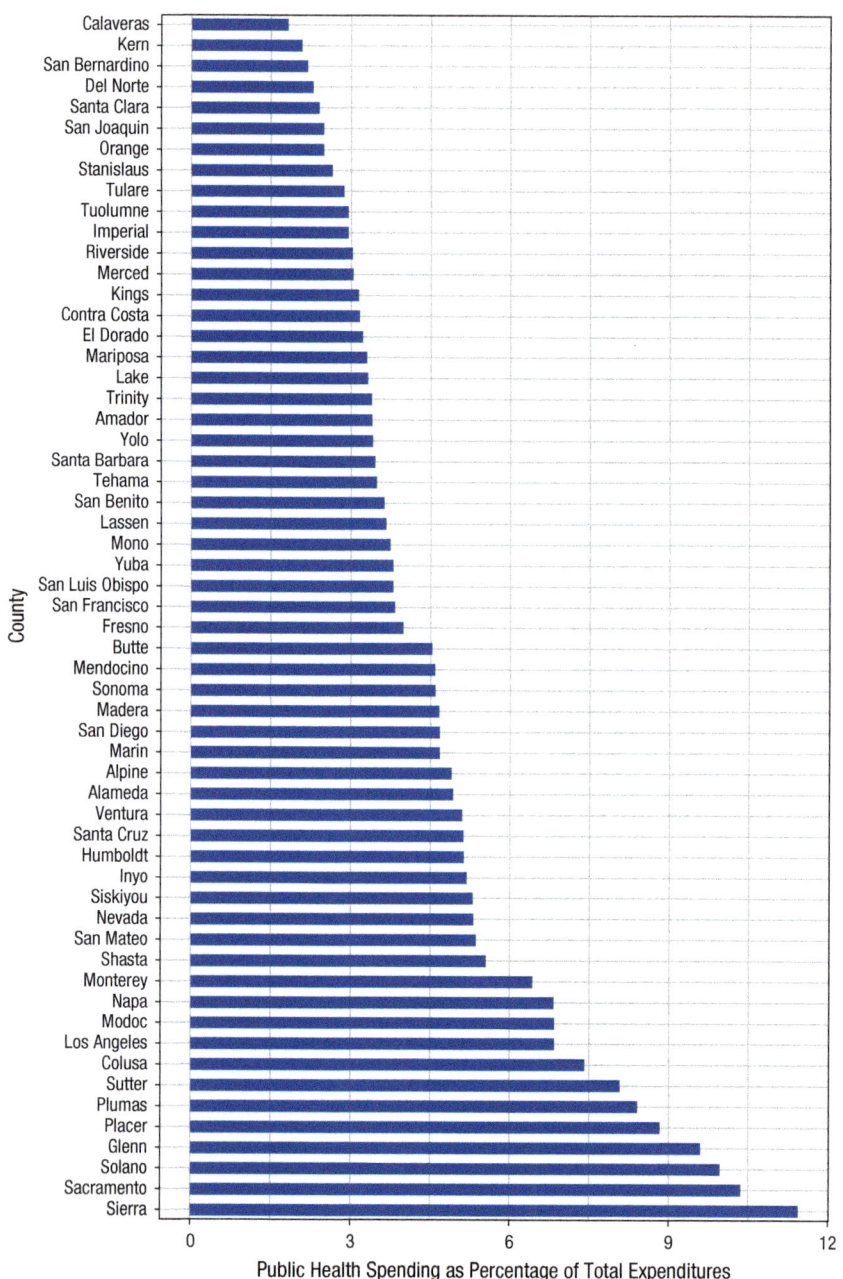

Figure 3.2. County-level expenditures on public health as percentage of total expenditures, 2019

Source: Data from the California State Controller's Office.

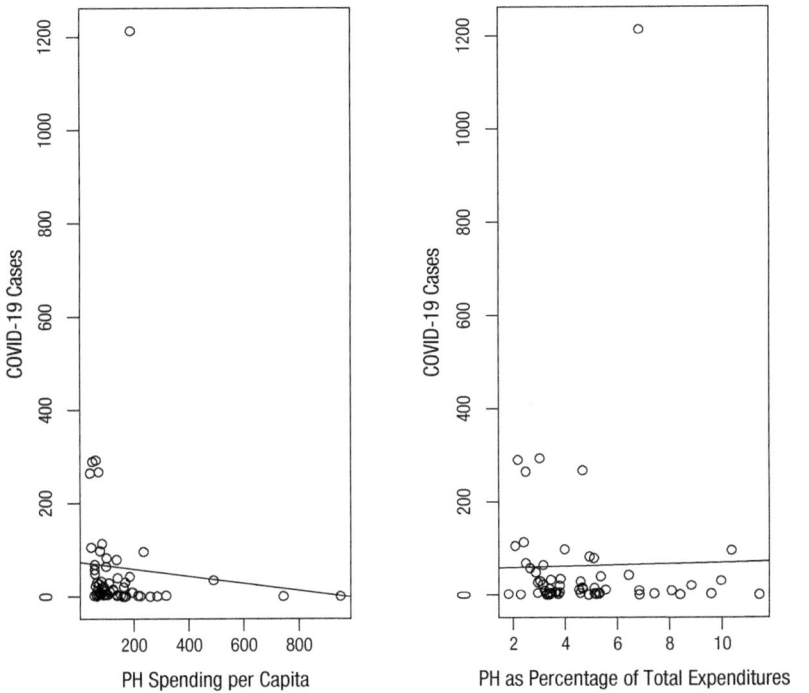

Figure 3.3. Relationship between public health (PH) spending and COVID-19 cases
Source: Data from the California COVID data repository, https://covid19.ca.gov.

cases it had. There is only so much we can interpret from this data, since COVID cases are determined by numerous factors unrelated to the budget of a health department. I therefore turn to other important factors that contribute to public health governance.

Determinants of Public Health Capacity

Funding alone does not ensure good public health outcomes. Public health budgets have been on the decline for well over a decade, with an estimated $4.5 billion shortfall in funding nationwide.[21] There have been over fifty thousand staffing cuts to local public health departments and ten thousand staffing cuts to state health departments in the decades after 9/11, with a shift in federal funding going from public health to individual health care provision. Funding for the nation's Public Health Emergency Preparedness Program declined by $256 million between 2002 and 2020.[22] Although the pandemic has shown how necessary public health expertise can be, the CDC's Epidemic Intelligence Service (EIS) officer training is at some of its lowest levels in recent years. Because of funding cuts, the EIS has gone from training around eighty people a year to sixty a year.[23] And since the pandemic began, hundreds of public health officials have left their positions, both voluntarily and involuntarily.[24]

In addition to funding, there is ample scholarship showing that other factors contribute to good public health outcomes, including pandemic preparedness. In a measure of local public health capacity, the Centers for Disease Control and Prevention designates six determinants: preparedness planning and readiness assessment, surveillance and epidemiology capacity, laboratory capacity, health alert network (communications and information technology), risk communication and health information dissemination, and education and training.[25] While some of these relate to formal state capacity, others relate instead to the ability of the state to work with nonstate actors, particularly when disseminating information or working through partners.

Public health critically relies on the state's relationship with other actors in order to develop capacity. Public health services are divided among the state and external groups, including private health providers and nongovernmental organizations. Public health agencies must be able "to inform, influence, communicate, and collaborate" with other actors in order to be successful.[26] Local public health capacity is informed by a local jurisdiction's existing medical and health services, as well as community health partnerships.[27] Empirically, public health systems that show high levels of formal capacity (i.e., public health agencies that have expertise to formulate and implement policy), *combined with* high levels of coordination with local organizations, outperform systems that share capacities across governmental and nongovernmental groups.[28] These are not just enablers of effective public health service delivery; instead, they are crucial elements of public health capacity.

In a review of public health capacities at the national and regional levels, Aluttis et al. lay out reasons that partnerships are just as important to capacity as factors like financial resources or workforce- and knowledge-development.[29] They emphasize the interorganizational relationships between governments and health care providers, academic institutions, the private sector, and socioeconomic groups. They also coordinate with other public health bodies across different levels of government. The partnerships are more effective when they are formalized across the public and private sectors, through policies and legal mechanisms.

The COVID pandemic has forced a reckoning with the state of America's public health infrastructure, and how it can be improved in the future. The National Academy of Sciences declared the state of American public health "in disarray" in a decades-old report, with tensions existing between politicians and public health officials.[30] Public health itself is also subject to boom-and-bust funding cycles in response to crises, shifting agendas, and interest-group concerns. Joshua Sharfstein and Georges Benjamin noted recently that public health infrastructure in the United States is notoriously weak, since it relies on collective action that is hard to mobilize.[31]

For "public health 3.0," experts stress greater engagement between public health officials and sectors such as finance, technology, transportation, real estate, and social services.[32] One example from the pandemic was Challenge Seattle, which brought together the Seattle and King County health departments with businesses from companies like Starbucks, Microsoft, and Amazon. This grew out of individual relationships—on March 4, 2020, Dow Constantine, King County's executive, convened a call with executives of Seattle corporations. He asked them to keep their workforces home in response to the spread of the coronavirus in the Seattle area, including a positive case of an Amazon employee. By then, executives themselves, relying on in-house experts, had come to similar conclusions. (An in-house specialist on workforce health at Microsoft, Colleen Daly, has a PhD in public health and reported directly to Microsoft CEO Satya Nadella and president Brad Smith beginning the night of February 29.)[33]

On March 5, Amazon and Microsoft—both of which are headquartered in Seattle—as well as Facebook and Google, which have large offices there—asked employees to work from home. This was a drastic measure that was viewed as risky for the companies, which would be losing revenues from lost productivity, canceled events, and disrupted supply chains.[34] Challenge Seattle formalized these relationships by creating a forum for shared data, best practices, and decisions about reopenings.[35]

Aside from stakeholder engagement and partnerships across historical silos, other factors that create public health capacity include regional cooperation and partnerships with academic institutions. Regional cooperation and information sharing fosters trust across different levels of government and creates efficiencies, whereas competition and conflict among neighboring departments is likely to undermine public health goals.[36] Partnerships with research and academic communities unite data and practice and create opportunities for career exchange and service learning.

It is challenging to gather systematic data on these elements of public health capacity. The next section therefore turns to a case study of the Bay Area, where many county health officers worked together in the earliest moments of the pandemic. This section tries to understand how health officers worked in their communities to formulate and communicate policy decisions, and how they interpreted and utilized their legal authority.

The Bay Area and Public Health Capacity

The San Francisco Bay Area has been widely credited for its swift and decisive action in response to COVID. On March 16, 2020, health officers of six Bay Area counties—San Francisco, Santa Clara, Marin, Alameda, Contra Costa, San Mateo—and the city of Berkeley jointly issued stay-at-home orders affecting over seven million residents. These orders limited nonessential activities outside the home; residents were allowed to visit only grocery stores and pharmacies. Businesses, schools, and workplaces were deemed nonessential and temporarily closed. Households were not permitted to interact, and individuals could spend time outdoors only for exercise or limited recreation. This initial order also asked individuals to maintain six feet of distance at all times but did not require face coverings.

At the time, there were 258 reported cases of COVID in the Bay Area, with four deaths.[37] The CDC had documented the first case of community spread of COVID in Santa Clara County in late February; on February 25, San Francisco mayor London Breed declared a state of emergency. By March 11, Santa Clara and San Francisco Counties banned large gatherings. The events leading up to the shelter-in-place order involved constant discussions between the health officers of the Association of Bay Area Health Officials (ABAHO) about the best way to respond collectively to the impending pandemic. The story of the Bay Area's early shutdowns has been breathlessly covered by the national press, often in contrast to comparatively worse management on the East Coast.[38]

Prior to 2020, San Francisco and its neighboring counties in the Bay Area were not particularly known for their robust public health agencies. Instead, the San Francisco Bay Area is similar to many other urban and metropolitan areas in the United States. It is home to three large cities and booming sectors of the economy, such as the technology industry. It has long been a stronghold of liberal politics, with an educated population. The Bay Area also has problems related to unaffordable housing (and a resulting homelessness crisis), economic inequality, and risk of natural disasters, including wildfire and earthquakes. Like many cities, there are sterling medical schools—the University of California San Francisco (UCSF) and Stanford—with strong research programs. There are competing hospital systems and private medical providers alongside public and nonprofit medical providers.

But the speed and autonomy with which the Bay Area health officials acted set the region on a path that became somewhat singular in the COVID pandemic. Because of a history of regional cooperation across counties, epidemiological expertise, and a history of outreach to the private sector and nonprofits, the Bay Area highlights the need for capacity along multiple dimensions.

Regional Cooperation: The Association of Bay Area Health Officials

The county public health departments in Northern California cooperate on regional public health decisions through an organization, the Association of Bay Area Health Officials, or ABAHO. ABAHO was formed in 1985 to coordinate health policies across thirteen county and city health departments.[39] That year, the San Francisco health officer, Dr. David Werdegar, invited health officers from neighboring counties to dinner to discuss sharing data on AIDS cases as they collectively tried to understand the new disease. ABAHO continued operation as a formal organization in the decades since. In 2005, ABAHO created a team focused on pandemic preparedness. Dr. Mitch Katz, director of San Francisco's Department of Public Health at the time, convened a working group to address influenza preparedness. Among the issues the working group would need to consider were isolation and quarantine policies, vaccine prioritization, and the use of N95 masks.[40] In 2008, ABAHO received a grant from pharmaceutical company Gilead to hire a coordinator for the pandemic group. The coordinator helped promulgate directives for pandemics, including protocols calling for different levels of local interventions. In interviews, many health officers noted that this was critical to helping the Bay Area through the H1N1 influenza response in 2009.

Even the H1N1 pandemic, however, could not prepare a health agency against the novel coronavirus. Its protocols were almost a decade old, and H1N1 was managed successfully. However, the regional cooperation activated by ABAHO was critical to formulating a policy in February 2020. ABAHO members maintain a Slack group and meet monthly. It was directly responsible for the development of the shelter-in-place order, through a series of text messages and emergency calls in the first weeks of March.

The story of the initial days of the pandemic are at this point well known locally. Dr. Sara Cody, the Santa Clara County health officer, had been watching the virus in Wuhan and Western Europe. A lockdown order—or something that could keep residents at home and significantly curtail interactions—could curb the spread of the virus, but nothing on the scale of a lockdown had been implemented before. Dr. Tomás Aragón, the health officer of San Francisco, was also studying the data and coming to the conclusion that a lockdown was necessary.

The weekend of March 14–15, county health officers worried about St. Patrick's Day parades despite the fact that the counties had issued bans on large gatherings. Through a flurry of text messages, health officers across the Bay Area counties decided that drastic and immediate action was necessary. They spoke early on the morning of Sunday, March 15, and decided that a shelter-in-place order would need legal enforcement and collective effort with local elected officials. That afternoon, Santa Clara County organized the lawyers of each of the six counties to draw up the orders, which included fines and misdemeanor charges.[41]

In June 2021, Sara Cody delivered the McCoy Family Center for Ethics in Society's Arrow Lecture at Stanford University. In it, she explained how California empowers its local public health officers to act unilaterally. She stressed that the health and safety code includes a "duty" to act—not just an ability. The code specifies that in infectious disease emergencies, officers "shall take all measures as necessary" to protect the public health. Dr. Cody read the use of the word *shall* as a mandate to act to prevent the spread of the disease.

When the counties issued their shelter-in-place decisions on March 16, they did so with a unified voice. Not only were the counties in agreement that the Bay Area as a whole would need to be locked down, but they also enlisted the support of all elected officials, as well as local law enforcement. The mayors of San Francisco, San Jose, and

Oakland all supported the orders. The sheriff of San Francisco spoke publicly when shelter-in-place orders were issued, asking citizens for voluntary compliance so that the police would not have to enforce punitively.

Tomás Aragón, in an interview, spoke of the culture of "radical humility" that permeates the ABAHO.[42] Not all of its members are epidemiologists (crucially, as will be explained below, some are), but they make a point to defer to specialization and expertise. The health officer of Santa Cruz County, for example, an ob-gyn, cited ABAHO's "bank of knowledge and wisdom and experience" when explaining making policy for her own county.[43]

There has been business opposition to the shutdowns—leaders of local hospitality and retail associations protested at San Francisco City Hall in autumn 2020 and voiced some relief at Aragón's upcoming departure—but thus far, the Bay Area health officers have avoided the vitriolic pushback from county supervisors and residents that their counterparts in other parts of the state have received.[44] They have retained consistency in the strictness of their lockdown rules and have also remained more conservative than the state.

Partnerships with Stakeholders

Many of the individuals at the heart of public health decision making had long-standing ties to the scientific community as well as to politicians. Unlike Southern California, where many health officers have resigned after threats of job termination or threats from the community, the Bay Area's health officers have kept their jobs or even been promoted to visible state roles.[45]

The Bay Area's effective response is partly due to its strong ties to the medical research community, which helped in the creation of public health policies. The director of the San Francisco Department of Public Health, Dr Grant Colfax, completed a medical residency at UCSF. Dr. Colfax began working in the San Francisco Department of Public Health in 1997 as its director of HIV Prevention and Research.

(He later served as the director of the Office of National AIDS Policy under President Obama.) Tomás Aragón, now director of the California Department of Public Health but previously the longtime San Francisco health officer, was a medical resident at UCSF as well and entered the San Francisco Department of Public Health in 1996. He also had a degree in public health and was assigned to work on epidemiology and infectious diseases for the city's Office of Public Health Emergency Preparedness and Response. Sara Cody, health officer of Santa Clara County, completed training as an Epidemic Intelligence Service (EIS) officer with the Centers for Disease Control and Prevention.

In the early weeks of the pandemic, the Bay Area was vulnerable to the novel coronavirus that was spreading in Wuhan, given high levels of travel to and from Asia. But Bay Area health officers were particularly prepared, since two of them had worked specifically on pandemics and infections: Tomás Aragón had worked on SARS, while Sara Cody had worked on E. coli and salmonella outbreaks.[46]

The ties between the medical community and public health departments were forged during the AIDS/HIV crisis of the 1980s, when the federal government was completely unresponsive to the deaths of gay men from a new virus. Researchers at the University of California San Francisco worked to understand the virus, and created deep ties to public health officials and the city's communities—particularly marginalized communities—as a result.[47]

In February and March of 2020, the Bay Area was similarly prepared to conduct its own research in the absence of federal government involvement. Dr. Robert Wachter, head of medicine at UCSF, and George Rutherford, chair of Infectious Disease and Global Epidemiology at UCSF, are both veterans of the AIDS/HIV crisis. As they conducted research on HIV, they worked closely with the city's public health officials to determine policies such as closure of movie theaters and bathhouses. UCSF's research was implemented through the city's public hospital, Zuckerberg San Francisco General Hospital.

When SARS-CoV-2 appeared in Washington State, UCSF researchers began testing samples. Drs. Wachter and Rutherford spearheaded the effort to understand viral transmission, while Drs. Colfax and Aragón, their former medical residents, stood ready to draft policies in response. By April, for example, San Francisco issued a mask ordinance requiring all individuals within thirty feet of others to wear a mask. The State of California did not issue mask guidelines until June, and when it did, it kept the mask ordinance to individuals within six feet.[48] UCSF epidemiologists sit on policy advisory groups with the city. They organized testing drives in the Mission District, with many Hispanic residents, to understand disease rates and transmission across different ethnic groups.[49]

Conclusion

The pandemic's local public health response has highlighted the crucial role that public health officers play in formulating and implementing policies, particularly in emergencies. This chapter explained the history of public health authority and why it tends to be fragmented and decentralized. Even when bureaucracies are designed to insulate public health officials from politicization, public health institutions are often underresourced. The pandemic is also likely to change these institutional arrangements and allow greater political control over public health decisions.

Although this was a study of one state, California, it illustrates the general issues raised by the process of implementing emergency orders in a decentralized federal system. These include democratic accountability, and whether or not unelected officials should be granted wide discretion to act unilaterally during emergencies. California delegates statutory authority to local health officers to respond to public health emergencies, which has pitted public health officers against politicians, businesses, and citizens.

The pandemic has also shown that public health capacity is critical. Public health institutions need expertise and financing, and public health officials need to work with local politicians and law enforcement when devising policy. Further, they are more effective when there is trust and coordination between regional and community partners. Building public health infrastructure for the future will require more than simply stripping authority. Instead, integrating public health with broader governing and policy goals is likely to strengthen the public health response in future emergencies.

Notes

1. See, e.g., the Network for Public Health Law and the National Association of County and City Health Officials Report, 2021, "Proposed Limits on Public Health Authority: Dangerous for Public Health," and the Association of State and Territorial Health Officials Report, 2020, "Legal Challenges to State COVID-19 Orders." A description of lawsuits facing public health officials is available at Ballotpedia: https://ballotpedia.org/Lawsuits_about_state_actions_and_policies_in_response_to_the_coronavirus_(COVID-19)_pandemic,_2020-2021.

2. Christopher Adolph, Kenya Amano, Bree Bang-Jensen, Nancy Fullman, and John Wilkerson, "Pandemic Politics: Timing State-Level Social Distancing Responses to COVID-19," *Journal of Health Politics, Policy, and Law* 46, no. 2 (2021): 211–33.

3. Donald F. Kettl, "States Divided: The Implications of American Federalism for COVID-19," *Public Administration Review* 80, no. 4 (2020): 595–602; Alan Greenblatt, "America's Governments Are at War with Each Other," Governing.com, July 23, 2020.

4. California COVID Response: https://covid19.ca.gov.

5. CDC COVID Data Tracker: https://covid.cdc.gov/covid-data-tracker.

6. Russell Berman, "The City That Has Flattened the Coronavirus Curve," *The Atlantic*, April 12, 2020; Jay Caspian Kang, "What the San Francisco Bay Area Can Teach Us about Fighting a Pandemic," *New Yorker*, January 4, 2021.

7. The Network for Public Health Law and the National Association of County and City Health Officials, *Proposed Limits on Public Health Authority: Dangerous for Public Health*, 2021, https://www.networkforphl.org/wp-content/uploads/2021/06/Proposed-Limits-on-Public-Health-Authority-Dangerous-for-Public-Health-FINAL.pdf.

8. Network for Public Health Law, *Proposed Limits*.

9. From "A History of the University of California, San Francisco," https://history.library.ucsf.edu/1868_hospitals.html.

10. Michael R. Cousineau and Robert E. Tranquada, "Crisis and Commitment: 150 Years of Service by Los Angeles County Public Hospitals," *American Journal of Public Health* 97 (2007): 606–15.

11. California State Assembly Committee on Health, hearing on SB 1360, July 11, 1995.

12. Health Officers Association of California (HOAC), "Appointing a Local Health Officer: A Guide for Cities," http://www.calhealthofficers.org/documents/City%20Guide%20to%20Appointing%20a%20Local%20Health%20Officer.pdf.

13. See SB 1630, Part 3—Local Health Departments, Chapter 2—Powers and Duties of Local Health Officers and Local Health Departments.

14. See Health and Safety Code, Division 101, Administration of Public Health, Part 3, Local Health Departments, Chapter 2, Powers and Duties of Local Health Officers and Local Health Departments, https://leginfo.legislature.ca.gov/faces/codes_displayText.xhtml?lawCode=HSC&division=101.&title=&part=3.&chapter=2.&article=1.

15. Health and Safety Code, Section 101040.

16. Angela Hart and Anna Maria Barry-Jester, "The Inside Story of How the Bay Area Got Ahead of the COVID-19 Crisis," *Kaiser Health News*, April 21, 2020.

17. HOAC, "Appointing a Local Health Officer."

18. Jorge E. Galva, Christopher Atchison, and Samuel Levey, "Public Health Strategy and the Police Powers of the State," *Public Health Reports* 120, no. 1 (2005): 20–27.

19. California Senate Committee on Public Safety, hearing on SB104, April 12, 2005.

20. California Senate Committee on Public Safety, hearing on SB104, April 12, 2005.

21. Nason Maani and Sandro Galea, "COVID-19 and Underinvestment in the Public Health Infrastructure of the United States," *Milbank Quarterly* 98, no. 2 (2020): 250–59.

22. Karen DeSalvo, Bob Hughes, Mary Bassett, Georges Benjamin, Michael Fraser, Sandro Galea, J. Nadine Gracia, and Jeffrey Howard, "Public Health COVID-19 Impact Assessment: Lessons Learned and Compelling Needs," *National Academy of Medicine: Perspectives*, April 7, 2021.

23. Nathaniel Smith and Michael R. Fraser, "Straining the System: Novel Coronavirus and Preparedness for Concomitant Disasters," *American Journal of Public Health* 110, no. 5 (2020): 648–49.

24. Nadia Kounang, "The Pandemic Has Pushed More Than 250 Public Health Officials Out the Door," *CNN.com*, May 23, 2021.

25. Julia F. Costich and F. Douglas Scutchfield, "Public Health Preparedness and Response Capacity Inventory Validity Study," *Journal of Public Health Management Practice* 10, no. 3 (May–June 2004): 225–33.

26. Glen P. Mays, F. Douglas Scutchfield, Michelyn W. Bhandari, and Sharla A. Smith, "Understanding the Organization of Public Health Delivery Systems: An Empirical Typology," *Milbank Quarterly* 88, no. 1 (2010): 81–111.

27. See both Stephen M. Shortell, Gloria J. Bazzoli, Nicole L. Dubbs, and Peter Kralovec, "Classifying Health Networks and Systems: Managerial and Policy Implications," *Health Care Management Review* 25, no. 4 (2000): 9–17; and Glen P. Mays, Paul K. Halverson, and Arnold D. Kaluzny, "Managed Care, Public Health, and Privatization: A Typology of Interorganizational Arrangements," in *Managed Care and Public Health*, ed. Paul K. Halverson, Arnold D. Kaluzny, and Curtis P. McLaughlin (Gaithersburg, MD: Aspen Publishers, 1998), 185–200.

28. Mays et al., "Understanding the Organization of Public Health Delivery Systems."

29. Christoph Aluttis, Stephan Van den Broucke, Cristina Chiotan, Caroline Costongs, Kai Michelsen, and Helmut Brand, "Public Health and Health Promotion Capacity at National and Regional Level: A Review of Conceptual Frameworks," *Journal of Public Health Research* 3, no. 1 (2014): 199.

30. Institute of Medicine, *The Future of Public Health* (Washington, DC: National Academies Press, 1988).

31. Joshua Sharfstein and Georges Benjamin, "The Exceptional American Relationship to Public Health," *Foreign Affairs*, August 6, 2020.

32. Brian E. Dixon, Virginia A. Caine, and Paul K. Halverson, "Deficient Response to COVID-19 Makes the Case for Evolving the Public Health System," *American Journal of Preventive Medicine* 59, no. 6 (2020): 887–91; DeSalvo et al., "COVID-19 Impact Assessment."

33. Karen Wiese, "Ahead of the Pack: How Microsoft Told Workers to Stay Home," *New York Times*, March 15, 2020.

34. Shannon Bond, "Amazon, Facebook, Google, Microsoft Tell Seattle Workers to Stay Home," NPR.org, March 5, 2020.

35. DeSalvo et al., "COVID-19 Impact Assessment," 13.

36. John Hoornbeek, Michael Morris, Patrick Libbey, and Gianfranco Pezzino, "Consolidating Local Health Departments in the United States: Challenges, Evidence, and Thoughts for the Future," *Public Health Reports* 134, no. 2 (2019): 103–8; DeSalvo et al., "COVID-19 Impact Assessment."

37. Santa Clara County California, Press Release, "Seven Bay Area Jurisdictions Order Residents to Stay Home," March 16, 2020, https://www.sccgov.org/sites/phd/news/Pages/press-release-03-16-20.aspx.

38. Adam Nagourney and Jonathan Martin, "The East Coast, Always in the Spotlight, Owes a Debt to the West," *New York Times*, April 13, 2020.

39. Adam W. Crawley and Wayne T. Enanoria, "The Association of Bay Area Health Officials: Advancing Public Health through Regional Networks," UC Berkeley: Center for Infectious Diseases & Emergency Readiness, April 27, 2012, https://escholarship.org/uc/item/39m462r5.

40. Crawley and Enanoria, "Association of Bay Area Health Officials."

41. Hart and Barry-Jester, "The Inside Story of How the Bay Area Got Ahead of the COVID-19 Crisis."

42. Zoom interview with Tomás Aragón, August 17, 2020.

43. Hart and Barry-Jester, "The Inside Story of How the Bay Area Got Ahead of the COVID-19 Crisis."

44. On the views of the business community, see Alex Barreira, "Departing S.F. Public Health Officer Leaves Mixed Legacy with Local Business Leaders," *San Francisco Business Times*, December 7, 2020.

45. Erica Pan, Alameda County's Interim Health Officer, was promoted to state epidemiologist and deputy director of the Center for Infectious Diseases in August after the resignation of Sonia Angell. Angell resigned in the wake of a backlog in coronavirus tests and issues around reporting data.

46. Perri Smith, "Disease Detectives: An Inside Look at the Epidemic Intelligence Service," *Stanford Journal of Public Health*, February 8, 2012, https://web.stanford.edu/group/sjph/cgi-bin/sjphsite/.

47. Ryan Kost, "How SF Battle with HIV/AIDS Shaped Today's Coronavirus Response," *San Francisco Chronicle*, April 4, 2020.

48. Interview with Tomás Aragón.

49. Kang, "What the San Francisco Bay Area Can Teach Us."

Chapter 4

Texas and COVID-19 Emergency Orders

Miranda E. Sullivan and David L. Leal

On March 4, 2020, the state of Texas declared its first presumptive positive case of COVID-19.[1] This travel-related case was located in Fort Bend County, which is in the Houston area, but many Texans had undoubtedly been infected before this date.[2] The commissioner of the Texas Department of State Health Services (DSHS), Dr. John Hellerstedt, observed that "having a COVID-19 case in Texas is a significant development in this outbreak," although he also noted that at this early stage "it doesn't change the fact that the immediate risk to most Texans is low."[3] The state also created a website dedicated to the pandemic, dshs.texas.gov/coronavirus.

The appearance of COVID in Texas was not unexpected. According to the DSHS, Texas agencies "have been preparing for the arrival of COVID-19 since it was first identified in China and began spreading to other countries. Planning has been going on continuously for laboratory testing, public health investigation and isolation and care for people who test positive." Governor Greg Abbott stated, "Over the past month, the state of Texas has been preparing for this moment, and we are confident in the steps we have taken to safeguard our communities against the coronavirus."[4]

This initial case was announced only a week prior to the World Health Organization's (WHO) designation of COVID-19 as a pandemic, and nine days prior to both the federal government's declaration of a national emergency and Texas governor Greg Abbott's declaration of a state disaster.[5] The federal government did not implement an immediate, clear, and centralized set of policies, however, so state and local governments were left to design and implement their own responses to the pandemic.

This chapter examines how policy makers and the public in Texas responded to the COVID pandemic. It describes the public health context, the content and timing of state and local policies, divergences between the approaches of Texas and the federal government, conflicts between state and local governments, the varying actions and statements of statewide elected officials, and public opinion about state and local actors.

Facing a health crisis unprecedented in modern memory, elected officials had multiple priorities to balance, little experience with infectious diseases, and no easy answers. Whereas future accounts of COVID will undoubtedly include a great deal of Monday-morning quarterbacking, this chapter focuses on what happened, how state and local officials explained their decisions at the time, and the complexities caused by a federal system of government. We see a story of different policy responses across levels of government, policy changes over time, variations in messaging, and shifting public reactions. Partisan polarization also played a role, as it eventually mapped onto the pandemic response via federal–state disagreements and attempted state preemptions of local policies.

The Texas Context

Texas is a state with an independent spirit, so we might expect to see different policy approaches vis-à-vis the federal government and other states. For instance, it is the only continental state not on the national power grid, which was consequential during the freeze in February 2021.[6] On the other hand, state politics is also shaped by the growing partisan polarization that is visible across the nation. For instance, the state has been increasingly active in opposing initiatives from Democratic presidential administrations. As governors and attorneys general from "red" and "blue" states have banded together to oppose federal laws and policies,[7] Texas has often been in the vanguard of such efforts.[8] As the pandemic response involved both national and state policy makers, and across two very different presidencies, how Texas reacted may help illustrate this new development in federalism.

In addition, the state of Texas has increasingly been in conflict with its own cities in a variety of policy realms, ranging from immigration to ride sharing.[9] As we see across the nation, Republican state policy makers have engaged in a policy of preemption by curtailing the policy-making options of primarily Democratic local officials.[10] Such dynamics can also work in the opposite partisan direction, with Democratic states telling Republican localities what they can and cannot do. For instance, California's AB 103 law prevents local governments from entering into new contracts with immigrant detention facilities.[11] How preemption in Texas played a role in state and local pandemic responses helps to better understand this emergent topic.

More generally, this chapter and the book project to which it contributes help to advance the unfortunately neglected study of state politics. Political scientists have long focused on national dynamics, despite state and local governments being consequential actors. For example, the amount of research on the presidency and presidential elections overwhelms and overshadows the small literature on governors and gubernatorial elections.[12] This imbalance is problematic for our understanding of politics and policy in a constitutional system that gives considerable sovereignty and autonomy to the states. Across a wide variety of policy areas, the states can choose paths of cooperation, conflict, or independence from the federal government. In recent years, controversies around "sanctuary cities" and the Affordable Care Act have brought into relief how federalism can create a patchwork of policies across the nation, although whether for better or worse is for individuals to decide.

Texas is also unique as a state that might be on the cusp of partisan change. While a number of states have become more "red" or "blue" in recent history, Texas is one of the largest prizes in an Electoral College system where thin margins of victory can have outsized effects. Often labeled a "red" state, Texas is politically diverse across multiple dimensions. Although all elected statewide officials are currently Republicans and both legislative chambers are controlled by the GOP, politicians with the same party label are not always on the same political page—as was the case historically when Texas was dominated by the Democratic Party.

In addition, Texas is not a state with a single large liberal city surrounded by conservative suburbs, small towns, and rural areas. It contains multiple large urban centers, along with a border region that has traditionally supported Democratic candidates. More recently, the suburbs have become less Republican, which complicates how the two parties approach political dynamics ranging from elections to redistricting.[13] At the presidential level, Democrats have been slowly but steadily eroding the Republican advantage since 2000, with Joe Biden losing by a relatively small six percentage point margin. While many see "turn Texas blue" as more a Democratic rallying cry than an accurate prediction of the immediate future, the future politics of the state are the subject of growing speculation. Few political observers will be surprised if elements of Texas politics become more "purple" in subsequent years.

This changing political landscape raises the stakes for all years. actors, as any missteps could prove costly in an increasingly competitive electoral environment. For example, consider the belief that the state's response to the freeze of 2021 could have implications for the 2022 Texas elections.[14] One-party rule means one-party responsibility, which can be problematic as electoral margins narrow. Another indicator is the attention paid to the actor Matthew McConaughey's potential interest in running for governor. One poll even found him nine points ahead of Governor Abbott.[15] This suggests that politics in Texas may be a political Jenga puzzle, with the right person capable of disrupting business as usual.

This chapter begins by discussing the COVID context in Texas, beginning with the first diagnosed case and continuing with the rise and fall of cases and fatalities across 2020 and 2021. We then detail how local and state officials initially responded to the pandemic. What policies were implemented, and who implemented them?

The next section examines statewide University of Texas/*Texas Tribune* polling data to see how Texans evaluated the role of Governor Greg Abbott and local governments in responding to the pandemic. Texas initially trailed the federal government in utilizing its emergency powers but eventually acted as a trailblazer in the reopening processes, moving before the federal government. In addition, Texas state and local governments were often in conflict over health policies like mask mandates and shutdowns.

We then examine the reopening stage of the pandemic, followed by how Texans viewed state and local governments in this changing context. The section also addresses issues of messaging, preemption, and enforcement and how they affected the public health response of the state. Finally, we highlight the larger lessons learned from the pandemic about the use of emergency powers in Texas.

The Public Health Context

The first COVID case in Texas was announced on March 4, 2020. The infected individual had previously traveled abroad and presumably contracted COVID during his travels. Just over a week later, cases began to appear in Harris, Travis, and Dallas Counties, raising alarm about the possibility of community transmission within the state.

This shows the rise and fall in COVID cases and fatalities in Texas from early 2020 through the end of 2021. We see three major peaks: in the summer of 2020, the winter of 2020–21, and the fall of 2021.

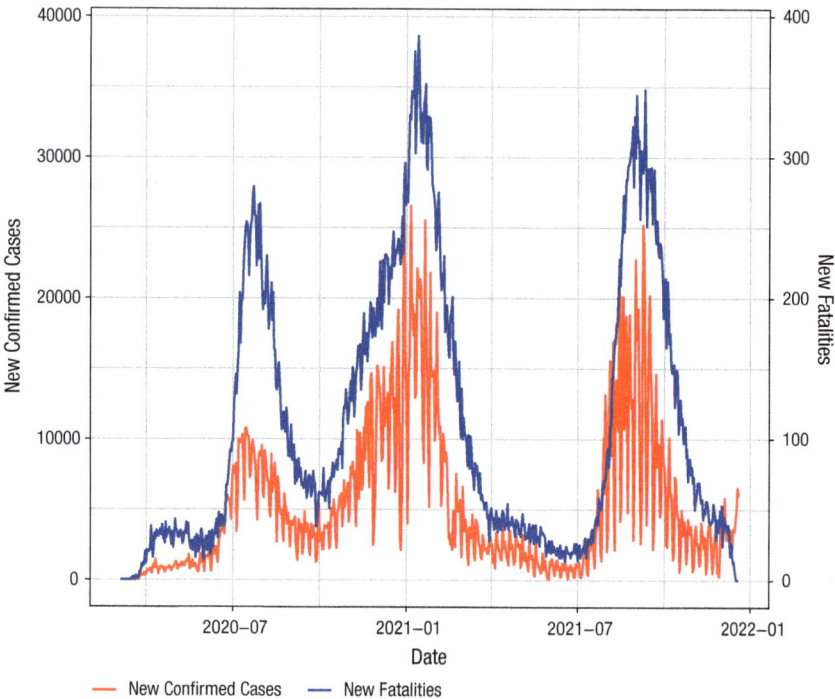

Figure 4.1. Texas COVID cases and fatalities by date

Sources: Centers for Disease Control and Prevention (CDC), COVID Data Tracker, US Department of Health and Human Services, accessed September 29, 2021, https://covid.cdc.gov/covid-data-tracker.

Early 2020: Texas Closes

As COVID began to spread around Texas in March 2020, there was no centralized, comprehensive emergency response from the federal government, which created a policy gap that state officials began to fill. President Trump emphasized this approach a few weeks into the pandemic, telling governors, "You are going to call your own shots. I've gotten to know almost all of you, most of you I've known and some very well. You are all very capable people, I think in all cases, very capable people. And you're going to be calling your shots."[16] In the case of Texas, this meant that much of the COVID response would be initiated by Governor Greg Abbott as well as by city and county officials.

What was the legal basis for public health directives from the governor? In Texas, gubernatorial emergency powers are primarily derived from the Texas Disaster Act of 1975, which outlines the authority of state and local governments during a declared emergency in the state. One of the most notable contributions of this act is the creation of the Division of Emergency Management, under the direction of both the governor and the Texas Department of Public Safety, which helps to coordinate state and federal resources and agencies to best respond to an emergency.[17]

Additionally, based on the Texas Health and Safety Code, the state government has been able to claim the power to quarantine and generally restrict the movement of Texans during an emergency.[18] Specifically, a court case in New Jersey during the threat of Ebola helped establish a model response to challenges to a state's quarantine powers. *Hickox v. Christie* upheld the state of New Jersey's right to enforce quarantine should it be deemed necessary for public health.[19] Although not every emergency power used to mitigate the COVID pandemic was clearly outlined in state policy, the historical trend is generally one of state court approval of more expansive emergency orders.[20]

In March 2020, the concern about community-spread COVID-19 heightened around the country, including Texas. The first state action was Greg Abbott's declaration of a state of disaster ("I . . . do hereby certify that COVID-19 poses an imminent threat of disaster") on March 13, which was the same day that President Trump declared a national emergency.[21] Abbott's order made available state resources to help better finance COVID response measures, such as increasing testing capacity and expanding the supply of personal protective equipment. It also urged institutions that house high-risk individuals, such as prisons and nursing homes, to implement measures, such as limited visitation, to keep their communities safe.[22] It did not include a stay-at-home order, although by this point thirty-nine states, with both Democratic and Republican governors, had already issued one.[23]

On March 14, the day after Abbott's declaration, local governments in Texas began to take their own approach to the crisis. For the next few days, Governor Abbott stated that local governments could respond as they saw fit, as they proceeded to do, and he would therefore not implement statewide closures of schools and businesses as many states had already done.[24]

In Texas, the county judge is broadly considered to be the highest executive and judicial authority within the county. County judges often lead the county commissioners court and distribute information to the public, among other responsibilities.[25] For example, after Abbott's declaration, Harris County judge Lina Hidalgo ordered bars and clubs to be temporarily closed and for restaurants to offer take-out service only.[26]

The next day, the first known death from COVID occurred in Texas. The patient was in his late nineties and lived in Matagorda County. According to Dr. Hellerstedt, "A death in Texas shows the gravity of the situation. It's critically important for us all to take actions that will help protect our most vulnerable citizens. By working together, we can slow the spread of COVID-19 and help ensure the health care system will be able to care for those who need it most." Texas Department of State Health Services gave the following advice to Texans: "Public health officials are further advising residents to limit their risk of exposure by avoiding large gatherings and crowded places, practicing good personal hygiene, and continuing their own preparations in case they need to stay home for two weeks. DSHS also urges people to follow the advice of local leaders for other community actions that will help stop the spread of the disease."[27]

On March 19, Governor Abbott adjusted course and issued Executive Order GA-08. This ordered the closing of bars, schools, and gymnasiums, and it required restaurants to offer takeout only until at least April 3, 2020.[28] On the same day, the Texas Supreme Court issued its Fourth Emergency Order, which was one of many emergency orders by the court that would address complications introduced by the COVID-19 pandemic.[29] This order suspended eviction proceedings for a month.[30] Governor Abbott said the ruling "offers a lifeline to many

Texans who are beginning to feel the economic impact of COVID-19, the disease caused by the new coronavirus."[31]

The Texas Supreme Court action followed in the footsteps of local governments across the state and country. For more information about local government actions regarding evictions, for instance, see chapter 5 in this volume by Farris, Holman, and Sullivan. March 19 was therefore a crucial day in Texas's initial pandemic response, and notably, the policy response was contained in two orders from two branches of state government.

The governor also created the Texas Eviction Diversion Program in September 2020, which was intended to fund "rental assistance and legal services for Texans facing eviction" via funding from the federal CARES Act. The original expiration date was in July 2021, but this was extended by the Texas Supreme Court through its Thirty-Fourth Emergency Order. The Texas Department of Housing and Community Affairs reported that over eighty thousand households received assistance, and that over ninety million dollars was received by over ten thousand households. According to the *Texas Tribune*, "Fred Fuchs, an attorney with Texas RioGrande Legal Aid, said that although he has seen the statewide rent relief program make a difference in clients' lives, evictions are still a worry because a federal eviction moratorium is set to expire on July 31."[32]

Once these initial measures were in place, state and local governments changed their focus to ensuring that hospitals and health care workers had sufficient resources and supplies. The first action was taken by Dallas County, where elective medical procedures were banned on March 21 in hopes of conserving capacity and resources for COVID patients.[33] The next day, Governor Abbott extended this policy to the entire state when he ordered the postponement of elective procedures.[34] His March 22 order prohibited any procedures that were not "medically necessary," in an effort to conserve resources for COVID-19 patients.

The first shelter-in-place order was issued on March 23 by Judge Clay Jenkins of Dallas County, which temporarily closed nonessential businesses and asked the community to stay home unless purchasing essential goods or going outside for exercise, such as walking.[35] Although this action by Dallas County was controversial, other local governments followed suit the next day. On March 24, the following counties issued shelter-in-place orders: Tarrant (Dallas-Fort Worth), Harris (Houston), Bexar (San Antonio), Collin (Dallas-Fort Worth), and Travis (Austin), among others.[36] These counties encompassed the largest cities in the state.

One week later, on March 31, Governor Abbott signed Executive Order GA-14, which asked Texans to stay home as much as possible. At this point in the pandemic, Texas had recorded 3,266 confirmed cases.[37] According to an *Austin American-Statesman* editorial, "His latest executive order tells Texans to minimize contact with other people unless they are providing or receiving 'essential services,' such as going to the grocery store or pharmacy, seeing a doctor, taking a jog or going to work at a critical job that can't be done from home." Although he did not term this a "stay-at-home" order, the editorial argued that "it largely mirrors stay-at-home mandates already passed by dozens of counties and cities, including Austin and Dallas, which provide similar exceptions for essential outings."[38]

The executive order stated that "every person in Texas shall, except where necessary to provide or obtain essential services, minimize social gatherings and minimize in-person contact with people who are not in the same household." It defined "essential services" as "everything listed by the U.S. Department of Homeland Security in its Guidance on the Essential Critical Infrastructure Workforce, Version 2.0, plus religious services conducted in churches, congregations, and houses of worship."

Furthermore, when carrying out essential services, "people and businesses should follow the Guidelines from the President and the CDC by practicing good hygiene, environmental cleanliness, and sanitation, implementing social distancing, and working from home if possible. In particular, all services should be provided through remote telework from home unless they are essential services that cannot be provided through remote telework."[39]

The topic of religion and the pandemic would gain political attention, as several local closure orders included religious institutions. In the following year, Texas voters approved Proposition 3, a constitutional amendment with the following language:

> Sec. 6-a. This state or a political subdivision of this state may not enact, adopt, or issue a statute, order, proclamation, decision, or rule that prohibits or limits religious services, including religious services conducted in churches, congregations, and places of worship, in this state by a religious organization established to support and serve the propagation of a sincerely held religious belief.

The amendment had been previously passed by the Texas State Senate (28–2) and the Texas House of Representatives (108–33). It was approved by Texas voters on November 2, 2021, by a large margin (62.42 to 37.58 percent), although not without some opposition.[40]

State–Federal Comparisons

The initial pandemic response in Texas can be characterized as delayed in comparison to that of the federal government. Figure 4.2 uses the Oxford COVID-19 Government Response Tracker, a database that represents the presence, or lack thereof, of COVID mitigation actions at federal and state levels. The policies accounted for within this measure include, but are not limited to, the presence of a mask mandate, school closures, and limitations on business operations. Based on the COVID mitigation policies implemented within the state during a given day, a numerical value is assigned to the state to represent its overall COVID mitigation policy level during that day. This graph illustrates the totality of key COVID policies enacted during this early time in the pandemic (March and April 2020) by the federal government and the state of Texas.

According to these data, Texas initially had fewer response measures than did the federal government, albeit for a relatively short period of

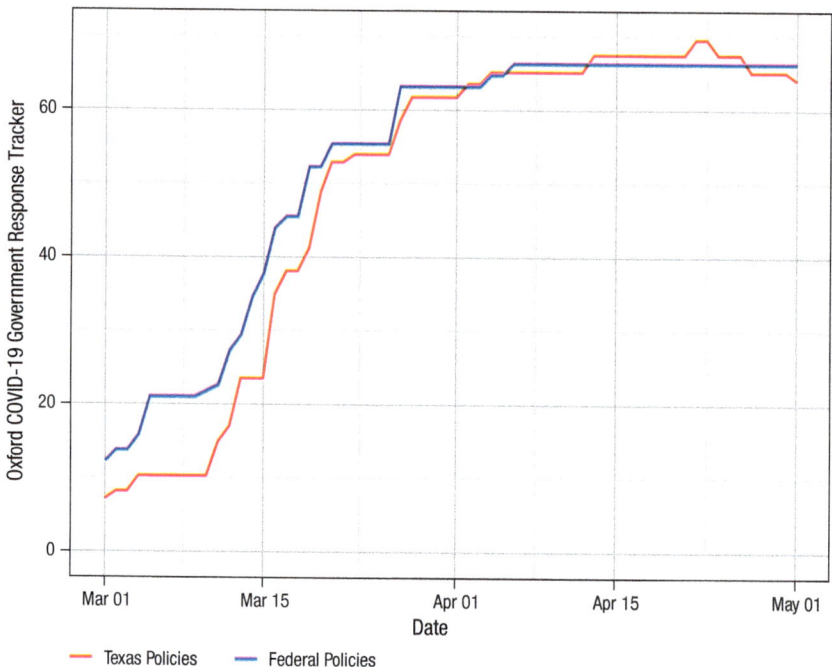

Figure 4.2. Texas and national and government response index
Data for March and April 2020.

Source: Oxford COVID-19 Government Response Tracker, accessed September 29, 2021, Blavatnik School of Government, University of Oxford.

time. By early April, Texas reached the national government response index score. For a brief time in April, the Texas figure was higher than that of the national government.

These data represent a time when Trump was in the White House, so they do not reflect partisan policy differences. Also, the presentation of such data is not to imply that Texas should or should not have had a higher or lower index score than did the national government. Those are policy choices for elected and appointed officials.

We also wanted to compare the Texas response with that of other states in 2020–21. Figure 4.3 compares Texas to four other states traditionally considered "red," thereby taking partisanship into account.

These states are Arizona, Florida, Georgia, and Oklahoma. We see that all five increased their overall policy responses initially, and with much the same numerical pattern. We then see a general decline in index scores, although Arizona was something of an outlier with the earliest decline followed by approximate stability within the 50 to 60 range. Florida and Georgia had the highest index numbers in the summer, but then both declined, with Florida's the steepest. Oklahoma also showed a very steep decline, as by mid-summer it had the lowest index score. All state scores moved upward toward the end of the year, which undoubtedly reflected the increasing COVID numbers at that time. All five states ended the year somewhere in the 50 to 60 range.

In general, Texas was in the middle range of this five-state group. It moved upward with all states (excepting the early Arizona decline), and

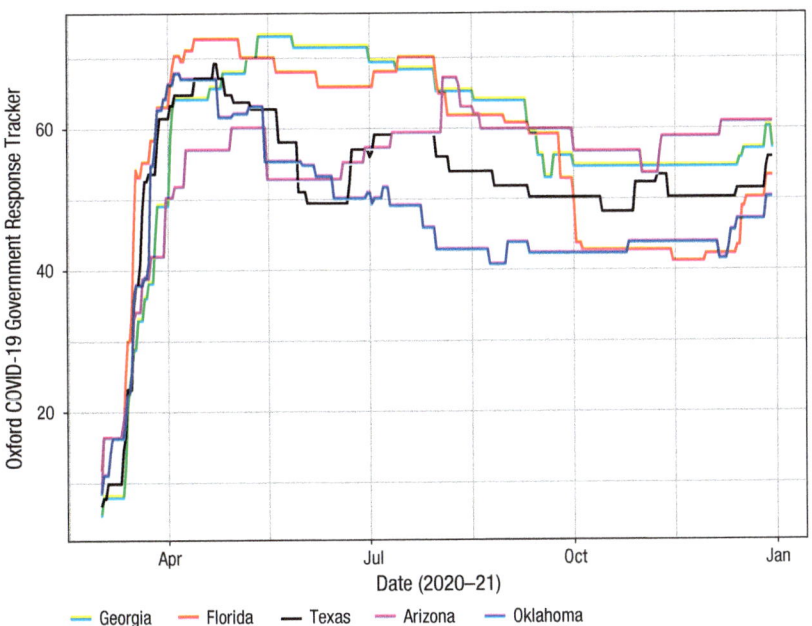

Figure 4.3. Policy response in red states
Source: Oxford COVID-19 Government Response Tracker.

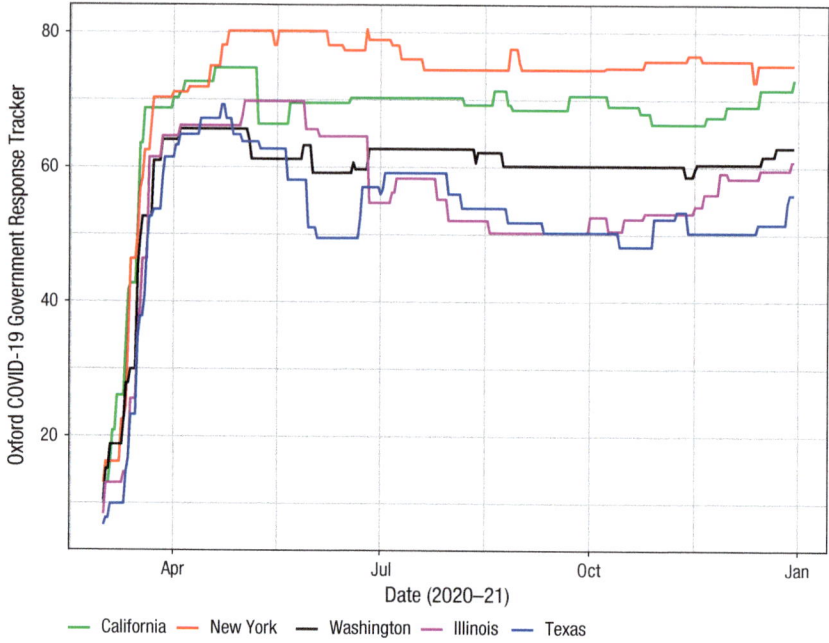

Figure 4.4. Policy response in Texas and blue states
Source: Oxford COVID-19 Government Response Tracker.

then declined sharply and had the lowest score at points in June. The state's score then increased during the remainder of the summer and began to decline in the fall, where it remained at approximately 50.

Figure 4.4 compares Texas with four large "blue" states—California, New York, Washington, and Illinois. Texas largely maintains a lower policy response level than these blue states, though Illinois and Texas remain close and exchange leads at times. After Texas's large dip at the beginning of its reopening phase in April and May 2020, we see a general pattern of stability among these blue states and Texas after the summer. The main substantive difference is that Texas continues to remain at a lower policy level than most blue states even as it follows this general pattern.

Other State Officials and Policies

Abortion and COVID

On March 23, Attorney General Ken Paxton issued an interpretation of Abbott's nonessential medical procedure order. Paxton declared it to include any procedure that would not be immediately necessary to prevent adverse effects or death, thereby encompassing most abortion procedures. According to the *Austin American-Statesman*, he said, "We must work together as Texans to stop the spread of COVID-19 and ensure that our health care professionals and facilities have all the resources they need to fight the virus at this time." In addition, "No one is exempt from the governor's executive order on medically unnecessary surgeries and procedures, including abortion providers." He noted that the order allowed for abortions "medically necessary to preserve the life or health of the mother."[41] He also added that violating a gubernatorial executive order could result in a fine of up to one thousand dollars and up to 180 days in jail.

Abortion providers, including Planned Parenthood, promptly challenged this on the grounds that abortion procedures require very little staff or personal protective equipment and that the order violated the Fourteenth Amendment of the US Constitution.[42] While Paxton's order was initially blocked by US District Court judge Lee Yeakel of Austin, the Fifth Circuit Court would ultimately overturn the lower court decisions and thereby leave in place this ban on most abortions throughout this early phase of the pandemic.[43]

On April 17, Governor Abbott issued a new order that would have the effect of allowing some abortions to resume. Technically, it allowed nonessential procedures to resume as long as this "would not deplete the hospital capacity or the personal protective equipment needed to cope with the COVID-19 disaster" or if the facility certified that "it will reserve at least 25% of its hospital capacity for treatment of COVID-19 patients" and "will not request any personal protective equipment from any public source, whether federal, state, or local, for the duration of the COVID-19 disaster."[44]

According to the *Texas Tribune*, "Abbott demurred when asked last week if abortions could proceed under his latest directive, saying it was a decision for the courts and 'not part of this order.' But abortion providers said they meet the criteria he laid out—and the state did not dispute that in its filing Wednesday."[45]

Nevertheless, "the state asked the [US] Supreme Court to keep the appeals court rulings on the books," but on January 25, 2021, the high court voided the Fifth Circuit rulings. While the state argued that the Fifth Circuit decisions "have been cited hundreds of times in courts across the country" in COVID restriction cases, Planned Parenthood responded that because Abbott's new rule prevented a continued court challenge, the Fifth Circuit decisions should be vacated lest they "tie petitioners' hands in future cases."[46]

Economics and Reopening

Not long into the crisis, variations of opinion developed across and within levels of Texas government. While many elected officials and health professionals urged Texans to stay home to protect the vulnerable, a debate emerged about the trade-offs between public health and the economy.

In a Fox News interview with Tucker Carlson on March 24, Lieutenant Governor Dan Patrick stated the following: "No one reached out to me and said, 'As a senior citizen, are you willing to take a chance on your survival in exchange for keeping the America that all America loves for your children and grandchildren?' And if that's the exchange, I'm all in. And that doesn't make me noble or brave or anything like that."[47]

At that point, the context was both national and local. On that same day, President Trump said in a Fox virtual town hall meeting, "You can destroy a country this way by closing it down. . . . You're going to lose more people by putting a country into a massive recession or a depression." He added that he wanted the nation "open for business" by April 12.[48]

Responding to Trump, Patrick said, "My heart is lifted tonight by what I heard the president say because we can do more than one thing at a time. We can do two things. So you know, my message is that: Let's get back to work. Let's get back to living. Let's be smart about it, and those of us who are 70-plus, we'll take care of ourselves, but don't sacrifice the country. Don't do that. Don't ruin this great American dream."[49]

Other responses to Trump were less positive. According to *US News & World Report*, New York governor Andrew Cuomo said, "My mother is not expendable. Your mother is not expendable. We will not put a dollar figure on human life. We can have a public health strategy that is consistent with an economic one. No one should be talking about social darwinism for the sake of the stock market." And Liz Cheney (R-WY) tweeted the following, but without mentioning Trump: "Letting the virus spread to your parents and grandparents to protect your 401k is not pro-life."[50] In Texas, Beto O'Rourke (the Democratic candidate for US Senate in 2018 and, later, for governor in 2022) tweeted, "This kind of numbnuttery will kill people in Texas. Young as well as old. We need a state-wide shelter in place order to stop the spread of coronavirus and save hundreds of thousands of lives."[51]

At this point, local governments in Texas were moving in the opposite direction. According to the *Texas Tribune*, "Even as Patrick made those comments, mayors of most of Texas' largest cities heeded the calls of most scientists, doctors and other health care professionals. One by one, beginning Sunday and moving into Tuesday, many Texas mayors ordered or were in the process of ordering their cities' residents to stay home."[52]

A week later, Governor Abbott issued the above-noted Executive Order GA-14. In attendance was Dan Patrick, House Speaker Dennis Bonnen, and various state health and education officials. The governor's office also invoked Trump, noting that "Today's Executive Order follows the decision by President Trump and the Centers for Disease

Control and Prevention (CDC) to enhance social distancing guidelines and extend the deadline for these guidelines to April 30th."[53]

A month later, Patrick would double down, telling Tucker Carlson "I'm sorry to say I was right on this and I'm thankful that now we are now [sic] finally beginning to open up Texas and other states because it's been long overdue." He also said, "I don't want to die, nobody wants to die, but man we've got to take some risks and get back in the game and get this country back up and running."[54] These statements received much attention, and the *Texas Tribune* noted that "he is not alone in his pleas to reopen Texas' doors. Hardline conservatives in the state, including some members of the Texas House Freedom Caucus, have begged the governor to allow businesses to open their doors."[55]

The chair of the Texas Democratic Party, Gilberto Hinojosa, took a different perspective on reopening: "Texas Republicans like Greg Abbott and Dan Patrick would put Texans at-risk to enrich themselves and their stock portfolios. The lives of our families, our friends, and our communities have no dollar amount."[56]

This debate illustrates the different perspectives of state and local actors about how to best mitigate the spread of COVID. Dan Patrick's initial comments appeared one day after the largest counties issued shelter-in-place orders and a week before Governor Abbott urged Texans to stay home. Noting this divergent rhetoric is not to take sides or engage in any Monday-morning quarterbacking. Instead, we show that at this early stage in the pandemic, Texans heard varying messages both across and within levels of government.

Public Opinion in the Early Stages

How did Texans view these emergency orders implemented early in the pandemic? The University of Texas/*Texas Tribune* fielded a statewide survey in mid-April, immediately before Governor Abbott announced the beginning of the reopening process in Texas. After nearly a month of unprecedented (and sometimes varying) emergency orders, what did

Texans think of how the governor and local governments were handling the crisis?

As discussed above, Texas's emergency orders were initially fewer than those of the federal government but quickly caught up; by contrast, state efforts began and remained less vigorous than those of its local governments. What were the attitudes of Texans toward Greg Abbott's handling of the COVID pandemic up to this point? More specifically, were Texans from large cities more or less favorable toward Greg Abbott, given that they had witnessed a more extensive use of local emergency orders? Finally, what were Texans' attitudes toward their local government's handling of the pandemic, and did this differ by city and region?

The University of Texas/*Texas Tribune* poll not only shows statewide opinion but also reveals some differences between respondents in Houston, Dallas-Fort Worth, San Antonio, Austin, and other areas. Recall that each of these large cities implemented a number of emergency orders both prior to, and stricter than, those enacted at the state level. However, Governor Abbott would also attempt to impose limitations on local emergency orders, and such preemptions became an important part of the debate.

Figures 4.5 and 4.6 illustrate how Texans viewed Governor Abbott's handling of the COVID crisis. Respondents were given five options: strongly disapprove, disapprove, neither, approve, and strongly approve. Figure 4.5 displays the opinions of the state as a whole, and figure 4.6 demonstrates these opinions broken down by metropolitan statistical area (MSA) to see which cities in Texas displayed which levels of support.

In figure 4.5, the modal response was "strongly approve," while "approve" was the second most popular option. A smaller share expressed strong disapproval or disapproval, and relatively few Texans were in the middle. The graph is approximately U-shaped, which suggests a degree of polarization. It is possible that partisanship played a role, despite the question asking specifically about the governor's handling of COVID, and not overall approval or disapproval.

Figure 4.6 breaks down opinion according to region. Each bar represents the percentage of respondents who chose that option, with the

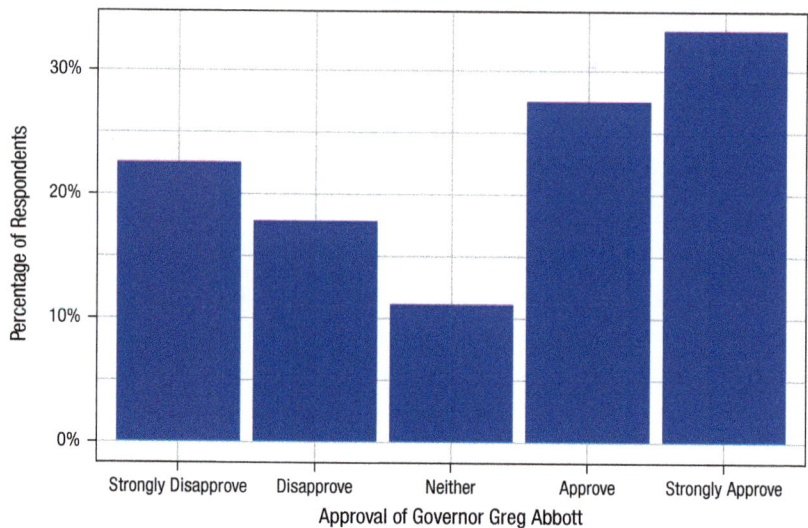

Figure 4.5. Statewide Approval of Governor Abbott in April 2020

Source: University of Texas/*Texas Tribune* Poll, April 2020, https://texaspolitics.utexas.edu/polling-data-archive.

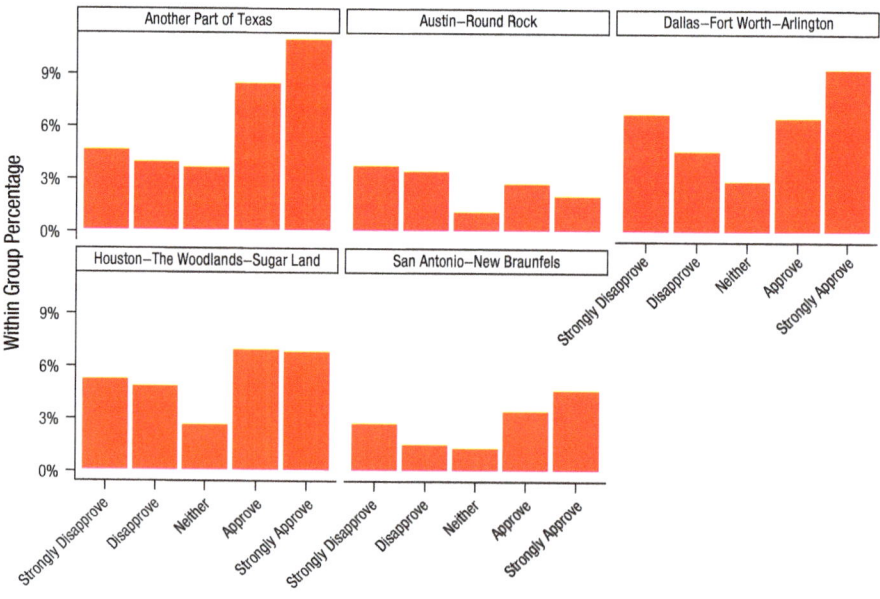

Figure 4.6. Approval of Governor Abbott's handling of COVID-19 by MSA in April 2020

Source: University of Texas/*Texas Tribune* Poll, April 2020.

y-axis representing the percentage of the entire group of Texans that falls into that category, which allows us to see the sampling variation between these metropolitan statistical areas. As we can see, with the exception of Austin, a Democratic Party stronghold, Texans largely reported more approval than disapproval of Greg Abbott's handling of the pandemic. The governor also had much more approval than disapproval among Texans who did not call these large urban areas home.

We again see additional evidence of polarization, as the graphs generally have a U-shaped pattern; more respondents reported "strongly approve" or "strongly disapprove" than gave the "neither" response. While the shapes of the "U" vary in the five regions, the beginning of the pandemic saw more support than opposition for the governor, and with relatively few Texans in the middle.

How did Texans view their local governments, which often implemented orders that were both earlier and stricter than those implemented by the state? Figure 4.7 indicates strong support for such governments at this stage of the pandemic. We also see less polarization, as the graph is no longer U-shaped. This may reflect the fact that local units of government are more likely to reflect the partisanship of their respondents than a state government is to represent residents of the whole state.

In figure 4.8, all regions show much higher levels of approval than disapproval of the handling of the pandemic by local governments. This approval of local governments is considerably larger than the corresponding approval of Governor Abbott. A Pearson's chi-squared test, which tests whether the relationship we see between standard metropolitan statistical areas and Abbott approval is likely to occur by random chance, indicates a statistically significant difference ($p = 0.0002$) in attitudes by region.

However, we might note that the questions are not equivalent, as the state question is asked in terms of an individual (Abbott) whereas the local question is asked about these institutions in general. Furthermore, localities are likely to be more politically homogenous than is a state. We therefore cannot rule out that partisanship led to this greater

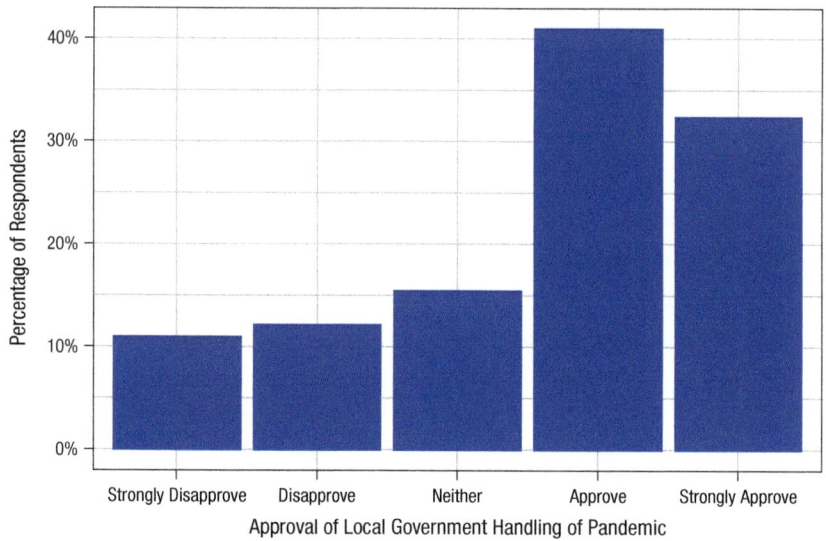

Figure 4.7. Statewide approval of local government in April 2020
Source: University of Texas/*Texas Tribune* Poll, April 2020.

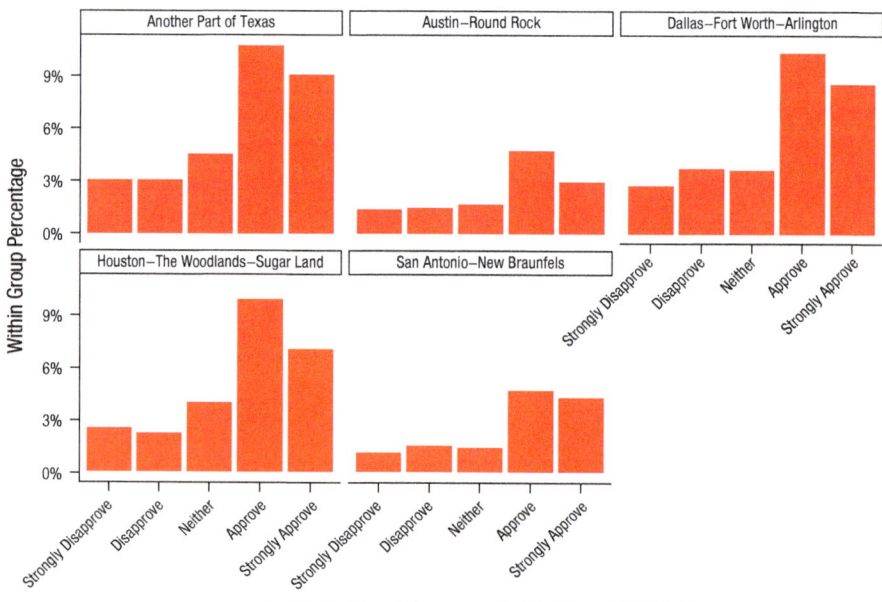

Figure 4.8. Approval of local government's handling of COVID–19 by MSA in April 2020
Source: University of Texas/*Texas Tribune* Poll, April 2020.

support for local governments than for a statewide leader (who has a specific party affiliation).

We should also note that these respondents were surveyed immediately before Governor Abbott announced the state's reopening plans. A majority of Texans reported approving of his COVID policies when the state's strictest emergency orders were in place, but did their attitudes change when the reopening process began? And how did respondents react as local governments across the state maintained their emergency orders while the state government moved to reopen?

Before we turn to these reactions, let us consider the elements of this reopening process. In the section that follows, we outline the actions by Governor Abbott and other officials that began to unwind the emergency orders in place across the state.

Texas Reopens

In this section, we outline which state emergency orders were lifted and which orders remained in place. We then examine how local governments navigated these changes: which emergency policies did they attempt to continue, and what limitations did the state attempt to impose? We also examine instances when localities, particularly school districts, tried to defy the state. Finally, we review University of Texas/*Texas Tribune* polling data about the exposure of Texans to COVID and the reported financial effects.

On April 27, 2020, Greg Abbott announced that on May 1 he would begin easing the restrictions implemented by his emergency orders. This took place right after the fielding of the April wave of the University of Texas/*Texas Tribune* survey. Figure 4.9 demonstrates the changes in federal and Texas policy responses during this time period. In early April, the COVID policy index was essentially the same for these two levels of government. Beginning around mid-month, the Texas numbers are even higher than those of the federal government (see figure 4.2). Toward the end of April, however, we see a decrease

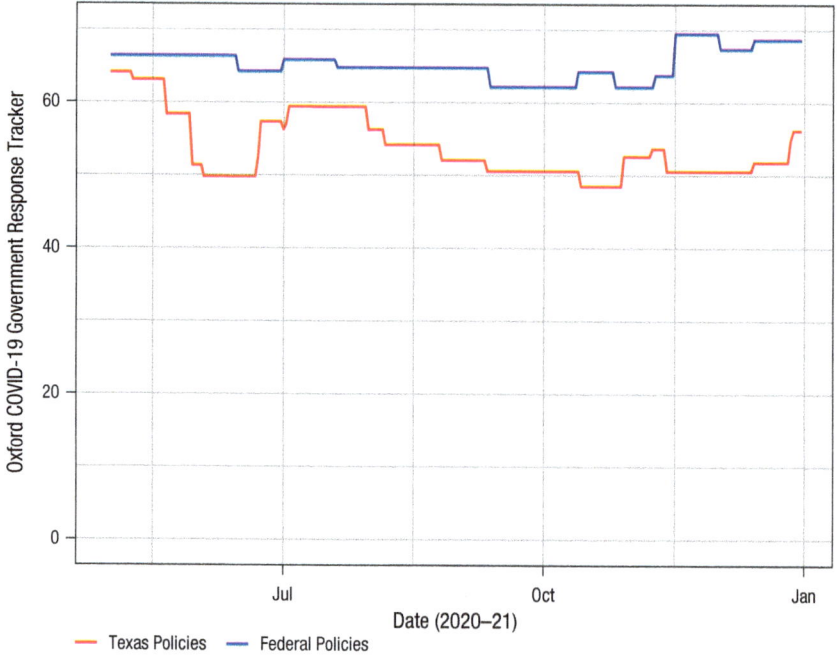

Figure 4.9. Texas and national government response index
Source: CDC, COVID Data Tracker.

in the Texas index, whereas the federal response remained fairly constant. Although the Texas index showed some subsequent fluctuation, it remained below the figure for the federal government in 2020.

Most emergency orders were only partially lifted, given that the pandemic was still continuing at this time, and many orders remained in place, depending on the risk levels associated with a business. For example, on May 1, Abbott allowed restaurants, retail, libraries, movie theaters, and similar businesses to reopen but limited their capacities to 25 percent in an attempt to continue to limit the risk of spreading COVID. Businesses that were considered to pose a higher risk of transmission, such as gymnasiums and bars, were still ordered to remain closed.[57]

Some experts across the state saw this action as too early.[58] The interim health authority of Austin, Mark Escott, stated, "This is too soon for us. As we're still preparing contact tracing, ramping up testing, working to protect vulnerable populations, now is not the time to flip on the light switch."[59] Other public health experts were not necessarily critical of Abbott's phased reopening plan so long as testing was increased; however, they suggested that the state might encounter setbacks along the way. The president of the Baylor College of Medicine, Dr. Paul Klotman, warned the public that they would likely see "two steps forward and one step backward as outbreaks occur."[60]

At this time, Abbott did not impose a mask mandate, as did about a third of the other states. While these states collectively had leadership on both sides of the aisle, more states with Democratic governors issued mask mandates than those with Republican governors.[61] Moreover, Republican-led states with similar outbreaks to Texas, like Georgia and Florida, also did not issue mask mandates at this point in the pandemic.[62] Therefore, it is not surprising that Governor Abbott refrained from imposing a mask mandate.

Once Texas's phased reopening began, the phases moved quickly. Within a week of ordering that salons remain closed, Abbott allowed them to reopen and begin providing services. A week later, Abbott began phase two of reopening and doubled the capacity of retail stores, restaurants, and other lower-risk businesses to 50 percent capacity; he also allowed higher-risk businesses, such as bars, to reopen at 25 percent capacity. With phase two beginning only two weeks after phase one, Texans may not have been able to witness the effects of the phase one reopening before the state changed to phase two, which could have implications for the public opinion data discussed below.

On June 3, only a few weeks after the initiation of phase two, Governor Abbott moved to phase three. This consisted of allowing most businesses in the state of Texas to reopen at 50 percent capacity. Nine days after this announcement, restaurants were permitted to reopen to 75 percent capacity.

The reopening measures were associated with an increase in COVID cases, however, which put a temporary halt to the state's reopening plans.[63] On June 25, Abbott lowered the allowed capacity of restaurants back to 50 percent in order to address this rise in cases. When this proved insufficient to reduce the surge of cases that Texas was experiencing, Abbott implemented a mask mandate a week later, a policy that he had previously opposed.[64] This required Texans to wear a mask in public spaces and businesses in all counties with twenty or more COVID cases.[65]

Moving forward, Governor Abbott added few new emergency orders, although he did follow the earlier actions of numerous local governments by postponing all elective medical procedures in order to maintain hospital capacity for COVID patients, as noted above. While Abbott was reluctant to put new emergency orders in place, he also seemed hesitant in lifting the emergency orders that were already in place. On June 26, reassessing his order from the day before on June 25, he once again limited restaurant capacity to 50 percent and did not allow capacity to move back to 75 percent until September 17.

According to figure 4.9, emergency orders then largely leveled out for the remainder of 2020, although with a few dips and spikes. In addition, these emergency orders were at a lower response level than those of the federal government. The variation in policy levels continued on with the changes in COVID cases and hospitalizations. Finally, at the beginning of March 2021, Greg Abbott announced a fully reopened Texas, which would take effect on March 10. This total reopening included a removal of all capacity restrictions and an end to the state mask mandate, effectively ending all substantive COVID-related emergency orders at the state level in Texas.

Some local governments continued to utilize emergency orders to try to limit the spread of COVID as new variants emerged, such as Delta and Omicron. However, the state government largely stepped aside and refrained from implementing any emergency orders at this stage of the pandemic. For this reason, the story of the Texas state government's emergency orders during the COVID pandemic largely ends here.

Texas Opinion: Health and Economic Impact

Throughout this period of reopening, Texans faced a number of health and financial challenges. We compiled descriptive statistics using the 2020 Texas Media and Society Survey, which was conducted by the Annette Strauss Institute for Civic Life at the University of Texas at Austin in October 2020. This survey includes both a nationally representative sample and a significant over-sample of Texans. We subset the data to include only respondents living in Texas in order to capture how Texans experienced the COVID pandemic and viewed the state's response. Once we filtered and subset the data, we had 1,116 respondents, and we examine how they reported the financial and health effects of COVID at this point in the reopening phase of the pandemic.

Figure 4.10 includes responses about employment and finances (which were not mutually exclusive). Over 5 percent of the respondents reported that they had lost their job permanently as a result of the pandemic, and another 5 percent were temporarily laid off. Nearly 15 percent had their hours reduced, and about 5 percent had their hours restored by October. Finally, 30 percent of Texans experienced financial concern due to the pandemic. Taken together, the pandemic collectively upended the financial security of no small share of Texans, even if many of the specific effects were in the single digits.

By this point in the pandemic, many Texans either had contracted COVID or knew a loved one who had. Figure 4.11 shows that although only roughly 3 percent of respondents had contracted COVID, many more reported knowing someone who had. Overall, Texans reported either having COVID or knowing someone who did at a higher rate than did the national average in the survey, though these differences were substantively small.

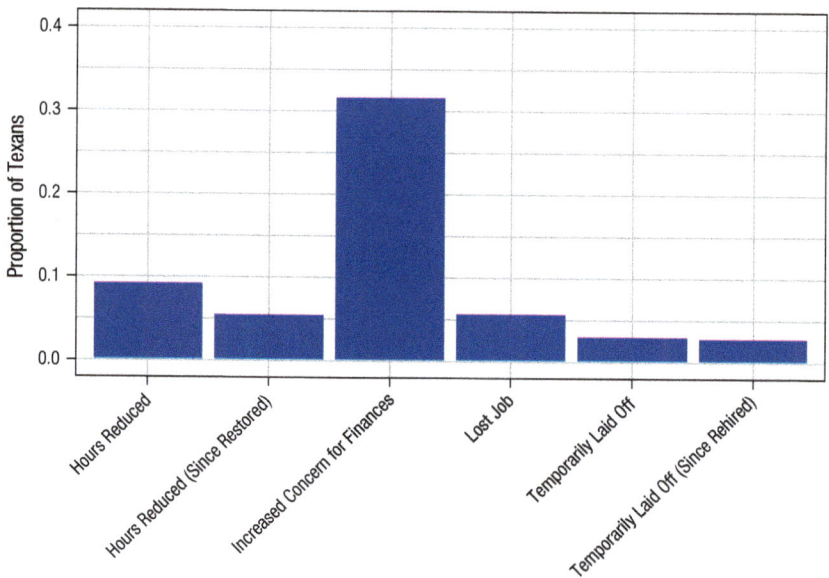

Figure 4.10. Texas and financial impact of COVID-19 in October 2020

Source: Texas Media & Society Survey (2020), Annette Strauss Institute for Civic Life, Moody College of Communication, University of Texas at Austin, https://utexas.app.box.com/v/TMASS-OCT2020.

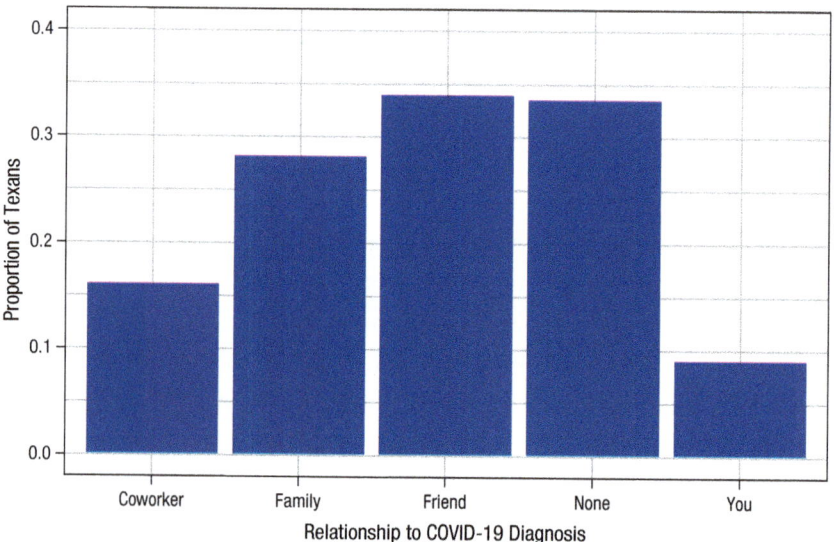

Figure 4.11. Texas and relationship to COVID-19 response in October 2020
Source: Texas Media & Society Survey (2020).

Public Opinion, Part II: How Texans Reacted to Reopening

The University of Texas/*Texas Tribune* survey conducted another wave in late September and early October 2020, which included several measures identical to those used in April. This allows us to compare how attitudes about the governor and local governments persisted or changed as Texas experienced the reopening phase.

As noted above, most Texans in the April survey approved of how Abbott as well as local governments were handling the pandemic. Although local government approval was somewhat higher, the data showed that Texans were generally positive about both.

As before, we are primarily interested in three questions. First, how did Texans view Abbott's handling of the pandemic up to this point, and how did this vary by region? Second, how did Texans view the handling of the pandemic by their local governments, and how did this vary by region? Third, how did opinions about local government compare to evaluations of the governor's handling of the pandemic?

First, in figure 4.12, we see that the modal response about Abbott's handling of the pandemic is now "strongly disapprove." In contrast to the April numbers (figure 4.5), the majority of Texans in October expressed more disapproval than approval of Abbott's performance.

It can also be informative to look more closely at which regions of Texas these levels of approval and disapproval are found. In figure 4.13, we see a general decline in evaluations of the governor's pandemic response. The y-axis represents the percentage out of all respondents that fall within a given category, which helps visually demonstrate that some regions were more prominent in the sample than others. Although the modal response in the four urban areas went from "strongly approve" in April to "strongly disapprove" in October, this obscures much variation. For instance, Austin respondents gave largely the same evaluation pattern. In the other four regions, the share of "strong approval" declined while "approval" remained approximately

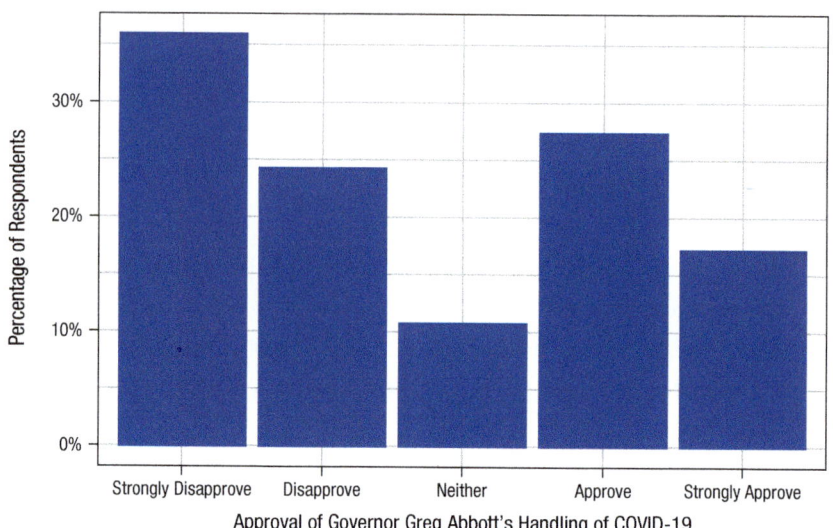

Figure 4.12. Statewide approval of Governor Abbott's handling of pandemic in October 2020

Source: University of Texas/*Texas Tribune* Poll, October 2020.

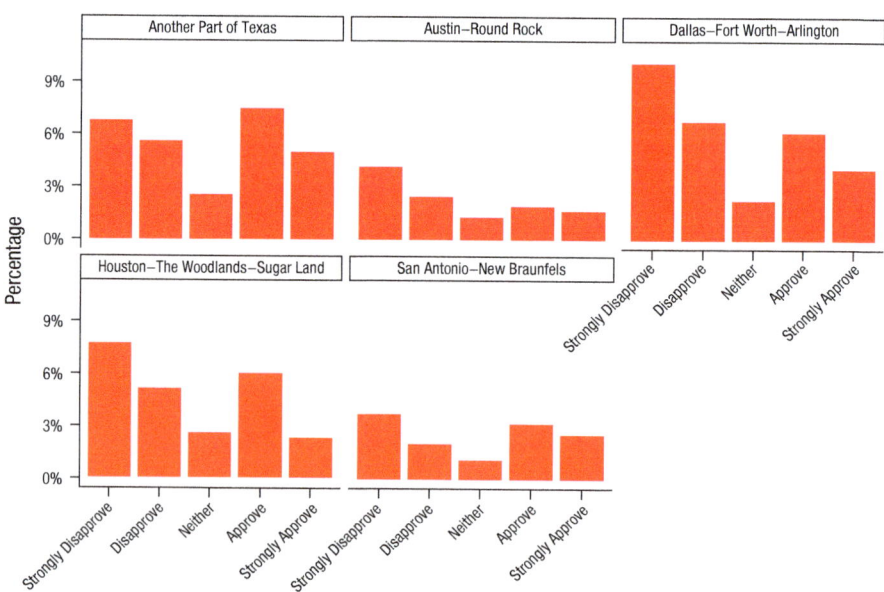

Figure 4.13. Approval of Governor Abbott's handling of COVID-19 by MSA in October 2020

Source: University of Texas/*Texas Tribune* Poll, October 2020.

the same. "Strong disapproval" and "disapproval" ratings increased, while "neither" remained about the same.

Explanations can always be found to explain shifts in the public approval of prominent elected officials, but two notable changes between April and October were the increase in COVID cases and the decrease in emergency orders by the Texas state government. We cannot disentangle one from the other, so Texans may have been expressing frustration with the continuing pandemic or the specific policies enacted by the governor. Governors, like presidents, can electorally benefit during good times but find themselves blamed in difficult times. Whether presidents and governors are responsible for these conditions may matter less than the "retrospective" question voters often ask: "Are we better off now than we were before?"

Adding more context to the earlier data are the results in figures 4.14 and 4.15, which show that Texas also became less positive about the responses of their local governments. In the state as a whole and across all regions, we now see more disapproval than approval of the handling of the COVID pandemic by local governments. At the state level, "approve" was the predominant response in the initial survey (figure 4.7), with "strongly approve" not far behind. In the second survey, "disapprove" was now the modal response, with the other responses approximately the same.

In figure 4.8, which showed regional variation in the initial survey, the relatively high share of respondents who chose "strongly approve" or "approve" was striking, but those choices flattened while "strongly disapprove" and "disapprove" grew considerably. This differs from the patterns we observed in Abbott approval, but the end result—lower approval—is the same in both instances.

If we calculate approval using statistical averages instead of interpreting graphics, we see notable trends. Overall, the approval gap between Abbott and local governments decreased over time, in that both lost support as the pandemic persisted throughout the summer and fall. In April 2020, the average statewide level of approval for Greg Abbott was 3.27 and the average level of approval for local governments was

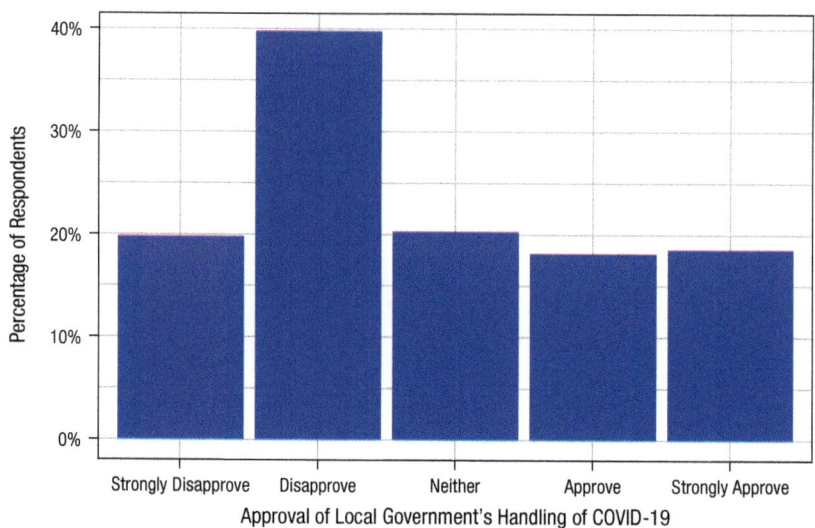

Figure 4.14. Statewide approval of local government's handling of COVID-19 in October 2020

Source: University of Texas/*Texas Tribune* Poll, October 2020.

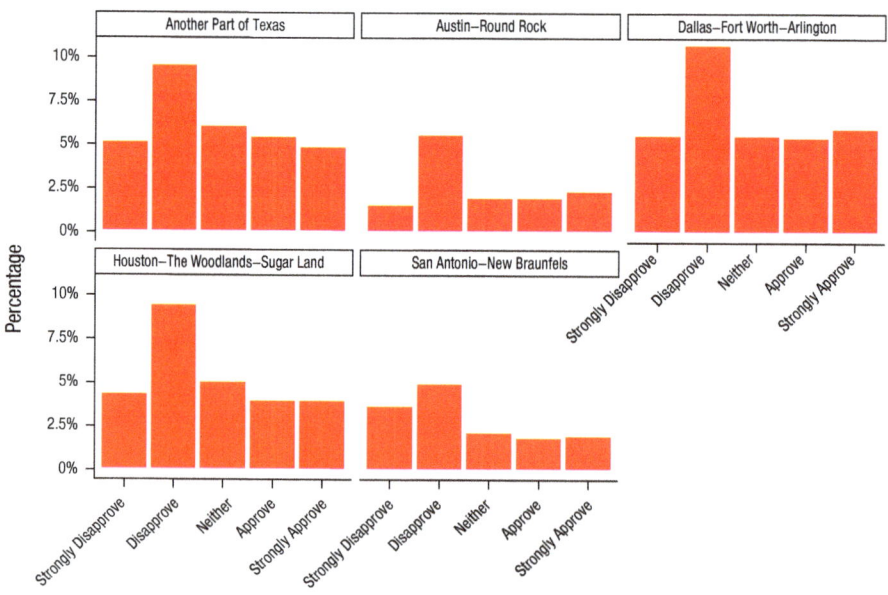

Figure 4.15. Approval of local government's handling of pandemic by MSA in October 2020

Source: University of Texas/*Texas Tribune* Poll, October 2020.

3.64. Both lost approval by October; the average level of approval in that month for Greg Abbott's handling of the pandemic was 2.7, and the average level of approval for local government handling of the pandemic was 2.79—essentially a tie. One possible conclusion about these declines to a similar level is that they reflected public unhappiness with the pandemic itself and were not necessarily a reflection of specific officials or institutions.

Finally, we examine data from the University of Texas/*Texas Tribune* survey from September–October of 2021, approximately a year later. In figure 4.16, we see several notable patterns in Abbott approval. First, the share of "strongly disapprove" responses has increased while those for "disapprove" declined. In a similar way, the "strongly approve" response option increased while "approve" responses declined. The share of respondents in the middle also decreased. This indicates that "strong" responses became more prominent over the year, while the

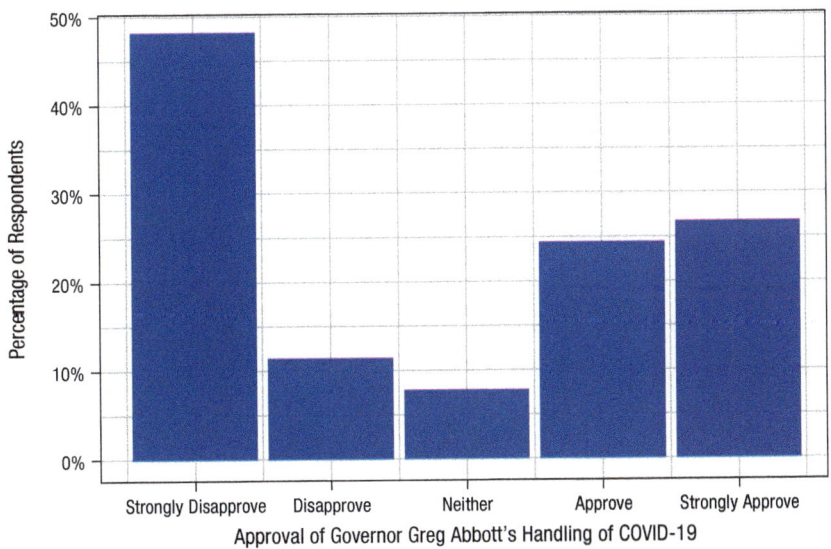

Figure 4.16. Approval of Governor Abbott's handling of COVID-19 in October 2021
Source: University of Texas/*Texas Tribune* Poll, October 2021.

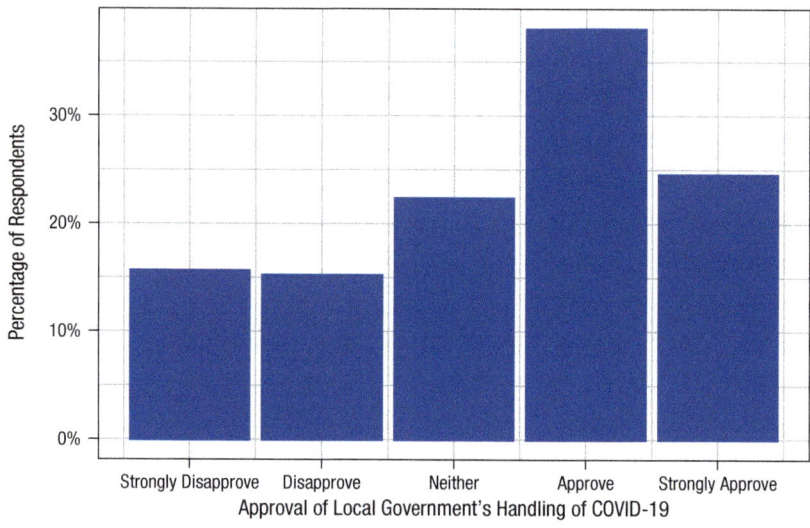

Figure 4.17. Approval of local government's handling of COVID-19 in October 2021
Source: University of Texas/*Texas Tribune* Poll, October 2021.

number of more middle-ground responses declined, which indicates a polarization of opinion about the governor.

A different pattern emerges for evaluations of local governments, as indicated by figure 4.17. The "approve" response option increased considerably, which largely reflects a decline in the share who responded "disapprove." Nevertheless, as noted elsewhere in this chapter, it is difficult to directly compare evaluations of one statewide elected official with those of an entire level of government. A governor can only represent one political party, whereas local governments are more likely to be in partisan alignment with survey respondents. We therefore cannot rule out a partisan effect as opposed to a COVID-management effect.

To further explore partisan dynamics is beyond the scope of this chapter, but we note the following analysis by the Texas Politics Project.[66] It examines February 2022 survey data and finds considerable opinion variation by party on Governor Abbott's handling of COVID. Not unexpectedly, Democrats were highly likely to "strongly disapprove"

(63 percent) or "disapprove" (10 percent), whereas Republicans were the most likely to "strongly approve" (39 percent) or "approve" (34 percent). Taken together, these numbers are mirror opposites: Democrats expressed 73 percent total disapproval, whereas Republicans expressed 73 percent total approval. Lastly, independents were slightly more likely to give one of the two approval responses (42 percent combined) than the two disapproval responses (39 percent combined). Independents were also the most likely to give the "neither" response (17 percent), in comparison to 7 percent of Democrats and 12 percent of Republicans.

The report suggests that Abbott's "middle-ground political strategy of downplaying state action while leaving the work of managing the response to surges to tightly-leashed local authorities played well enough with most of his Republican base." It also concludes that "for all the noise made by Abbott's also-ran primary challengers about his handling of the pandemic, the lion's share of Republicans in the February 2022 UT/TXP Poll (73%) approved of the governor's handling of the pandemic, though the intensity of their approval has decreased over its duration."

Local Governments and Preemption

As we noted above, the pandemic saw variations between state and federal policies, as well as some differences among statewide officials in Texas. However, the nation as a whole had little experience with pandemics, so there was a great deal of uncertainty about what policies were necessary, when they should be implemented, and what the trade-offs might be in other policy realms (such as the economy and K–12 education).

This context left room for Texas local governments to enact policies tailored to the wishes and needs of their communities. However, local governments do not have the same authority as do state governments. In our federal system, the concept of Dillon's Rule means that local governments are "creatures of the state" and therefore only possess those powers allocated by state governments. Local governments have no federal constitutional right to exist or to possess any specific powers. Nevertheless, rather than micromanage localities, the states devolve varying levels of authority to local governments to implement their own policies. For instance, when a state provides "home rule," local governments receive de facto autonomy rather than only exercising the powers specifically allowed by the state. Nevertheless, the state can later restrict any local ordinances it wishes.[67]

When state governments overturn or restrict the policies of local governments, this is termed *preemption*, and in Texas it gave Governor Abbott a powerful role in determining what local governments could and could not do in response to COVID. More generally, preemption is often in the news, typically in the context of Republican-led states limiting the more progressive policies of their big cities.[68] We see examples in various policy domains ranging from immigration to guns.[69] These scholars show that Texas has a history of constraining the power of local governments, well before COVID. During the pandemic, a national-level study found that the greater the partisan and ideological differences between governors and city officials, the more likely state preemptions were to occur.[70]

Starting early in the pandemic, state officials attempted to limit how local governments could respond. For instance, one of the earliest attempts at a local mask mandate occurred in Laredo, Texas, but Governor Abbott issued an order that prevented localities from enforcing penalties for violating a mask order; while the order remained in place, violators received information sheets instead of a fine.[71]

In November 2020, Attorney General Paxton successfully sued to block El Paso County's attempt to close nonessential businesses from late October to early December.[72] In October 2021, Governor Abbott stepped in to limit organizations—governmental or not—from imposing their own vaccination requirements. He maintained that Texans should have the right to decide for themselves whether or not to get the vaccine without being compelled to do so by their employer.[73]

In some cases, the clash between state and local governments led to mixed results. For instance, in late 2020, Paxton sued the City of Austin and Travis County over a New Year's weekend curfew. Although the courts found in his favor, the case was decided after the holiday, so the curfew took place.[74]

Furthermore, as discussed below, the question of whether the state of Texas can prevent school districts from enacting a mask mandate has been working its way through the state courts for some time. The issue is not whether a state can in theory preempt its local jurisdictions but whether state law enabled the governor to do so in this specific circumstance. At issue is whether the Texas Disaster Act gives the governor that power, and as of March 2022, the Texas Supreme Court had yet to definitively rule. Of course, the legislature could always amend the law to give the governor this power, although it did not do so in the 2021 legislative session. On the contrary, state legislators (from both sides of the aisle) seemed more interested in limiting gubernatorial power than expanding it (also discussed below).

Enforcement

The public health benefit of emergency orders is potentially limited when such directives are not enforced, or are unevenly enforced. Such variation could also confuse the public, which may become unclear about whether directives from elected officials have the force of law or are merely recommendations. As noted above, Laredo was prevented from enforcing a mask mandate, so it instead distributed information sheets to violators.

Enforcement can also become a political issue, which may lead to yet another complexity in a federal system that can produce different national, state, and local policies. The enforcement issue was studied by Curley, Harrison, and Federman, who found that state executive orders in response to COVID contained varying approaches to enforcement.[75]

Furthermore, a governor's political risks were related to the presence of language on enforcement within these orders.

Early in the pandemic, the media reported the arrest of a Dallas salon owner who resumed her business in defiance of COVID emergency orders.[76] Greg Abbott swiftly acted to ensure that Texans would not be arrested as a result of refusing to comply with such orders: "Throwing Texans in jail who have had their businesses shut down through no fault of their own is nonsensical, and I will not allow it to happen. That is why I am modifying my executive orders to ensure confinement is not a punishment for violating an order."[77] Abbott's communications director would note that "fines and license suspension or revocation still apply."[78]

Adding to the patchwork nature of health policy in a federal system is disparate enforcement at local levels.[79] According to a May 2020 report by the *Texas Tribune* and ProPublica, "Cities and counties arrived at dramatically different interpretations of Abbott's emergency orders. Austin, so far, has issued just two citations, while others like Laredo and Dallas have written hundreds of tickets, in addition to arresting a handful of business owners who defied orders to close." They also noted, "The erratic pattern foreshadows the struggles cities and counties now face as they interpret an entirely new set of regulations on reopening. That's further complicated as enforcement has become a political hot-button issue across Texas and the U.S. Abbott, a Republican, has repeatedly changed his guidance as his party base grows more agitated."[80]

While much of the public debate suggests that the main issue was the state vs. localities, this viewpoint may have obscured variation at the local level. For instance, Beauvais et al. noted that "Abbott and the state's other Republican leaders have blasted local officials in Dallas and Houston for what they called overzealous enforcement of COVID-19 regulations." In response, guidance to prosecutors by the Texas District and County Attorneys Association argued, "If the governor is going to keep changing the tune he plays as he leads the state out of this pandemic, there is little incentive to put your own necks on the line to enforce an order that could be invalidated the next day."[81] However, on the ground, a key issue may have been the varying interpretations of local officials and not just state vs. locality tug-of-war.

Local Resistance

As noted above, the issue of preemption in Texas was put to the test when some school districts resisted or even ignored the governor's mask orders. Rather than a direct attack on preemption, districts claimed that state officials were overreaching in a way that challenged the legitimate power of local authorities in a pandemic. This led to pushback from state elected officials, resulting in legal cases that made their way from local courts to the Texas Supreme Court.

That story began on March 2, 2021, when the governor ended his statewide mask order (GA-34). The following statement from his office explained the reasoning:

> With the medical advancements of vaccines and antibody therapeutic drugs, Texas now has the tools to protect Texans from the virus. We must now do more to restore livelihoods and normalcy for Texans by opening Texas 100 percent. Make no mistake, COVID-19 has not disappeared, but it is clear from the recoveries, vaccinations, reduced hospitalizations, and safe practices that Texans are using that state mandates are no longer needed. Today's announcement does not abandon safe practices that Texans have mastered over the past year. Instead, it is a reminder that each person has a role to play in their own personal safety and the safety of others. With this executive order, we are ensuring that all businesses and families in Texas have the freedom to determine their own destiny.[82]

This could in theory be interpreted to mean that school districts were free to make their own policies, and some announced a mask mandate would continue.[83] Attorney General Ken Paxton then sued Austin and Travis County. Paxton tweeted: "I told Travis County and the City of Austin to comply with state mask law. They blew me off. So, once again, I'm dragging them to court. Adler will never do the right thing on his own. His obstruction won't stop me from keeping Texas free and open." Mayor Steve Adler responded, "We are not aware of any Texas court that has allowed state leadership to overrule the health protection rules of a local health authority."[84]

The result was a somewhat complicated set of state orders, local defiance, state injunction requests, and court cases that involved various jurisdictions. In the above case, District Judge Lora Livingston denied Paxton's injunction request that would have blocked these jurisdictions' mask mandates. According to the *Texas Tribune*, at the March 26 trial "discussion broadly centered around the question: What powers do local public health departments have, and how do the governor's emergency powers affect them?" The judge also questioned the state's arguments about individual freedom: "I'm trying to understand why the person with the deadly virus should have more power than the person trying to stay alive and not catch the deadly virus." Lastly, she also raised the issue of the mixed messages that localities may have been receiving: "It's got to be pretty confusing for local officials to know when they are charged, in the governor's mind, and have the responsibility to react locally and take charge locally—and when they shouldn't."[85]

In May, Abbott issued an executive order that would seem to have ended this discretion, starting on June 5. It banned any jurisdiction, which included local governments and schools, from requiring masks. In the order, Governor Abbott stated, "The Lone Star State continues to defeat COVID-19 through the use of widely-available vaccines, antibody therapeutic drugs, and safe practices utilized by Texans in our communities. We can continue to mitigate COVID-19 while defending Texans' liberty to choose whether or not they mask up."[86]

An issue for schools was that the vast majority of children had not been vaccinated at that point. On the other hand, at the time of Abbott's order, the school year was either finished or about to end in most districts, so the issue was almost moot until the fall.[87] Nevertheless, a variety of school districts either sued the governor or just ignored his new executive order.[88]

According to the *Texas Tribune*, Abbott and Paxton argued that state law makes Abbott the disaster response's "commander in chief," and he can therefore override local mask mandate rules. However, "Abbott and Paxton also have argued that neither one of them has the authority to enforce Abbott's ban—a power that lies with district attorneys." For their part, some localities argued that state law does not give the governor total authority during a disaster, nor to prevent localities from enacting health-related policies.[89] In addition, Abbott asked the Texas Legislature to give him the authority to stop schools from imposing mask mandates, but it did not.[90]

The story also notes the ideas and politics associated with this debate; although Abbott argued "that the path forward relies on personal responsibility rather than government mandates," Abbott and Paxton were "also under considerable political pressure from their right flank to bring the hammer down on local officials who enact measures like mask mandates—which are highly unpopular among hard-right conservatives. Both men have drawn primary challengers from their right in their 2022 reelection bids."[91]

As cases made their way through the Texas courts, the school mask mandates remained. The Texas Supreme Court denied a request from Paxton, ruling that he could not skip the appellate step.[92] The Third Court of Appeals then refused to overturn a local court injunction against Paxton involving Houston mask mandates. Judge Chari Kelly wrote, "The Governor does not possess absolute authority under the Texas Disaster Act to preempt orders issued by local governmental entities or officials that contradict his executive orders" and the act "does not give the governor carte blanche to issue executive orders empowering him to rule the state in any way he wishes during a disaster."[93] The same appeals court would later uphold an injunction that allowed eighteen other school districts to have mask mandates.[94]

Because all state judges are elected in Texas (with governors making appointments to vacancies), partisanship may be playing a role in court decisions. Media stories have pointed out that local court judges in the largest cities are predominantly Democrats, while the Texas

Supreme Court is all Republican. In the above case, the Third Court of Appeals consists of Democrats. Nevertheless, according to the *Austin American-Statesman*, the arguments both parties are making involve issues of gubernatorial power, not arguments about health policy effectiveness; both sides quoted from the Texas Disaster Act.

For instance, "Local officials across Texas, particularly Democrats, beg to differ, arguing that state law creates a power-sharing arrangement that lets them craft area-specific safety measures in a huge state with diverse regions and needs. The Texas Disaster Act, they argue, did not create a governor-dictator." By contrast, "Abbott and Paxton say the 1975 Texas Disaster Act lets the governor set health and safety policies that protect the economy and personal freedoms, not just prevent the transmission of COVID-19—an interpretation the Supreme Court supported in earlier challenges to Abbott's executive orders."[95]

In addition, the courtroom dynamics in Texas have not simply featured Democrats versus Republicans. The *Austin American-Statesman* noted that the governor has received a great deal of backing from the Texas Supreme Court, including when his orders were challenged from the right. For example, a conservative legal challenge to Abbott's 2020 closure order failed because the court ruled that "state law bars courts from ordering the governor to abandon his directives." The court also overturned a conservative suit against Abbott's order that added six days to early voting as a means of reducing polling place density. The court ruled that with an election approaching, the plaintiffs waited too long to file suit.[96]

Legislative Response

Governor Abbott's issuing of emergency orders during the pandemic was questioned by elected officials on both sides of the aisle. This led to attempts during the 2021 legislative session to limit his power. The context is that the Texas Legislature is a part-time or "citizen" body, not a full-time or "professional" legislature. It typically meets once every two years for a "session," which can last for months.

Senate Bill 1025, which was filed in March 2021, would have reserved to the state legislature the power to close businesses or limit their hours of operations, among other provisions.[97] It was approved 30–1 but ultimately died in a House committee.

According to the *Austin American-Statesman*, "Although Gov. Greg Abbott took heat from conservative Republicans about his now-rescinded orders that closed businesses and required face masks to be worn during the pandemic, the bill's author insisted that the legislation was not a rebuke of Abbott's leadership or decisions." Brian Birdwell (R-Granbury) said, "By all accounts and by my own rigorous, detailed analysis, Gov. Abbott acted clearly within the letter of the law, and further the governor demonstrated a sincere desire to protect his fellow Texans while coordinating a well-organized response." He added, "I am adamant that only the Legislature be able to close businesses. The state legislative branch must make the most seminal decision about (people's) livelihood."[98]

House Bill 3 would have provided checks on the governor's power by allowing an oversight board to override a gubernatorial order. According to the *Texas Tribune*, "The committee, which would consist of the lieutenant governor and speaker—who would serve as joint chairs—and a number of committee chairs from both chambers, could in certain cases terminate pandemic disaster declarations, orders or other rules issued by the governor or local governments. It would only be able to act though when the Legislature is not convened for a regular or special session."[99] An amendment to prohibit mask wearing orders by the state or localities failed on a 71–72 vote. The bill passed the House 104–39, but the House and Senate could not come to agreement, so it died.

Although neither bill became law, the legislative efforts reflected that "For roughly the past year, Republicans and Democrats have picked apart the state's response to the coronavirus pandemic—and particularly how Gov. Greg Abbott has wielded his power along the way."[100] According to the *Austin American-Statesman*, "Many conservative Republicans chafed at Abbott's coronavirus restrictions, which followed the recommendations of public health experts, including state health officials and the governor's medical advisers. Abbott's pandemic performance, however, was not a central feature of debate about the [House] bill."[101]

The legislation therefore received both support and opposition from across the aisle. Steve Adler, the Democratic mayor of Austin, criticized the bill, claiming that "HB 3 would add an unneeded level of bureaucracy and put at risk the ability for cities to respond in a locally meaningful way." Furthermore, "Abbott has been buffeted by attacks from fellow Republicans, including state GOP Chair Allen West and Agriculture Commissioner Sid Miller, who argued that Abbott's rules were too restrictive."[102]

Conclusions

The Texas response to the COVID pandemic provides insights into federalism, local preemption, intraparty competition, and public opinion about state and local officials. When the crisis began, the state and nation had not experienced a parallel public health emergency since the Spanish flu a century ago. There were consequently few widely accepted or uncontroversial approaches to containing the spread of COVID or balancing competing economic and educational priorities. This gave rise to a variety of actions, sometimes contradictory, among national, state, and local governments. This chapter discussed such dynamics in Texas, not only chronicling state and local decisions over time but also highlighting the challenges of policy making in a federal system.

For local governments, the pandemic was both a health crisis and a political obstacle course. City and county officials would find themselves in disagreement with state officials over mask mandates, closings, and enforcement. This mapped onto the long-standing issue of preemption, whereby states attempt to limit the policy options of their localities. Often associated with "red" states attempting to control "blue" cities, it raises the more general question of what type of federalism we want. Although Dillon's Rule gives the final word to the states, both conservatives and progressives have rhetorically claimed to value local decision making.

In particular, we saw conflicts between local school districts and the state. The conflicts may have reflected the party differences between these levels of government, but they also involved the interpretation of the Texas Disaster Act and the power it gives to state and local officials. Some local districts ignored orders from Abbott and Paxton, and subsequent lawsuits made their way through the Texas court system. Whereas local courts, which have predominantly Democratic judges, have supported local school officials, the all-Republican Texas Supreme Court has yet to make a definitive decision as this book goes to press.

At stake are also issues of who has the power to make policy in Texas. In particular, the pandemic brought to light differences of opinion about the power of the governor to declare emergencies and institute policies. In both the state House and Senate, bills were introduced with considerable bipartisan support that would have limited gubernatorial power in various ways. While Governor Abbott expressed a willingness to discuss this issue, the legislature ultimately did not approve any legislation, which made the point moot for the time. However, this issue could be revisited in the next legislative session.

Although all statewide elected officials in Texas are Republicans, this does not mean they have identical policy views. Governor Abbott was the most prominent policy actor during the pandemic, but we also saw Lieutenant Governor Dan Patrick and Attorney General Ken Paxton playing roles. Patrick gained publicity for his discussion on Fox News of the hypothetical question "As a senior citizen, are you willing to take a chance on your survival in exchange for keeping the America that all America loves for your children and grandchildren?" This discussion was consistent with a statement that day by President Trump but took place a day after the largest counties issued shelter-in-place orders; it was also one week before Governor Abbott urged Texans to stay home.

Texans therefore saw messaging that showed variation depending on the level of government and the elected official.

Further complicating the politics were lawsuits against Governor Abbott from his political right. As noted above, such conservatives sued against his closure order in 2020 as well as his extension of early voting for six days to avoid density at the polls. Both suits lost, which illustrate the high level of support Abbott received throughout the pandemic from the State Supreme Court.

Paxton was in the spotlight for his ruling that Governor Abbott's order banning nonessential medical procedures applied to abortions. This was contested in federal court, and although the Fifth Circuit upheld his decision, this verdict was ultimately vacated by the US Supreme Court in early 2021. Nevertheless, this order served to ban most abortions in an early stage of the pandemic, which was consistent with a long-standing goal of GOP policy makers.

In terms of public opinion, views about the governor and local governments became less positive from April to October 2020. The University of Texas/*Texas Tribune* survey asked Texans across the state about how they thought these actors and institutions handled the COVID crisis, and while both began with fairly high levels of approval in April, this support had declined by October. Although the data still showed some support for both, the public had, on balance, become more negative than positive over time. In the second survey, the governor and local governments ended up at almost the exact same level of public support.

This decline went beyond partisanship; whereas a governor is clearly a member of one party, the term *local governments* encompasses both Democratic and Republican officials, who are more likely to be congruent with the views of survey respondents. We did see some evidence of partisanship in the data, such as the relatively negative views of Governor Abbott in the Democratic stronghold of Austin. Nevertheless, partisanship did not prevent Austinites from becoming more negative about their local (and almost entirely Democratic) government's handling of the crisis in 2020.

By October of 2021, statewide approval of localities was more positive, while opinions about the governor were more polarized. However, we also noted a Texas Politics Project study of early 2022 survey data showing considerable partisan effects in gubernatorial approval.

In the future, research could further examine how Texans view national, state, and local emergency orders; how they apportion responsibility for outcomes among state, local, and national governments and officials; and how they viewed the actions of the different statewide officials during the pandemic. In addition, researchers might investigate whether partisanship, location, and COVID numbers shaped such attitudes. We also need to know more about how the public wants responsibility to be apportioned between the governor, the legislature, and the courts. As part of this question, what do Texans think about state preemptions of local policies, and particularly the conflicts between school districts and state officials? While the Texas Supreme Court may rule on the Texas Disaster Act and the relative powers of the governor and school boards, the pandemic brought such issues into relief and could be the subject of lawmaking and litigation into the future.

Lastly, the issue of gubernatorial powers overlaps with the discussion earlier in this chapter about the potentially shifting nature of Texas politics. Although it is unlikely that Democrats will soon "turn Texas blue," it is possible that future election cycles could see the emergence of a more "purple" state politics. In particularly, it would be ironic if Republican state officials and justices strengthened the emergency powers of the governor or legislative leaders in a way that ultimately redounded to the advantage of a future Democratic state legislature or governor.

Notes

1. The surveys analyzed in this chapter are the 2020 Texas Media and Society Survey by the Annette Strauss Institute for Civic Life (https://straussinstitute.moody.utexas.edu/research/texas-media-society-survey); and the University of Texas/*Texas Tribune* polls for April and October 2020 and October 2021 (https://texaspolitics.utexas.edu/research-data-archive). A presumptive positive case

indicates that a person has tested positive for COVID-19 based on a laboratory test, but that the case has not yet been confirmed by the CDC. See Centers for Disease Control and Prevention, "CDC Announces Additional COVID-19 Infections," media release, March 3, 2020.

2. The area is known as the Houston-The Woodlands-Sugar Land Metropolitan Statistical Area (MSA). See Tony Plohetski, "Coronavirus Was Here before We Knew It, Austin Officials Conclude," *Austin American-Statesman*, May 16, 2020.

3. Texas Health and Human Services, "DSHS Announces First Case of COVID-19 in Texas," March 4, 2020.

4. Texas Health and Human Services, "DSHS Announces First Case."

5. Christopher Adams, "Timeline: How Coronavirus in Texas Unfolded since First Case One Year Ago," KXAN, March 4, 2021.

6. Claire McInerny, "Why Is Texas on Its Own Electric Grid?" KUT, July 22, 2021.

7. Alan Greenblatt, "How Governors, Not Congress, Emerged as Trump's Main Opposition," *Governing*, April 27, 2020.

8. Dan Frosch and Jacob Gershman, "Opponent: Obama Administration; Former Attorney General, Now Governor, Has Led a Red-State Revolt against the White House," *Wall Street Journal*, June 24, 2016.

9. Alex Samuels, "Uber, Lyft Return to Austin as Texas Gov. Abbott Signs Ride-Hailing Measure into Law," *Texas Tribune*, May 29, 2017; Ballotpedia, "Sanctuary Policy Preemption Conflicts between the Federal and Local Governments," last updated April 8, 2022.

10. Lori Riverstone-Newell, "The Rise of State Preemption Laws in Response to Local Policy Innovation," *Publius: The Journal of Federalism* 47, no. 3 (2017): 403–25.

11. Committee on Budget. Public Safety: Omnibus,"California Assembly Bill no. 103 (2017), Chapter 17.

12. But see Larry Sabato, *Goodbye to Good-Time Charlie: The American Governor Transformed, 1950–1975* (Lexington, MA: D. C. Heath, 1978); Thomas M. Carsey, *Campaign Dynamics: The Race for Governor* (Ann Arbor: University of Michigan Press, 2001); David L. Leal, *Electing America's Governors: The Politics of Executive Elections* (New York: Palgrave Macmillan, 2006); Thad Kousser and Justin H. Phillips, *The Power of American Governors: Winning on Budgets and Losing on Policy* (New York: Cambridge University Press, 2012).

13. Alex Samuels and Geoffrey Skelley, "Why Democratic Gains in Texas's Big Metro Areas Could Outweigh Republican Success in South Texas," *FiveThirtyEight*, October 19, 2021.

14. Ross Ramsey, "Analysis: 2022 Primary Elections in Texas Merit a Severe Weather Alert," *Texas Tribune*, November 19, 2021.

15. Dan Solomon, "Matthew McConaughey Isn't Running for Governor. But We Still Have Questions about His Interest in Politics," *Texas Monthly*, November 30, 2021.

16. Kevin Liptak, Kristen Holmes, and Ryan Nobles, "Trump Completes Reversal, Telling Govs 'You Are Going to Call Your Own Shots' and Distributes New Guidelines," CNN, April 16, 2020.

17. James A. Marten, "Emergency Management," *Handbook of Texas Online*, Texas State Historical Association, January 1, 1995, accessed April 21, 2022, https://www.tshaonline.org/handbook/entries/emergency-management.

18. Kevin Price, "Quarantine Authority in Texas: A COVID-19 Case Study," *Journal of Biosecurity, Biosafety, and Biodefense Law* 12, no. 1 (2021): 133–54, https://doi.org/10.1515/jbbbl-2021-2007.

19. Price, "Quarantine Authority."

20. Price, "Quarantine Authority."

21. See Greg Abbott, "Proclamation by Governor of the State of Texas," March 13, 2020; and Donald J. Trump, "Proclamation on Declaring a National Emergency concerning the Novel Coronavirus Disease (COVID-19) Outbreak," March 13, 2020.

22. Edgar Walters, "Texas Governor Declares Statewide Emergency, Says State Will Soon Be Able to Test Thousands," *Texas Tribune*, March 13, 2020.

23. Amanda Moreland, Christine Herlihy, Michael A. Tynan, Gregory Sunshine, Russell F. McCord, Charity Hilton, Jason Poovey, et al., "Timing of State and Territorial COVID-19 Stay-at-Home Orders and Changes in Population Movement," *Morbidity and Mortality Weekly Report* 69, no. 35 (September 4, 2020): 1198–1203.

24. Patrick Svitek, "Gov. Greg Abbott Resists Calls for Statewide Shelter-in-Place; Moves to Expand Hospital Capacity," *Texas Tribune*, March 22, 2020.

25. The role of the county judge in Texas differs slightly from county to county, however. For more information, see Texas Association of Counties, "2018 Guide to Texas Law for County Officials."

26. Stacy Fernández and Sami Sparber, "Coronavirus Prompts Dallas and Houston to Close Bars and Clubs, Make Restaurants Takeout Only," *Texas Tribune*, March 16, 2020.

27. Texas Department of State Health Services, "Texas Confirms First Death in COVID-19 Patient," news release, March 17, 2020.

28. Patrick Svitek, "Gov. Greg Abbott Closes Bars, Restaurants and Schools as He Anticipates Tens of Thousands Could Test Positive for Coronavirus," *Texas Tribune*, March 19, 2020.

29. Supreme Court of Texas, "Fourth Emergency Order regarding the COVID-19 State of Disaster," March 19, 2020.

30. Elvia Limón, "Here's How the COVID-19 Pandemic Has Unfolded in Texas since March," *Texas Tribune*, July 31, 2020.

31. Chuck Lindell, "Texas Supreme Court Halts Most Eviction Proceedings in State," *Austin American-Statesman*, March 19, 2020.

32. Allyson Waller, "Texas Supreme Court Extends State Program to Help Tenants Avoid Eviction until Oct. 1," *Texas Tribune*, July 19, 2021.

33. Brandon Formby, "Dallas County Bans Elective Medical Procedures to Focus Resources on Climbing Coronavirus Cases," *Texas Tribune*, March 21, 2020.

34. Svitek, "Abbott Resists Calls."

35. Cassandra Pollock and Aliyya Swaby, "Dallas County Orders Residents to Shelter in Place as Coronavirus Cases There Spread," *Texas Tribune*, March 22, 2020.

36. Limón, "Here's How."

37. Limón, "Here's How."

38. "Whatever Abbott Calls It, Stay Home If You Can," editorial, *Austin American-Statesman*, March 31, 2020.

39. Greg Abbott, "Executive Order No. GA-14 Relating to Statewide Continuity of Essential Services and Activities during the COVID-19 Disaster," March 31, 2020.

40. Ballotpedia, "Texas Proposition 3, Prohibition on Limiting Religious Services or Organizations Amendment (2021)," accessed May 9, 2022.

41. Chuck Lindell, "Emergency Order Blocks Most Abortions in Texas, Paxton Says," *Austin American-Statesman*, March 23, 2020.

42. Erica Turret, Sara Tannenbaum, Blake N. Shultz, and Katherine Kraschel, "COVID-19 Does Not Change the Right to Abortion," *Health Affairs*, April 17, 2020.

43. See Chuck Lindell, "Federal Judge Blocks Texas from Enforcing Coronavirus-Related Abortion Ban," *Austin American-Statesman*, March 30, 2020; Cobb & Counsel PLLC, "Courts to Decide Whether Governor Has Unlimited Power in a Disaster," September 20, 2021; and Texas Attorney General, "Fifth Circuit Once Again Upholds Governor's Order Halting Unnecessary Medical Procedures, Including Abortion," news release, April 20, 2020.

44. Office of the Texas Governor, "Governor Abbott Issues Executive Order to Loosen Restrictions on Surgeries," April 17, 2020.

45. Shannon Najmabadi, "Texas Clinics Resume Abortion Services as State Acknowledges Ban Is No Longer in Place," *Texas Tribune*, April 22, 2020.

46. Pete Williams, "Supreme Court Wipes Out Lower Court Rulings in Texas Abortion Battle," NBC News, January 25, 2021.

47. Abby Livingston, "Texas Lt. Gov. Dan Patrick Says a Failing Economy Is Worse than Coronavirus," *Texas Tribune*, March 23, 2020.

48. Susan Milligan, "Trump's Choice: The Economy or Human Lives," *US News & World Report*, March 24, 2020.

49. Livingston, "Failing Economy."

50. Milligan, "Trump's Choice."

51. Aris Folley, "O'Rourke Slams Texas Official Who Suggested Grandparents Risk Their Lives for Economy during Pandemic," *The Hill*, March 24, 2020.

52. Livingston, "Failing Economy."

53. Office of the Texas Governor, "Governor Abbott Issues Executive Order, Implements Statewide Essential Services and Activities Protocols," news release, March 31, 2020.

54. Alex Samuels, "Dan Patrick Says 'There Are More Important Things than Living and That's Saving This Country,'" *Texas Tribune*, April 21, 2020.

55. Samuels, "'There Are More Important Things.'"

56. Samuels, "'There Are More Important Things.'"

57. Stephanie Lamm, "How COVID-19 Shut Down Texas," *Houston Chronicle*, September 27, 2020.

58. R. G. Ratcliffe, "'Doctors and Data' Suggest Abbott May Be Reopening Texas Too Early," *Texas Monthly*, April 28, 2020.

59. Emma Platoff, "Health Experts Give Abbott's Plan to Reopen Mixed Reviews, Warn State Should Revive Stay-at-Home Order If Surge Emerges," *Texas Tribune*, April 29, 2020.

60. Jeremy Blackman and Austin Bureau, "Gov. Abbott Sets May 1 Reopening for Most Businesses, Churches, Malls, Libraries," *Houston Chronicle*, April 27, 2020.

61. Bill Chappell, "More than 20 US States Now Require Face Masks in Public," NPR, July 10, 2020.

62. Chappell, "More than 20 US States."

63. Arelis R. Hernández, Frances Stead Sellers, and Ben Guarino, "Reopening Reverses Course in Texas and Florida as Coronavirus Cases Spike," *Washington Post*, June 26, 2020.

64. Patrick Svitek, "Gov. Greg Abbott Orders Texans in Most Counties to Wear Masks in Public," *Texas Tribune*, July 2, 2020; David Montgomery and J. David Goodman, "Texas Governor Reverses Course and Orders Face Masks," *New York Times*, July 2, 2020.

65. Svitek, "Abbott Orders Texans."

66. Jim Henson and Joshua Blank, "With Attention Elsewhere, Abbott Extends His Emergency Powers Related to COVID and the Border," Texas Politics Project, March 30, 2022.

67. Jesse J. Richardson, "Dillon's Rule Is from Mars, Home Rule Is from Venus: Local Government Autonomy and the Rules of Statutory Construction," *Publius: The Journal of Federalism* 41, no. 4 (2011): 662–85.

68. Richard Briffault, "The Challenge of the New Preemption," Columbia Public Law Research Paper No. 14-580, February 1, 2018; Luke Fowler and Stephanie L. Witt, "State Preemption of Local Authority: Explaining Patterns of State Adoption of Preemption Measures," *Publius: The Journal of Federalism* 49 (2019): 540–59; Riverstone-Newell, "Rise of State Preemption Laws."

69. For immigration, see Mark A. Hall, Lilli Mann-Jackson, and Scott D. Rhodes, "State Preemption of Local Immigration 'Sanctuary' Policies: Legal Considerations," *American Journal of Public Health* 111 (February 2021): 259–64, https://doi.org/10.2105/AJPH.2020.306018; for guns, see Riverstone-Newell, "Rise of State Preemption Laws."

70. Carol S. Weissert, Matthew J. Uttermark, Kenneth R. Mackie, and Alexandra Artiles, "Governors in Control: Executive Orders, State-Local Preemption, and the COVID-19 Pandemic," *Publius: The Journal of Federalism* 51, no. 3 (Summer 2021): 396–428.

71. Miles Moffeit, Sue Ambrose, and Allie Morris, "Texas Leaders Say You Should Wear a Mask, but You Don't Have to, Muddling Public Health Message," *Dallas Morning News*, May 9, 2020.

72. Julián Aguilar, "Appeals Court Again Halts El Paso County's Shutdown of Nonessential Businesses," *Texas Tribune*, November 13, 2020.

73. Katie B. Blakey, Kelley Edwards, David B. Jordan, Alexis C. Knapp, and Sherry L. Travers, "Texas Governor Abbott Bars Employers and Individuals from Compelling COVID-19 Vaccines," *Littler News & Analysis*, October 12, 2021.

74. Reese Oxner, "Austin and Travis County Officials Can Keep Enforcing Local Mask Mandate for Now, Judge Says," *Texas Tribune*, March 26, 2021.

75. Cali Curley, Nicky Harrison, and Peter Federman, "Comparing Motivations for Including Enforcement in US COVID-19 State Executive Orders," *Journal of Comparative Policy Analysis: Research and Practice* 23, no. 2 (2021): 191–203.

76. Christopher Hooks, "Showdown at the Salon: How Hairdressing Became the Thing We Fight about in the Middle of the Pandemic," *Texas Monthly*, May 8, 2020.

77. Office of the Texas Governor, "Governor Abbott Modifies COVID-19 Executive Orders to Eliminate Confinement as a Punishment," May 7, 2020.

78. Sally Beauvais, Lexi Churchill, Kiah Collier, Vianna Davila, and Ren Larson, "Gov. Greg Abbott Is Limiting Enforcement of COVID-19 Orders, but Many Cities Already Took a Lax Approach," *Texas Tribune* and ProPublica, May 14, 2020.

79. Beauvais et al., "Abbott Is Limiting Enforcement."

80. Beauvais et al., "Abbott Is Limiting Enforcement."

81. Beauvais et al., "Abbott Is Limiting Enforcement."

82. Office of the Texas Governor, "Governor Abbott Lifts Mask Mandate, Opens Texas 100 Percent," March 2, 2021.

83. Patrick Svitek, "Gov. Greg Abbott Says No Public Schools or Government Entities Will Be Allowed to Require Masks," *Texas Tribune*, May 18, 2021.

84. Chuck Lindell, "Delay Lets Austin, Travis County Enforce Mask Mandates for Now," *Austin American-Statesman*, March 12, 2021.

85. Oxner, "Austin and Travis County Officials."

86. Mike Copeland, "Waco Schools, Local Governments Scrambling to Comply with Abbott's Masking Order," *Waco Tribune-Herald*, May 19, 2021.

87. Svitek, "Abbott Says No Public Schools."

88. Joshua Fechter, "Gov. Greg Abbott Wanted State Lawmakers to Ban Mask Mandates in Public Schools. They Didn't," *Texas Tribune*, September 7, 2021.

89. Joshua Fechter, "Gov. Greg Abbott and Local Officials Are Fighting Several Legal Battles over Mask Mandates. Here's What You Need to Know," *Texas Tribune*, September 21, 2021.

90. Fechter, "Abbott Wanted State Lawmakers."

91. Fechter, "Abbott and Local Officials Are Fighting."

92. Chuck Lindell, "Texas Supreme Court Leaves Mask Mandate Orders in Place, for Now," *Austin American-Statesman*, August 19, 2021.

93. Chuck Lindell, "Ruling against Abbott, Austin Appeals Court Lets Harris County Impose Mask Mandate," *Austin American-Statesman*, January 6, 2022.

94. Chuck Lindell, "Appeals Court Upholds Mask Mandates for Austin, 18 Other Texas School Districts," *Austin American-Statesman*, March 17, 2022.

95. Chuck Lindell, "Who Has Power over Mask Mandates, Greg Abbott or Locals? Texas Supreme Court Asked to Decide," *Austin American-Statesman*, February 21, 2022.

96. Lindell, "Who Has Power."

97. Chuck Lindell, "Senate Approves Curtailing Texas Governor's Disaster Powers," *Austin American-Statesman*, April 13, 2021.

98. Lindell, "Senate Approves Curtailing."

99. Cassandra Pollock, Patrick Svitek, and Shawn Mulcahy, "Debate Ramps Up at Texas Legislature over Governor's Emergency Powers during Pandemic," *Texas Tribune*, March 4, 2021.

100. Pollock, Svitek, and Mulcahy, "Debate Ramps Up."

101. Nicole Cobler, "Texas House, Senate Fail to Reach Compromise on Bill Curtailing Governor's Pandemic Powers," *Austin American-Statesman*, May 30, 2021.

102. Nicole Cobler, "Texas House Approves Checks to Governor's Pandemic Powers," *Austin American-Statesman*, May 11, 2021.

Chapter 5

Using the *Emergency* in Emergency Orders
Municipal Policy Action and Federalism during the COVID-19 Crisis

Emily M. Farris, Mirya R. Holman, and Miranda E. Sullivan

In the spring of 2020, COVID-19, a novel, highly contagious respiratory illness caused by SARS-CoV-2, colloquially known as the coronavirus, spread unevenly across the United States. By March 17, COVID had been detected in every state, but early rates of infection varied dramatically, from ninety-one cases per million people in West Virginia to 3,941 cases per million in New York. The emerging health crisis was compounded by an economic crisis, as businesses shut down, schools moved online, and events were canceled in order to slow the spread of the virus. Again, the impacts of COVID on the economy were felt everywhere but were unevenly dispersed across the United States. The federal government initially failed to adequately respond to the dual health and economic crises; subsequent efforts were marred by dysfunction and delay. The localized impact of COVID on public health and the economy, in addition to the policy vacuum at the federal level, pushed local governments to take a variety of emergency actions to address the dual crises of the pandemic. In this chapter, we examine early efforts by local governments to limit the spread of COVID through shelter-in-place mandates. We then examine efforts by cities to address both the spread and the economic consequences of COVID through emergency eviction moratoriums.

We find that cities engaged in a wide set of "emergency" orders associated with addressing the rapid spread of COVID and the subsequent economic fallout. Yet, cities still do this within the structure of federalism, where they are restricted by state and federal rules. Focusing on shelter-in-place policies and eviction moratoriums, we find that cities construct these emergency policies within the context of what states are also doing and the characteristics of their populations. Our results suggest the need to understand emergency actions within the frame of local politics in addition to national events.

Federalism and the Initial COVID-19 Responses in the United States

The quick spread of the unprecedented health and economic crises of the COVID pandemic across the world and throughout the United States prompted a variety of government responses, depending in part on the authority, politics, and administrative capacity of various places. In other countries, national governments led COVID responses with centralized public health and emergency systems and leadership. For instance, after a delayed initial response, China reacted with an aggressive lockdown to try to contain the virus. A major outbreak in Italy led to the lockdown of a cluster of towns in the Lombardy region. Strong initial national responses in countries such as Iceland, New Zealand, and South Korea involved lockdowns, aggressive testing, and contact tracing protocols.

In the United States, the federal government's response to the pandemic was "disjointed, chaotic, and confusing."[1] Even as it became clear that sustained community transmission would contribute substantially to the spread of COVID across the United States, state and local leaders received a delayed and fragmented response from federal leaders.[2] For example, the Trump administration failed to distribute personal protective equipment and medical supplies from the Strategic National Stockpile to states, instead leaving states to compete with other states and the federal government in bids for necessary healthcare items such as ventilators and medical-grade face masks.[3] Federal inaction and disarray in the early response to the pandemic left a leadership vacuum for governors and mayors to try to fill during the emergency.

These federal failures and the unfolding crisis of the COVID pandemic quickly revealed both the nuances and difficulties of US federalism and the crucial role of state and local governments in public health and other pandemic-related issues. The United States' system of federalism includes a division of responsibilities between federal and state governments, with both separate and overlapping powers.[4] Under the US Constitution, state governments exercise police powers, which are broad powers reserved to states and the people in the Tenth Amendment to govern public health and safety.[5] States then grant and share powers with local governments via city charters and state legislation. In the context of the pandemic, this largely meant that many of the powers to address the pandemic devolved to state and local governments, where they had subnational authority to issue public health orders.

As nonentities in the US Constitution, local governments' power, authority, and policy control in the United States are important, yet highly fractured. State governments can limit local government autonomy, as well as overlap in policy, potentially causing conflict in state–local relations.[6] As a result, cities make policy decisions not just in the context of their own political and economic environments, but also within what states say cities can and cannot do. These restrictions can prove particularly challenging for cities if there are ideological mismatches between city and state political leadership.[7]

Facing political, societal, and economic pressures, cities adopt different policy solutions at different times to shared problems.[8] Local or state policy innovation is particularly common for new and emerging problems or when there is a policy vacuum because of inaction at the federal level; for example, local and state governments have taken the lead in addressing climate change as the national government has failed to act.[9] Within the federalism framework, policy diffusion is also often common, as other state and local officials learn by observing the outcomes of other locations trying out solutions and adopting or rejecting policies accordingly.[10]

Emergency Public Health Actions

The lack of federal action, the localized instances of outbreaks, and the economic consequences of these outbreaks pushed many state and local governments to engage in emergency actions to limit the spread of COVID.[11] These actions were unprecedented in many ways.[12] The initial response to the pandemic included a variety of public health interventions, such as closing schools and businesses, banning gatherings of certain sizes, and issuing shelter-in-place or stay-at-home orders.

Theoretically, a decentralized emergency management system can be ideal in some ways during crises, as it may allow agile responses to local problems.[13] However, in the US context, several challenges complicated state and local governments' initial responses to the pandemic. While federal systems in other countries were able to quickly react to localized problems, scholars argued that US federalism was particularly ill suited to address COVID, due to the lack of formal institutions that facilitate intergovernmental relations and coordination.[14] In addition, state and local government responses to COVID were disadvantaged by the limited fiscal capacities and resources, due to "chronic underinvestment in public health infrastructure as well as emergency preparedness."[15]

Looking to immediately curtail the rapid spread of COVID amid evolving concerns of transmission and capacity of healthcare providers, many local and state governments issued stay-at-home or shelter-in-place orders, which limited the public's travel in the community, other than for certain essential functions. These emergency actions typically mandated the temporary closing of nonessential businesses, restricted the size of group gatherings outside one's household, and required social distancing for interactions deemed to be essential. By March 19, only one state (California) had implemented a stay-at-home order; by March 22, Illinois, New Jersey, and New York had issued shelter-in-place mandates. Some places, such as local governments in the Bay Area in California, declared emergencies and issued initial stay-at-home orders prior to any state action, responding to the quick impact of community spread of COVID in the region. By the end of March, with 186,000 cases of COVID across the United States, thirty-two states had stay-at-home orders in effect.[16] In other states, such as Florida and Texas, the state governments left policy making initially up to local officials. Other governors resisted any kind of policy response, even going as far as preempting and limiting the ability of local governments to create policies to respond to COVID as the pandemic progressed.

For instance, the mayor of San Francisco, London Breed, declared a local emergency on February 25, 2020, under Sections 8550 et seq. of the Government Code, Section 3.100(13) of the San Francisco Charter, and Chapter 7 of the San Francisco Administrative Code.[17] San Francisco's board of supervisors passed a motion concurring with Mayor Breed's local emergency declaration on March 3, 2020. Given the quick community spread, a public health order went into effect on March 17 in San Francisco, requiring residents to remain in place initially until April 7. Mayor Breed noted the difficulty imposed by the shelter-in-place order and underscored its importance in a press release:

> We know these measures will significantly disrupt people's day to day lives, but they are absolutely necessary. This is going to be a defining moment for our City and we all have a responsibility to do our part to protect our neighbors and slow the spread of this virus by staying at home unless it is absolutely essential to go outside.[18]

Economic Crises and Emergency Orders

With stay-at-home orders shuttering businesses to control COVID's spread, cities and their residents additionally faced serious economic consequences during the pandemic. Cities engaged in a wide set of efforts to alleviate some of the economic side effects of the pandemic. These municipal policies ranged from setting up emergency food bank programs and free testing for the population to freezing utility shutoffs. Some policies were rolled out much later in the pandemic as federal aid money became available to cities as part of the CARES Act, and others were accomplished through public–private partnerships, such as a program in Birmingham, Alabama, that connected small businesses with temporary workers and protective equipment.[19] Eviction moratoriums by local governments represent one of the more common policies by local governments to address the economic consequences of COVID.[20]

An eviction crisis predated the pandemic, but business closures and widespread job losses during the pandemic dramatically increased the risk of eviction for a larger group of renters.[21] Because of this, public health workers and housing advocates lobbied local governments to issue eviction moratoriums, which would limit whether and how landlords could evict tenants for nonpayment of rent.[22] In September 2020, a full five months into the pandemic, the Centers for Disease Control and Prevention (CDC) issued a national eviction moratorium.[23] Several cities passed their own eviction moratoriums before this, often specifically focusing on these emergency orders as a public health measure that would both protect vulnerable renters and help reduce the spread of COVID. For example, Glendale, Arizona, adopted a resolution that stated,

> Glendale residents who are most vulnerable to COVID-19, including those 65 years and older and those with underlying health issues, are advised to self-quarantine, self-isolate, or otherwise remain in their homes to reduce the transmission of COVID-19 . . . because homelessness can exacerbate vulnerability to COVID-19, the City must take measures to preserve and increase housing security to protect public health and welfare.[24]

Many cities noted the emergency nature of these moratoriums. The moratorium order in Fremont, California, states,

> The City's Residential Eviction Moratorium provides that during the period of local emergency declared in response to COVID-19, no landlord shall endeavor to evict a residential tenant in either of the following situations: (1) for nonpayment of rent if the tenant demonstrates that the tenant is unable to pay rent due to financial impacts related to

COVID-19, or (2) for a no-fault eviction unless immediately necessary because of the existence of a hazardous condition affecting tenants or neighbors.[25]

Other cities specifically reference emergency declarations at the county or state levels in their own moratoriums. San Mateo, California, noted that the county "declared a local health emergency in response to the COVID-19 outbreak" and Augusta, Georgia, stated: "Governor Brian Kemp has declared a public health emergency in the state of Georgia."[26]

Two examples from Texas and Washington illustrate differences in cities' eviction policies and renters' protections. In mid-March 2020, the Texas Supreme Court suspended hearing eviction cases for approximately two months. In Austin, Texas, Mayor Steve Adler issued orders in late March requiring landlords to file a notice before they could ask the tenant to leave and giving tenants sixty days to respond. This effectively created a sixty-day eviction moratorium lasting until early May, at which time the mayor extended the past protections.[27] In Washington, the governor announced an eviction moratorium that prohibited the giving of notice, filing for, or enforcement of an eviction for nonpayment of rent in March 2020. Both Seattle and King County issued similar eviction moratoriums and offered additional protections beyond those in the state moratorium, on items such as the collection of late fees. As these cases illustrate, multiple policy approaches toward eviction policies were implemented to try to address the pandemic's crisis throughout 2020 and into 2021. Given both some of the quick emergency responses and the United States' often-puzzling system of federalism, renters could be covered by eviction moratoriums with overlapping jurisdictions or not at all.

Data and Methods

We are interested in better understanding cities' responses to the pandemic's public health and economic emergencies in the context of federalism. In the following section, we explore what influenced a city to adopt a shelter-in-place policy and/or an eviction moratorium as an initial response to the COVID pandemic in 2020.

Dependent Variables

Our dependent variables include whether a city issued a shelter-in-place policy and an eviction moratorium. Identifying local policies is difficult at any time but even more difficult during the emergency of a pandemic, so collecting cities' responses to COVID was a methodological challenge. There was no central database of how cities responded at the time, and with over one thousand municipalities (and three thousand counties and seven hundred special health districts), the manual data collection presents a significant obstacle to understanding local responses to the pandemic. Collecting time-sensitive data, such as which cities implemented a COVID emergency order at the beginning of the crisis, makes manual data collection by the authors almost impossible. For the first set of policies that we examine, we turn to a new crowdsourcing method that allows for a quick and reliable collection of a large set of data across a wide set of local jurisdictions.[28]

Shelter-in-Place Policies

For US cities with a population over five thousand, we asked at least three workers on Amazon's MTurk platform to perform the following task on March 19–21, 2020: "We are interested in how local governments are responding to the COVID and coronavirus pandemic in the United States. For this task, we are going to ask you to find information about the city of [name of city, state]." In addition to what policies were in place, workers were asked to provide which level of government had responded (local city, local county, appointed, or state-level). Because multiple workers collected information on each city, we established a "consensus" answer regarding whether a policy existed in a particular place at the time of study.[29] For those cities with policies, we verified the share of cities mandating shelter-in-place by using online searches and comparing against larger databases of local policies. Of the cities in our sample, we identified 10 percent that had a shelter-in-place policy.

Eviction Moratoriums

In general, cities were a bit slower to pass eviction moratoriums compared to shelter-in-place efforts, and policies were easier to find (typically stand-alone orders or resolutions) and were more similar across cities. As a result, we opted to collect this data by hand through internet searches by the authors. We marked a city as having an eviction moratorium if the city had attempted to limit evictions in either residential properties or public housing. For example, San Francisco implemented a moratorium that applied only if tenants could prove that their inability to pay rent stemmed from either the pandemic or policies implemented in response to the pandemic.[30] Other cities' moratoriums were less restrictive. For example, Seattle halted all evictions unless the landlord could prove that a tenant's behavior was "an imminent threat to the health or safety of neighbors."[31] We identified eviction moratoriums in 24 percent of the cities in our sample.

Results

We start by looking at whether local government COVID-related policies replicate state-level policies or fill a vacuum when states have not acted. Recall that, under federalism, US cities' behavior can be constrained by state policy decisions, or cities can generally act independently to craft policy. In the pandemic's emergency environment, we see cities and states act in response to concerns about COVID, sometimes in tandem and sometimes in isolation. Figure 5.1 explores the relationships between local and state policy for shelter-in-place policies, while figure 5.2 provides this analysis for eviction moratoriums.

For shelter-in-place policies, cities are likely to act in tandem with the state. Cities in states with shelter-in-place policies were 10 percent more likely to have a shelter-in-place policy themselves. Given what we know about both the spread of COVID at the beginning of the pandemic and the role of federalism in shaping local policy, this is perhaps unsurprising, as we would expect states and their cities to share political circumstances and interests. For eviction moratoriums, however, we do not find this same pattern: the probability that cities pass an eviction moratorium is not correlated with the presence of a state eviction ban. We replicate these findings with a state-level score from the Eviction Lab, which scored states on a five-point scale based on their protections and assistance to renters as of March 23 and May 11, 2020.[32] We again find no connection between state eviction policy (however we measure it) and local eviction moratoriums.

We also explore local context to understand these policies. It is intuitive to expect that the severity of a problem in a locale ought to drive policy focus and response. Cities may simply respond to infection rates and deaths from COVID. We can expect responses will be commensurate to the risk from the spreading pandemic and the medical capacity in the city. For example, in exploring Canadian municipal COVID policy, Armstrong and Lucas find that the aggressiveness of municipal COVID policy response relates to the city's case totals.[33] We look at the total number of infections reported in the urban area at the time of data collection, drawing on data from the COVID-19 Resource Center. We opt to use COVID cases in the urban area because cities operate in location-based economic markets that transcend their boundaries into nearby cities and counties; and because of this, COVID spreads across cities within the same metro area. To account for this pattern, we aggregate county COVID counts up to the urban area or urban cluster, a census designation based on residential population density, which creates a measure of COVID cases for the entire urban area assigned to each city within that urban area.[34] We do not find any evidence that COVID rates in the urban area directly correlate with the probability that a city places an emergency shelter-in-place policy or eviction moratorium.

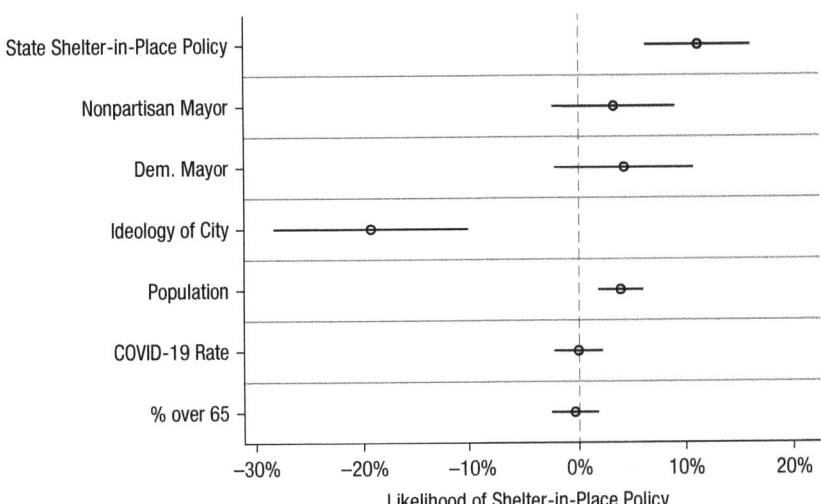

Figure 5.1. Emergency shelter-in-place policies

Note: Figure presents coefficients from multilevel logistic regression models predicting the presence of a local policy with clustered errors at the state level.

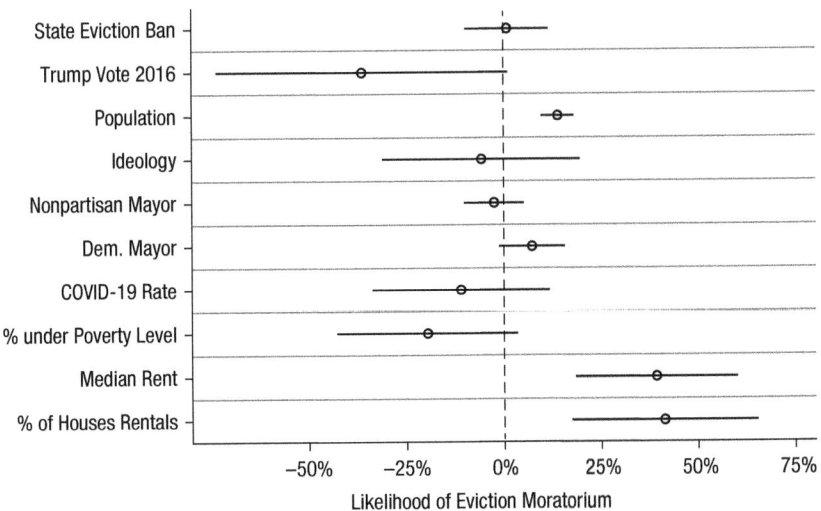

Figure 5.2. Correlates of city eviction moratoriums

Note: Figure presents coefficients from multilevel logistic regression models predicting the presence of a local policy with clustered errors at the state level.

High and accelerating levels of affective polarization in the United States in 2020 means that party affiliation shapes how people view a wide set of policy issues, how people process political information, and the degree to which individuals trust political actors. The general state of affective polarization was heightened by Donald Trump's reactions to the pandemic, particularly calling it a Democratic conspiracy, further politicizing the issue. A central outcome of this has been that party affiliation shapes views of the pandemic and willingness to comply with government recommendations.[35] Further, areas with more Republican voters saw less compliance with shelter-in-place policies during the early periods of COVID.[36]

Politics, ideology, and party affiliation shape all levels of politics in the United States, including pandemic policy responses.[37] Given the economic and political constraints cities face, mayoral party affiliation can impact fiscal policy and other local discretionary policies, such as public safety.[38] The lack of federal coordination during the pandemic may have accelerated these differences as Democratic mayors or cities with more Democratic voters may have been more likely to react quickly and aggressively. Republican governors acted more slowly to implement social distancing measures.[39] Given the partisan nature of COVID attitudes and policy, we control for the *party affiliation* of the mayor (Ballotpedia and internet searches), the party affiliation of the governor (Ballotpedia), and the ideology of the city's population.[40] We find mixed results here: more conservative cities (as measured through local ideology) are less likely to enact shelter-in-place policies, whereas ideology does not correlate with eviction moratoriums. We do not find evidence that the party affiliation of the mayor is correlated with either policy.

We also control for domain-specific factors. Given that COVID is particularly dangerous for individuals over the age of sixty-five, and that initial pandemic policies aimed to protect this population, we control for the share of the population that is over sixty-five.[41] While some cities referenced protections for the elderly population when they put shelter-in-place protections in place, we do not find that the share of the population over sixty-five is correlated with these policies.[42] Similarly, we examine local pressures that might shape eviction moratoriums. Given that evictions are affected by the characteristics of the housing market in a given place, we control for the share of houses occupied by renters and the median rent in each city.[43] Here, we find positive and significant effects: cities with more renters and higher rent are more likely (by almost 50 percent) to put an eviction moratorium into place.

Other Attempts at Local Pandemic Policy Making

Cities each responded to the public health and economic crises in many different ways, as the pandemic impacted practically all facets of social life. The methodological challenge of collecting and analyzing hundreds of cities' emergency responses to the pandemic limits our capacity to fully understand the wide range of policy responses that cities implemented to address the COVID crises. In this last section, we briefly detail one additional state and local policy issue, childcare access during the pandemic, which may be of interest to future scholars of local COVID emergency policy as the pandemic continues to have lasting societal implications, particularly for certain marginalized groups.

The pandemic and its economic crisis deeply impacted childcare availability and affordability, both for struggling families and childcare providers. With stay-at-home orders and school closures, the pandemic shifted considerable childcare responsibilities back to parents and other familial caregivers. Within the first two months of the stay-at-home orders, 60 percent of childcare centers in the United States had temporarily closed.[44] As a result, only 22 percent of essential workers were able to continue with the same childcare plans they had prior to the pandemic.[45] Increased family caregiving responsibilities fell on women—as it always has—and women disproportionately began to assume the additional caregiving and educational responsibilities during the pandemic, which added an estimated fifteen hours per week of labor to their workload and further declined workforce participation.[46] The challenges created by childcare closings were even more impactful on Black and Latino communities, many of which became childcare deserts because of sustained closures.[47] Moreover, the childcare workers affected by closures were largely women, people of color, and individuals without health insurance.[48]

In response to the pandemic's effect on the economy and childcare, some cities passed policies and provided funding that explicitly addressed the unfolding childcare crisis. Some policies were aimed to assist healthcare and frontline workers, such as Sacramento's program of free childcare for children of first responders, health care workers, and essential city employees and Chicago's partnership with local organizations that provided three months of free childcare for children of frontline workers.[49] Other programs were intended to support low-income residents, such as Miami's policy that provided free childcare to low-income families at certain local child care centers.[50] Finally, many cities, such as Milwaukee, partnered with local organizations, including the YMCA, to provide free childcare to families in their communities more broadly.[51] Some cities used CARES Act funding to fund childcare needs, such as Houston, which provided $3 million in relief funds to childcare centers serving low-income and underserved communities.[52] The variety of approaches and policies complicate comparisons across cities, but these nuances may also provide more interest to future scholars seeking to understand different COVID policy making.

Conclusion

As the pandemic quickly spread throughout the United States, cities responded to the public health emergency by issuing emergency orders for residents to stay at home, limiting evictions, and undertaking efforts to address the lack of childcare. We explore what factors shaped cities' efforts to slow the health and economic crises unfolding as a result of

COVID and find that different policy responses were influenced by different factors. Whether a state passed shelter-in-place policies mattered for a city's similar policy, but not so for eviction moratoriums. The rate of COVID infection and mayors' party affiliation did not influence either policy, and local ideology influenced only stay-at-home orders. Our work demonstrates the importance of examining the constraints on governments, even in an emergency. Cities operate in an environment where they cannot simply do whatever they want whenever they want; as a result, a quick response to COVID may have been hampered by the inability of cities to declare emergencies.

That we find different correlates for the shelter-in-place policies and eviction moratoriums also suggests that cities understand the policy tools that they easily control—and those that they do not. While cities and states traditionally share police powers, the federal government also engages in a broad set of policies relating to police powers. Thus, the ability of cities to impose a sweeping policy like shelter-in-place occurs in an environment where cities often are overruled by state and federal laws. In comparison, land use policy is almost entirely controlled by cities.[53] The differences between state action and local action for shelter-in-place and eviction moratoriums can thus potentially be traced to what powers cities actually have and use. At the same time, a wide set of cities in our sample did not put an eviction moratorium in place specifically because they were unable to do so per state law. For example, Boise passed a resolution asking for state action on evictions because the city was not empowered to pass its own moratorium. In other states, the authority for evictions rested with county leaders, some of whom passed their own moratoriums. Augusta–Richmond County in Georgia passed its own moratorium, noting that "Governor Brian Kemp has declared a public health emergency in the state of Georgia." The city then passed its own moratorium, reaffirming the county's action.[54] The tangled web of federalism, combined with the lack of any central database of policies and the quick nature of policy (especially during the early pandemic) makes studying these questions difficult.

Future research could work to further disentangle which levels of government act first in emergency contexts and how preemption, federalism, and emergency powers all shape quick policy responses in crises.

Notes

1. Cynthia J. Bowling, Jonathan M. Fisk, and John C. Morris, "Seeking Patterns in Chaos: Transactional Federalism in the Trump Administration's Response to the COVID-19 Pandemic," *American Review of Public Administration* 50, no. 6–7 (July 2020): 512–18; Greg Goelzhauser and David M. Konisky, "The State of American Federalism 2019–2020: Polarized and Punitive Intergovernmental Relations," *Publius: The Journal of Federalism* 50, no. 3 (2020): 311–43.

2. Donald F. Kettl, "States Divided: The Implications of American Federalism for COVID-19," *Public Administration Review* 80, no. 4 (2020): 595–602, https://doi.org/10.1111/puar.13243.

3. Clary Estes, "States Are Being Forced into Bidding Wars to Get Medical Equipment to Combat Coronavirus," *Forbes*, March 28, 2020.

4. Rebecca Bromley-Trujillo and Mirya R. Holman, "Climate Change Policymaking in the States: A View at 2020," *Publius: The Journal of Federalism* 50, no. 3 (2020): 446–72, https://doi.org/10.1093/publius/pjaa008.

5. Nancy J. Knauer, "The COVID-19 Pandemic and Federalism: Who Decides?" *New York University Journal of Legislation and Public Policy* 23, no. 1 (2002).

6. Katherine Levine Einstein and David M. Glick, "Does Race Affect Access to Government Services? An Experiment Exploring Street-Level Bureaucrats and Access to Public Housing," *American Journal of Political Science* 61, no. 1 (2017): 100–116.

7. Michael Barber and Adam M. Dynes, "City-State Ideological Incongruence and Municipal Preemption," *American Journal of Political Science*, forthcoming.

8. Charles R. Shipan and Craig Volden, "Bottom-Up Federalism: The Diffusion of Antismoking Policies from US Cities to States," *American Journal of Political Science* 50, no. 4 (2006): 825–43, https://doi.org/10.1111/j.1540-5907.2006.00218.x.

9. Bromley-Trujillo and Holman, "Climate Change Policymaking."

10. Katherine Levine Einstein, David M. Glick, and Maxwell Palmer, "City Learning: Evidence of Policy Information Diffusion from a Survey of US Mayors," *Political Research Quarterly* 72, no. 1 (2019): 243–58, https://doi.org/10.1177/1065912918785060; Rebecca Bromley-Trujillo, J. S. Butler, John Poe, and Whitney Davis, "The Spreading of Innovation: State Adoptions of Energy and Climate Change Policy," *Review of Policy Research* 33, no. 5 (2016): 544–65.

11. Mirya R. Holman, Emily M. Farris, and Jane Lawrence Sumner, "Local Political Institutions and First-Mover Policy Responses to COVID-19," *Journal of Political Institutions and Political Economy* 1, no. 4 (2020): 523–41, https://doi.org/10.1561/113.00000020.

12. John Kincaid and J. Wesley Leckrone, "Partisan Fractures in US Federalism's COVID-19 Policy Responses," *State and Local Government Review* 52, no. 4 (2020): 298–308.

13. Marijn Janssen and Haiko van der Voort, "Agile and Adaptive Governance in Crisis Response: Lessons from the COVID-19 Pandemic," *International Journal of Information Management* 55 (December 2020): 102180, https://doi.org/10.1016/j.ijinfomgt.2020.102180.

14. See both Mark J. Rozell and Clyde Wilcox, "Federalism in a Time of Plague: How Federal Systems Cope with Pandemic," *American Review of Public Administration* 50, no. 6–7 (2020): 519–25; and Philip Rocco, Daniel Béland, and Alex Waddan, "Stuck in Neutral? Federalism, Policy Instruments, and Counter-Cyclical Responses to COVID-19 in the United States," *Policy and Society* 39, no. 3 (2002): 458–77.

15. H. Daniel Xu and Rashmita Basu, "How the United States Flunked the COVID-19 Test: Some Observations and Several Lessons," *American Review of Public Administration* 50, no. 6–7 (2020): 568–76, p. 572, https://doi.org/10.1177/0275074020941701.

16. Jennifer Kates, Josh Michaud, and Jennifer Tolbert, "Stay-at-Home Orders to Fight COVID-19 in the United States: The Risks of a Scattershot Approach," *Kaiser Family Foundation*, April 5, 2020.

17. Office of the Mayor, San Francisco, "Proclamation by the Mayor Declaring the Existence of a Local Emergency," February 25, 2020, https://sfmayor.org/sites/default/files/Proclamation%20of%20Local%20Emergency%20re.%20COVID-19%202.25.2020.pdf.

18. Office of the Mayor, San Francisco, "San Francisco Issues New Public Health Order Requiring Residents Stay at Home Except for Essential Needs," news release, March 16, 2020, https://sfmayor.org/article/san-francisco-issues-new-public-health-order-requiring-residents-stay-home-except-essential.

19. Reniya Dinkins, "A Public-Private Partnership for Helping Small Businesses and Empowering Workers in Birmingham, Ala.," *Brookings* (blog), July 20, 2020.

20. Emily M. Farris, Mirya R. Holman, and Miranda E. Sullivan, "Representation and Anti-Racist Policymaking in US Cities during COVID-19," *Representation* (OnlineFirst), January 4, 2022.

21. Katherine Levine Einstein, Maxwell Palmer, Stacy Fox, Marina Berardino, Noah Fischer, Jackson Moore-Otto, Aislinn O'Brien, Marilyn Rutecki, and Benjamin Wuesthoff, "COVID-19 Housing Policy," Initiative on Cities, Boston University, 2020; Paul M. Ong, "Systemic Racial Inequality and the COVID-19

Renter Crisis," UCLA, Luskin Institute for Inequality and Democracy, August 7, 2020, https://challengeinequality.luskin.ucla.edu/2020/08/07/systemic-racial-inequality-covid-19-renter-crisis.

22. Emily A. Benfer, David Vlahov, Marissa Y. Long, Evan Walker-Wells, J. L. Pottenger Jr., Gregg Gonsalves, and Danya E. Keene, "Eviction, Health Inequity, and the Spread of COVID-19: Housing Policy as a Primary Pandemic Mitigation Strategy," *Journal of Urban Health* 98, no. 1 (2021): 1–12, https://doi.org/10.1007/s11524-020-00502-1; Anjalika Nande, Justin Sheen, Emma L. Walters, Brennan Klein, Matteo Chinazzi, Andrei H. Gheorghe, Ben Adlam, et al., "The Effect of Eviction Moratoria on the Transmission of SARS-CoV-2," *Nature Communications* 12, no. 1 (2021): 1–13; Mychal Cohen and Eleanor Noble, "Preventing Eviction Filings," *Urban Institute*, 2020.

23. CDC, "Temporary Halt in Residential Evictions to Prevent the Further Spread of COVID-19," Centers for Disease Control and Prevention, September 4, 2020, https://www.cdc.gov/coronavirus/2019-ncov/covid-eviction-declaration.html.

24. City of Glendale, "A Resolution of the Council of the City of Glendale, Maricopa County, Arizona, Placing a Temporary Moratorium on Evictions from Public Housing for Non-Payment of Rent Due to the Financial Impacts of Coronavirus Disease 2019 (COVID-19)," March 24, 2020, https://docs.glendaleaz.com/WebLink/DocView.aspx?id=7212732&dbid=0&repo=City-of-Glendale&cr=1.

25. City of Fremont, "An Executive Order of the Director of Emergency Services Imposing Regulations Related to Evictions from All Residential Rental Units Due to the Novel Corona Virus (COVID-19) Declared Emergency," March 25, 2020, https://www.fremont.gov/?navid=1034.

26. See both City of San Mateo, "Adopting an Emergency Ordinance Amending an Ordinance Imposing a Moratorium on Evictions for Non-Payment of Rent by Tenants Impacted by the COVID-19 Pandemic," March 23, 2020, https://www.cityofsanmateo.org/DocumentCenter/View/80318/Emergency-Ordinance---Commercial-Eviction-Moratorium-Extended-93020?bidId=; and Mayor of Augusta, Georgia, "Executive Order #2020-003," March 16, 2020, https://www.augustaga.gov/DocumentCenter/View/13365/EXECUTIVE-ORDER-BY-MAYOR-HARDIE-DAVIS-JR--COVID-19-RESPONSE?bidId=.

27. In Travis County, where Austin is located and part of its jurisdiction, the county government also suspended action on evictions, and county justices of the peace also stopped hearing cases on evictions for nonpayment during the pandemic.

28. Jane Lawrence Sumner, Emily M. Farris, and Mirya R. Holman, "Crowdsourcing Reliable Local Data," *Political Analysis* 28, no. 2 (2020): 244–62.

29. See Sumner, Farris, and Holman, "Crowdsourcing Reliable Local Data" for details on establishing consensus.

30. Office of the Mayor, San Francisco, "Second Supplement to Mayoral Proclamation Declaring the Existence of a Local Emergency Dated February 25, 2020," March 13, 2020, https://sfmayor.org/sites/default/files/Supplemental Declaration2_03132020_stamped.pdf.

31. City of Seattle, "Moratorium on Residential Evictions," March 14, 2020, https://durkan.seattle.gov/wp-content/uploads/sites/9/2020/03/Ex-B-Modified-EO-03162020-highlighted-FINAL.pdf.

32. Anne Kat Alexander and Sarah Lee, "Preliminary Analysis: A Year of Eviction Moratoria," *Eviction Lab*, March 29, 2021.

33. David A. Armstrong II and Jack Lucas, "Measuring and Comparing Municipal Policy Responses to COVID-19," *Canadian Journal of Political Science* 53, no. 2 (2020): 227–38.

34. US Census Bureau, "Qualifying Urban Areas for the 2010 Census" (report), 2012.

35. For party affiliation, see Shana Kushner Gadarian, Sara Wallace Goodman, and Thomas B. Pepinsky, "Partisanship, Health Behavior, and Policy Attitudes in the Early Stages of the COVID-19 Pandemic," *PLOS ONE* 16, no. 4 (2021): e0249596, https://doi.org/10.1371/journal.pone.0249596; for compliance, see Guy Grossman, Soojong Kim, Jonah M. Rexer, and Harsha Thirumurthy, "Political Partisanship Influences Behavioral Responses to Governors' Recommendations for COVID-19 Prevention in the United States," *Proceedings of the National Academy of Sciences* 117, no. 39 (2020), 24144–53.

36. Damon Roberts and Stephen Utych, "Polarized Social Distancing: Residents of Republican-Majority Counties Spend More Time Away from Home During the COVID-19 Crisis" (working paper), 2021.

37. Justin de Benedictis-Kessner and Christopher Warshaw, "Mayoral Partisanship and Municipal Fiscal Policy," *Journal of Politics* 78, no. 4 (2016): 1124–38, https://doi.org/10.1086/686308; Constantine Boussalis, Travis G. Coan, and Mirya R. Holman, "Climate Change Communication from Cities in the USA," *Climatic Change* 149, no. 2 (2018): 173–87, https://doi.org/10.1007/s10584-018-2223-1.

38. De Benedictis-Kessner and Warshaw, "Mayoral Partisanship."

39. Christopher Adolph, Kenya Amano, Bree Bang-Jensen, Nancy Fullman, and John Wilkerson, "Pandemic Politics: Timing State-Level Social Distancing Responses to COVID-19," *Journal of Health Politics, Policy, and Law* 46, no. 2 (2021): 211–33.

40. For partisan attitudes, see Gadarian, Goodman, and Pepinsky, "Partisanship." For party affiliation, see Chris Tausanovitch and Christopher Warshaw, "Representation in Municipal Government," *American Political Science Review* 108, no. 3 (2014): 605–41, https://doi.org/10.1017/S0003055414000318.

41. For COVID in people over age sixty-five, see Clara Bonanad, Sergio García-Blas, Francisco Tarazona-Santabalbina, Juan Sanchis, Vicente

Bertomeu-González, Lorenzo Fácila, Albert Ariza, Julio Núñez, and Alberto Cordero, "The Effect of Age on Mortality in Patients with COVID-19: A Meta-Analysis with 611,583 Subjects," *Journal of the American Medical Directors Association* 21, no. 7 (2020): 915–18. For population share of this cohort, see US Census Bureau, American Community Survey 2020, Sex and Age.

42. For example, Dallas's shelter-in-place order required that nursing homes and long-term care facilities prohibit nonessential visitors; see Dallas County, "Amended Order of Judge Clay Jenkins," March 24, 2020, https://www.dallas county.org/Assets/uploads/docs/judge-jenkins/covid-19/03242020-Amended Order-FINAL.pdf.

43. Richard M. Medina, Kara Byrne, Simon Brewer, and Emily A. Nicolosi, "Housing Inequalities: Eviction Patterns in Salt Lake County, Utah," *Cities* 104 (2020): 102804; Devin Q. Rutan and Matthew Desmond, "The Concentrated Geography of Eviction," *Annals of the American Academy of Political and Social Science* 693, no. 1 (2021): 64–81.

44. Medina et al., "Housing Inequalities"; Umair Ali, Chris M. Herbst, and Christos A. Makridis, "The Impact of COVID-19 on the US Child Care Market: Evidence from Stay-at-Home Orders," *Economics of Education Review* 82 (June 2021): 102094, https://doi.org/10.1016/j.econedurev.2021.102094; Andrew N. Hashikawa, Jill M. Sells, Peter M. DeJonge, Abbey Alkon, Emily T. Martin, and Timothy R. Shope, "Child Care in the Time of Coronavirus Disease-19: A Period of Challenge and Opportunity," *Journal of Pediatrics* 225 (October 2020): 239–45, https://doi.org/10.1016/j.jpeds.2020.07.042; Linda Smith and Sarah Tracey, "Child Care in COVID-19: Another Look at What Parents Want," *Bipartisan Policy Center*, August 26, 2020.

45. Hashikawa et al., "Child Care in the Time of Coronavirus"; Smith and Tracey, "Child Care in COVID-19."

46. Molly Wiant Cummins and Grace Ellen Brannon, "The Balancing Act Is Magnified: US Mothers' Struggles amidst a Pandemic," in *Mothers, Mothering, and COVID-19: Dispatches from the Pandemic*, ed. Andrea O'Reilly and Fiona Joy Green (Bradford, ON: Demeter Press, 2021), 211–20; Andrea O'Reilly, "'Certainly Not an Equal-Opportunity Pandemic': COVID-19 and Its Impact on Mothers' Care-work, Health, and Employment," in *Mothers, Mothering, and COVID-19: Dispatches from the Pandemic*, ed. Andrea O'Reilly and Fiona Joy Green (Bradford, ON: Demeter Press, 2021), 41–52.

47. Gina Adams and Margaret Todd, "Meeting the School-Age Child Care Needs of Working Parents Facing COVID-19 Distance Learning: Policy Options to Consider," *Urban Institute*, July 2021; Rasheed Malik, Won F. Lee, Aaron Sojourner, Katie Hamm, and Elizabeth E. Davis, "The Coronavirus Will Make Child Care Deserts Worse and Exacerbate Inequality," *Center for American Progress*, June 22, 2020.

48. Ali, Herbst, and Makridis, "The Impact of COVID-19."

49. City of Sacramento, "City Leaders Announce Free Childcare Plan to Help Those on Front Lines of Coronavirus Response," news release, March 20, 2020, https://www.cityofsacramento.org/Emergency-Management/COVID19/Media Releases; City of Chicago, "Childcare," https://www.chicago.gov/city/en/sites/health-care-workers/home/childcare.html.

50. City of Miami, "New Program Offering Free Childcare Services to Qualifying Residents," February 10, 2021, https://www.miamigov.com/Notices/News-Media/New-Program-Offering-Free-Childcare-Services-to-Qualifying-Residents.

51. Amy Schwabe, "How Does Social Distancing Work in Child Care? Here's What the Metropolitan Milwaukee YMCA Is Doing," *Milwaukee Journal Sentinel*, April 13, 2020.

52. Office of the Mayor, Houston, "City of Houston Offers Child Care Center Rental Assistance Funding Made Available by CARES Act Funding," news release, November 6, 2020, https://www.houstontx.gov/mayor/press/2020/child-care-center-rental-assistance.html.

53. Jessica Trounstine, *Segregation by Design: Local Politics and Inequality in American Cities* (New York: Cambridge University Press, 2018).

54. For more information, see Mayor of Augusta, Georgia, "Executive Order #2020-003."

Part III

RESPONSE TO THE EXERCISE OF EMERGENCY POWERS

Chapter 6

Public Opinion on the COVID-19 Pandemic
From Consensus to Conflict

Yiqian Alice Wang

Since the onset of the COVID-19 pandemic in March 2020, the United States has reported nearly 75.5 million cases of coronavirus infections and nine hundred thousand deaths as of February 2022.[1] The unprecedented nature of this public health crisis—both in terms of the speed with which outbreaks spread across the country as well as its associated human costs—has rendered it increasingly necessary for policy makers and public health experts alike to understand public attitudes toward COVID vaccinations and prevention.

Focusing on the fifteen-month period from March 2020 to June 2021, I examine trends in public opinion concerning the extent to which citizens perceived COVID to be a public health and economic threat. Specifically, I detail how public attitudes shifted from an initial consensus in support of restrictive policies to a more fragmented landscape characterized by demographic and political differences. Here, of particular interest is the development of a stark partisan divide separating Democratic and Republican publics in May 2020—this partisan divide not only would persist but would structure attitudes toward COVID policies going forward.

Next, I address changes in public opinion with respect to different state-level policies intended to reduce COVID spread. Here, I examine public attitudes toward (1) vaccine "passports," (2) mandatory vaccination requirements across educational and employment settings,

(3) restrictions on movement/gatherings, and (4) restrictions on school reopenings in the aggregate as well as across respondent subgroups. After mapping out the demographic and political divides in public attitudes toward COVID restrictions, I highlight some possible explanations for these observed differences. In particular, this section emphasizes how elite political cues and differences in risk perception may drive partisan and gender divisions.

After examining state-level variation in public opinion using California as a case study, I conclude by discussing how observed differences in attitudes among subgroups toward the pandemic may better inform how politicians and public health experts communicate COVID recommendations to the public more broadly.

American Attitudes toward COVID-19

By mid-March 2020, the World Health Organization officially declared COVID-19 a pandemic. This declaration was followed by President Trump's pronouncement on March 13 that the pandemic now constituted a national emergency. On the same day, the Trump administration would issue a travel ban prohibiting non-Americans who had visited any of twenty-six European countries in the Schengen Area within the last fourteen days from entering the United States. On March 19, California issued the nation's first stay-at-home order, which prohibited travel outside the home except for "essential" activities.

By the end of March 2020, the severity of the pandemic would become more pronounced—around this period, the US had reported more confirmed COVID cases than another other country. By then, a substantial portion of the population would have already come into some form of direct contact with national- or state-level institutions as they moved to contain COVID spread; indeed, by late March, nearly 75 percent of the population was under some form of state-mandated stay-at-home order. In light of this new reality, public perception changed accordingly. While the public continued to view COVID as a greater threat to the health of the nation than to themselves or to their families, the percentage of those who expressed concern over the pandemic was significantly higher now in comparison to early March. The share of the public that reported COVID to be a major threat to the economy increased by 18 percentage points (from 70 to 88 percent), while those who perceived it to be a threat to the health of the US population more generally increased by 19 percentage points, from 47 to 66 percent.[2] A similar—though slightly less pronounced—increase was observable among the share of respondents who viewed COVID to be a threat to their personal financial situation and personal health (a 15 and 9 percentage point increase, respectively).[3]

It was also around late March and early April that attitudes toward the pandemic began to converge even further across the general population, with approximately 75 percent of respondents indicating that they were "somewhat" or "very" concerned about COVID infection.[4] Arguably, public opinion was moving toward a political consensus.

Early public consensus concerning the severity of the pandemic also transferred into general compliance with CDC-recommended behaviors for reducing COVID spread as well as public support for

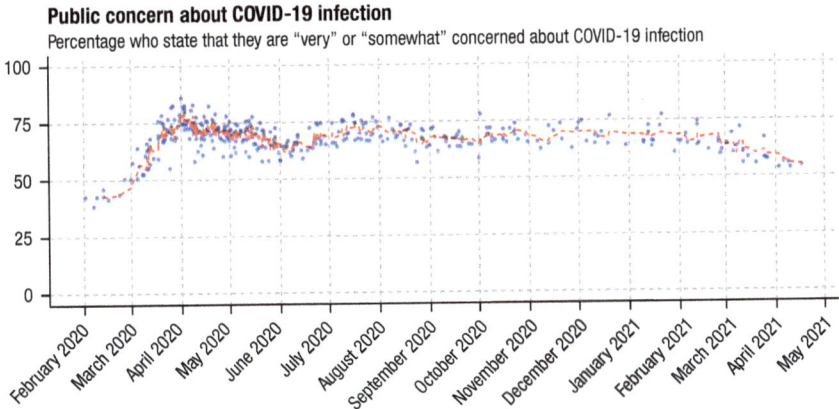

Figure 6.1. Public concern about COVID-19 infection
Source: FiveThirtyEight, 2021.

COVID-related restrictions. In early April 2020, 75 percent of the public stated that they had avoided public spaces within the past seven days, while 89 percent indicated that they had avoided unnecessary traveling. Meanwhile, 81 and 74 percent of the public said that they avoided small gatherings and large crowds, respectively. Yet, after public compliance hit its peak in April, the percentage of the public who reported taking these four precautions within the past week declined relatively steadily until July 2021. In August 2021, there was a temporary "bump" in public compliance that tapered off in October of the same year. This increase may be partially attributed to a temporary surge in COVID cases—in August 2021, the US averaged approximately one hundred thousand new COVID infections per day, a rate that had last been seen during the winter surge in 2020.

The only exception to this downward trend is with respect to mask wearing. While 64 percent of the public indicated that they wore a mask in April, the fraction of people who did so increased by 19 percentage

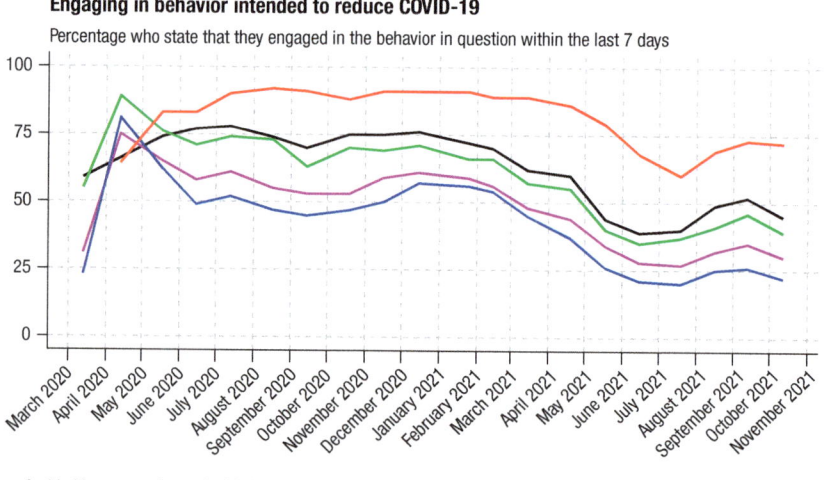

Figure 6.2. Behavior intended to reduce COVID-19 transmission
Source: Gallup, 2021.

points to 83 percent in May and hovered around 90 percent from July 2020 to April 2021. From April 2021 to late July 2021, the public reported less mask-wearing behavior, but opted to "mask up" again following the August surge.

Even more, at this point in time, there was near universal support for COVID restrictions including, among others, school closures, and nonessential interstate and international travel. Agreement over such protective measures was seemingly unaffected by individual-level characteristics—including party affiliation and state of residence—that often structure other attitudes toward public policies.

For instance, 95 percent of the public supported restricting international travel to the United States, while 91 percent supported canceling major sporting and entertainment events in order to slow the spread of the coronavirus outbreak.[5] Although some variation in support existed among Democratic and Republican respondents, these differences were minimal and generally fell within the 2 to 7 percentage points range. Nonetheless, despite these differences, the majority of the public (as well as the majority of Democrats and Republicans) supported some form of state-mandated shutdown measure.

During these initial stages of the pandemic, the main attitudinal differences that existed in the public were (1) among individuals who "strongly supported" COVID restrictions and (2) between partisans over the extent to which they believed the pandemic posed a major threat to public health. Across the board, the public's political identities were strongly correlated with their attitudes toward COVID restrictions as well as with the general threat that they considered the pandemic posed. Among the first group of persons who "strongly supported" COVID policies, Democrats were more likely to support restrictive regulations than Republicans. Among the second, more Democrats than Republicans (52 versus 78 percent, respectively) perceived COVID to be a major threat to the health of the US population; in contrast, 84 percent of Democrats and 92 percent of Republicans believed COVID to be a major threat to the US economy.[6]

From Public Consensus to Fragmentation

However, this early "March consensus" began to break down two months later as variation in support for COVID-related restrictions and belief in the severity of COVID increased over time. While a nascent partisan divide was evident in the early stages of the pandemic, it became increasingly visible in May and early June. As before, Democrats were more likely to express concern or strong concern over COVID than their Republican counterparts, regardless of the severity of the pandemic in their home states.[7] However, from March 2020 to August 2020, Democrat-identifying individuals became increasingly concerned about COVID as a health threat; in contrast, any comparable trend was not evident with respect to Republican attitudes.[8]

This partisan divide is also observable with respect to whether individuals engaged in behavior intended to reduce COVID spread and expressed willingness to endorse behaviors that do so. As figure 6.2 makes clear, more than 75 percent of the public reported engaging in some

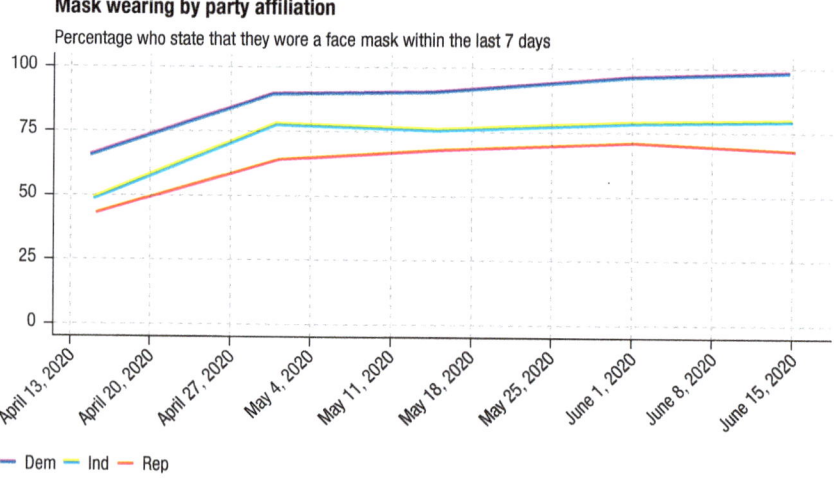

Figure 6.3. Mask wearing by party affiliation
Source: Gallup, 2020.

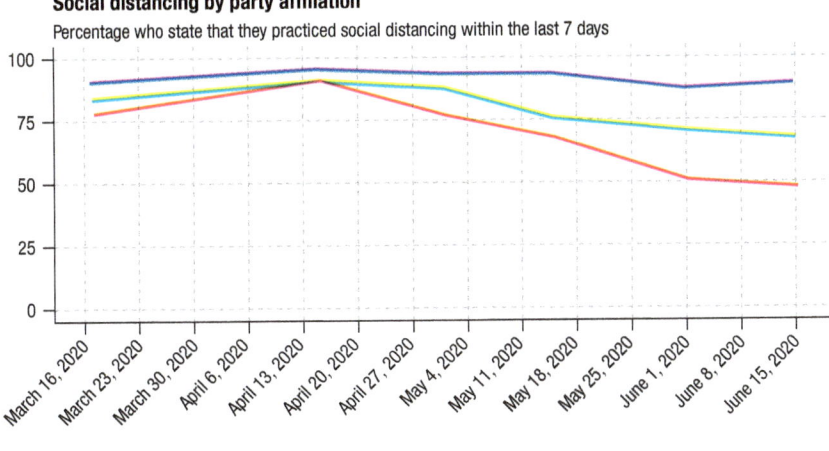

Figure 6.4. Social distancing by party affiliation
Source: Gallup, 2020.

form of social distancing behavior (whether avoiding large crowds or smaller gatherings), while 64 percent reported wearing masks. Yet, we observe a distinct partisan gap in mask wearing behavior—consistently, at least 20 percentage points more Democrats reported wearing a mask within the past week than their Republican counterparts. By August 2021, while 71 percent of Democrats reported wearing a mask in a store or business "all or most of the time" within the past month, only 30 percent of Republicans indicated that they did so.[9]

A similar partisan gap is evident for social distancing behaviors. Unlike partisan differences in mask wearing, where Democrats and Republicans maintained a relatively consistent 20 percentage point gap from April to June 2020, the gap between Democrats and Republicans with respect to social distancing increased over time. Indeed, the roughly 13 percentage point gap evident in March 2020 would triple in size by June of that same year.

Democrats and Republicans also differed significantly regarding whether they believe healthy individuals who do not exhibit COVID-related symptoms should stay at home as much as possible in order to

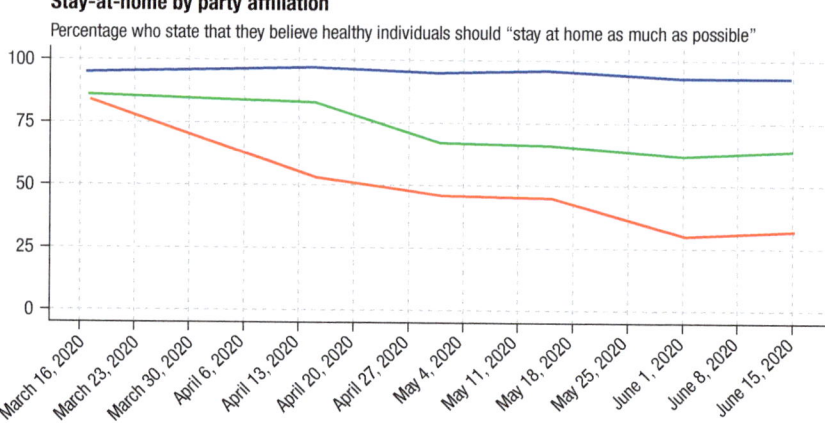

Figure 6.5. Stay-at-home by party affiliation
Source: Gallup, 2020.

help reduce COVID spread. Here, the increase in the partisan gap is even more stark than that observed with respect to social distancing. In March 2020, the partisan gap between Democrats and Republicans was approximately 10 percentage points; by June 2020, that gap would increase by nearly six times.

Republicans' reduced concern with regard to COVID and their decreased willingness to engage in COVID-mitigating behavior is also reflected in their changing attitudes toward the vaccine, which started before vaccines were made available. In general, public willingness to vaccinate against COVID remained relatively high. Vaccine hesitancy increased from July to September 2020, though this uncertainty might partially reflect the public's reaction to the "newness" of the vaccine. Beginning in October 2020, the percentage of individuals who were willing to vaccinate against COVID increased and remained relatively steady from March 2021 onward.

During this same period, Democrats expressed more favorable attitudes toward the COVID-19 vaccine than their Republican counterparts. Indeed, Republican-identifying respondents exhibited a decreasing time trend across these six months, whereby they became

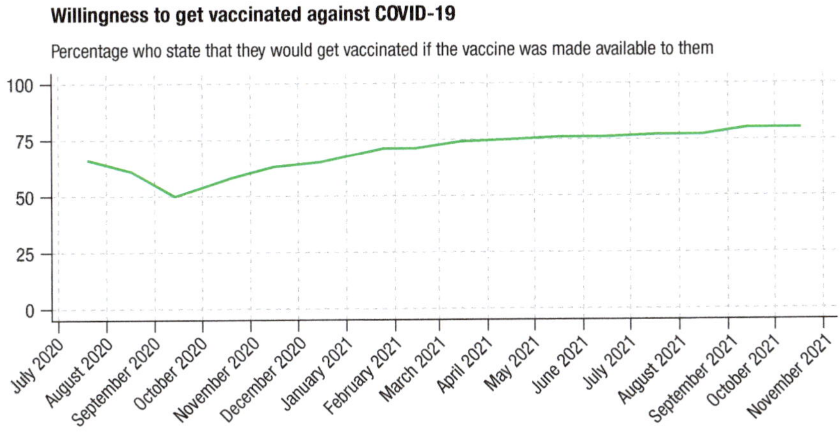

Figure 6.6. Public willingness to vaccinate against COVID-19
Source: Gallup, 2020–21.

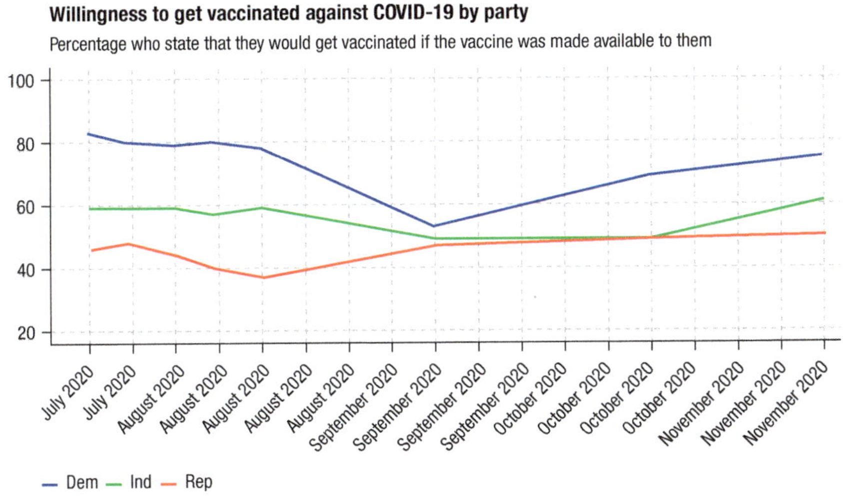

Figure 6.7. Public willingness to vaccinate by party
Source: Gallup, 2020.

less likely to express willingness to receive the vaccine once it became available to them. Meanwhile, no such time trend could be discerned for Democrats.[10]

As with the initial consensus over the degree to which COVID posed a national threat, public agreement over the necessity of COVID restrictions and lockdown measures also disappeared over time. As governors and other state-level officials started to grapple with the dilemma of balancing public health with other economic-oriented concerns, Democrats and Republicans began to diverge still further over the necessity of restrictions intended to reduce COVID spread. In early April 2020, 66 percent of the general public expressed concern that state-level restrictions would be lifted too quickly.[11] Even though the proportion of persons who expressed this view increased by 2 percentage points to 68 percent in early May, the increased divide between Republicans and Democrats on this issue became much starker. By then, the 30-percentage point gap in early April (51 of Republicans, 81 percent of Democrats) had increased to 40 by late April (47 of Republicans, 87 of Democrats).[12]

By August 2020, COVID became the third leading cause of death in the United States, surpassed only by cancer and heart disease. The US now reported more than 5.4 million confirmed coronavirus cases, with COVID-related deaths exceeding one thousand per day. While vaccines under development by Pfizer and Johnson & Johnson entered their phase 3 clinical trials by late September, COVID cases continued to rise, particularly in the Midwest.

As national and international responses to the pandemic ramped up in earnest, early consensus among the US public over the appropriate political course of action would break down even further that fall. By September 2020, 85 percent of Democrats believed COVID to be a major threat to the US population, while only 46 percent of Republicans reported similar sentiments.[13] Interestingly, despite their attitudinal divergence regarding nearly all COVID-related measures (from the severity of the pandemic to the necessity of COVID restrictions), Democrats and Republicans converged with respect to their beliefs that the pandemic posed a threat to the US economy. While 77 percent of Democrats and 62 percent of Republicans believed this to be the case in March 2020, that gap narrowed to a four percentage point difference by September of that year. By February 2021, this percentage had increased even further, to 83 and 81 percent, respectively.[14]

Attitudes toward Pandemic Restrictions

Just as public attitudes toward the severity of COVID shifted from an initial consensus to a more fragmented landscape characterized by stark partisan differences, opinions toward specific pandemic-related mandates were also marked by comparable changes. This section examines variations in public opinion regarding so-called vaccine passports and mandatory vaccination requirements (for travel and within the employment and educational contexts) as well as broader policy restrictions on movement/gatherings. It also briefly addresses how the ongoing pandemic has affected the public's attitudes toward health care and policy reform more generally.

Vaccine Mandates and "Passports"

Although definitions of "vaccine passports" may vary, they tend to refer to institutionalized programs in which the applicability of COVID restrictions is directly tied to an individual's vaccination status. Under such a system, COVID restrictions related to travel, entertainment events, dining, and the like may be lifted for those who are vaccinated, even though those restrictions would remain in place for unvaccinated persons. Public debate concerning the desirability of vaccine passports—ranging from arguments that question their ability to temper disease transmission to those that point toward their potential infringements on individual liberty—have become increasingly contentious. While their specific motivations for supporting or opposing vaccine passports may differ, persons tend to fall into one of two camps.

Opponents argue that vaccine passports functionally coerce people into getting vaccinated in order to access basic liberties, which may be especially pernicious when individuals hold religious or other personal objections to the COVID vaccine. Meanwhile, supporters argue that vaccine passports are crucial for controlling the spread of COVID and that passports successfully balance respect for individual liberties with state interests in protecting public health.

Overall, the idea of requiring vaccine documentation for entry into restaurants and other businesses remains deeply unpopular, with less than 30 percent of the public supportive of such policies.[15] As expected, there remained subgroup differences, and the level of support for vaccine passports varied across gender, party affiliation, vaccination status, education, race/ethnicity, and income level. A higher percentage of men than women expressed support for vaccine passports, particularly when passports are presented as optional measures (in the sense that businesses are allowed but not required to adopt them).

Reflecting broader partisan divides over the severity of the pandemic, a higher percentage of Democrats than Republicans supported vaccine passports (46 percent and 12 percent, respectively), which is especially the case when passports are characterized as optional.[16] Meanwhile, vaccinated and college-educated respondents are more supportive of vaccine passports than unvaccinated or less-educated respondents, while persons with higher income are more supportive of vaccine passports than those with lower income. Overall, support for vaccine passports is higher when they are presented as voluntary (i.e., permitted but not required); interestingly, the use of the term "vaccine passport" does not appear to have any negative effects on public support for such policies.

These partisan divides are also reflected in state-level policy. By November 2021, twenty states—all of which have Republican governors—prohibited vaccine passports wholesale. While eleven states enacted bans through executive others, the remaining nine passed bans through their state legislatures. As of December 2021, five states have allowed for some form of proof-of-vaccination policy, in which certain

COVID restrictions are entirely or partially lifted for vaccinated persons. Of these five states, all five have Democratic governors.

Mandatory Vaccinations

In September 2020, before a vaccine became available, approximately 40 percent of respondents supported state-level vaccination mandates for adults.[17] By late April and early May of 2021, a now-majority of the public (62 percent) expressed support for some form of local, state, or federal vaccination requirements, with subgroup variation persisting across gender, race/ethnicity, education, and income level. These figures stayed constant or rose slightly as summer arrived. By July, the percentage of respondents who supported such mandatory vaccine policies stood at 64 percent. With the exception of Republican-identifying respondents, all other subgroups included a majority of individuals indicating that they either approved or strongly approved of a vaccination mandate. Even so, although a minority of Republicans

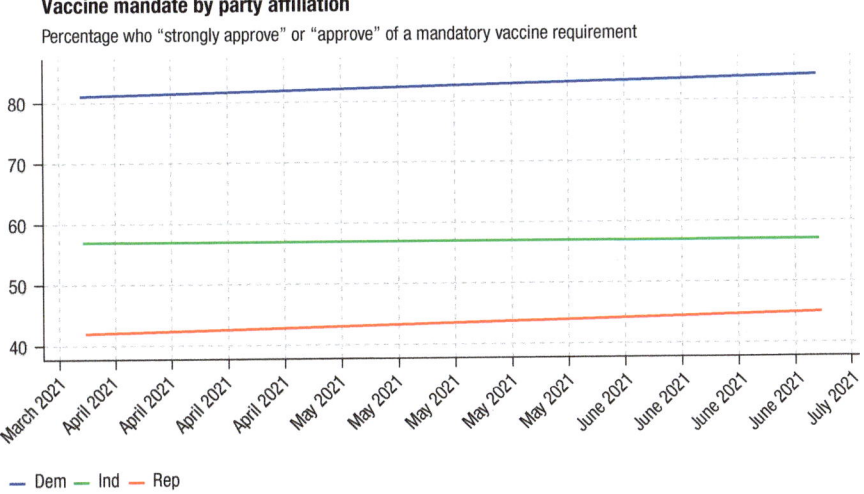

Figure 6.8. Support for mandatory vaccinations by party
Source: Gallup, 2021.

supported vaccination requirements, the percentage of those who did so increased from 42 to 45 percent between April/May and June/July of 2021. Meanwhile, the percentage of Democrats who supported similar policies also increased by 3 percentage points (from 81 to 84) during the same period, while the percentage of Independents remained the same at 57 percent.

As with the abovementioned subgroup trends for vaccine passports, men were more supportive of across-the-board mandatory vaccination measures than women. Older persons tended to express greater support for mandatory vaccine policies than their younger counterparts, while support for these policies increased more generally with educational attainment and income level.[18]

Mandatory Vaccinations for Airline Travel

In April/May 2020, a majority of the public (67 percent) expressed support for mandatory vaccinations prior to airline travel, with variation across gender, race/ethnicity, education, and income level. By July, approximately 70 percent of the public indicated support for such policies. Although partisan differences persisted, the gap in support between Democratic and Republican individuals is slightly smaller than the partisan gap evident for other policies (such as across-the-board mandatory vaccine requirements). In the intervening two-month period, the percentage of Republicans who supported vaccine requirements prior to airline travel increased by 3 percentage points, from 49 to 52 percent. Meanwhile, the percentage of Democrats who expressed similar sentiments increased from 84 to 87 percent; the percentage of Independents increased slightly, from 63 to 64.[19] By August 2021, 90 percent of Democrats supported some form of vaccination requirement for airline travel. In contrast, 50 percent of Independents and 29 percent of Republicans expressed similar sentiments.

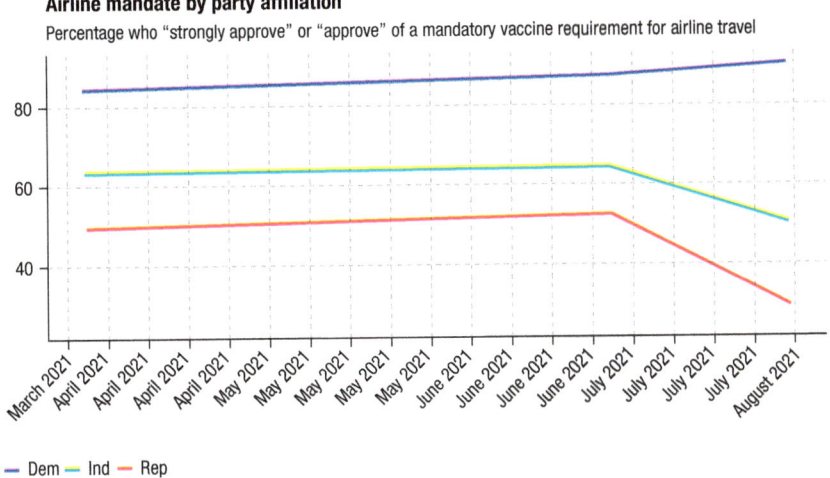

Figure 6.9. Support for mandatory vaccinations (travel) by party
Source: Gallup, 2021.

Mandatory Vaccinations in Educational and Employment Settings

As fall and the traditional start of the academic year approached, public debate turned toward the reopening of K–12 schools and colleges and universities. In September 2020, when the majority of educational institutions had adopted some form of virtual or remote learning requirement, close to half (49 percent) of all respondents supported some form of vaccine requirements for children in educational settings.[20] By late April and early May of the following year, a majority of the public (58 percent) expressed support for mandatory vaccinations as a prerequisite for K–12 school attendance.[21] By June and July of that same year, public support had increased by another 3 percentage points, to 61 percent. As with the other policies described above, similar variations persisted across demographic groups: men were more supportive than women, and support for mandatory vaccinations for K–12 students increased as educational attainment and income levels increased.

Reflecting broader political divisions, a partisan gap was also evident: in April/May 2021, 38 percent of Republicans and 76 percent of

Democrats supported some form of mandatory vaccine requirement for K–12 students. This gap not only persisted but increased slightly by June/July of that year: 81 percent of Democrats approved or strongly approved of these policies, whereas the percentage of Republicans who expressed similar attitudes was 40 percentage points lower.[22] As for mandatory vaccinations within the university context, a majority of the public (66 percent) expressed approval or strong approval for such policies. Unlike public opinion for K–12 reopening, however, the percentage of respondents who indicated their support did not change between April/May and June/July of 2021. Attitudes among Republicans did not change between April and July, remaining at 47 percent. Meanwhile, support among the Democrat-identifying public increased by 2 percentage points, from 83 to 85 percent.

Perhaps reflecting fragmented public opinion on this issue, school-related COVID policies also exhibit significant variation. As of November 2021, seventeen states (plus Washington, DC) had face mask requirements, while twenty-seven did not and six prohibited them altogether. Ten states and Washington, DC, required school employees to be vaccinated, while forty states did not.

Interestingly, rather than deciding through state-level policy whether schools must conduct screening tests and provide in-person or hybrid instruction, a majority of states allowed local school districts to make that determination themselves. Here, forty-five states allowed local school administrations to decide whether they wished to conduct screening tests, and twenty-nine states permitted local districts to decide between hybrid versus fully in-person instruction. It is unclear, however, whether this decision to devolve decision-making power to local school districts was due to state policy makers' belief that local administrators are better equipped to respond because of their knowledge of on-the-ground COVID conditions or out of reluctance to legislate on an issue that deeply divides the public.

By August 2021, 88 percent of Democrats supported some form of vaccination requirement for work-related purposes. In contrast,

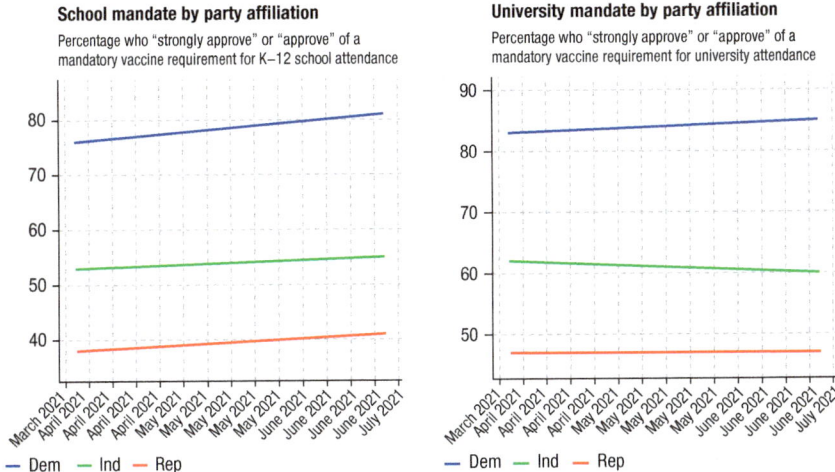

Figure 6.10. Support for mandatory vaccinations (education) by party
Source: COVID States Project, 2021.

43 percent of Independents and 24 percent of Republicans expressed similar sentiments. As before, all variations across demographic groups persisted in the same directions, with men, persons with higher income, and persons with higher levels of education more likely to support vaccine requirements/regulations.[23] With respect to vaccine mandates in the workplace, partisan differences in public opinion are again evident in state-level policy. As of November 2021, twenty-one states and Washington, DC, have some form of employee mandate in place (either among state, health care, or educational employees); meanwhile, seventeen states have no such mandate and another twelve prohibit such requirements altogether. Of the twenty-seven states with Republican governors, only Maryland, Massachusetts, and Vermont had some form of vaccine mandate in place. Interestingly, twenty-four of these twenty-seven states (again, with the exception of Maryland, Massachusetts, and Vermont) were involved in a lawsuit challenging federal vaccination requirements as of December 2021.

Restrictions on International and Nonessential Travel

Even across other policy domains, the divide between Democrats and Republicans concerning how best to combat the pandemic increased throughout 2021. Reflecting again the initial March 2020 consensus, partisans did not greatly differ in terms of their support for restrictions on international and nonessential travel. During the initial stages of the pandemic, 94 percent of Democrats and 96 percent of Republicans supported restricting international travel to the United States.[24] Although a majority of Republicans still supported policies restricting international travel to the US, in February 2021 those percentages were lower than they were in March 2020 and exhibited a greater gap in comparison to Democratic attitudes. Whereas 71 percent of Republicans wished to restrict international travel to the US, 87 percent of Democrats expressed similar policy preferences in February 2021.

Similarly, in March 2020, 83 percent of Democrats and 76 percent of Republicans supported policies restricting nonessential travel. Across

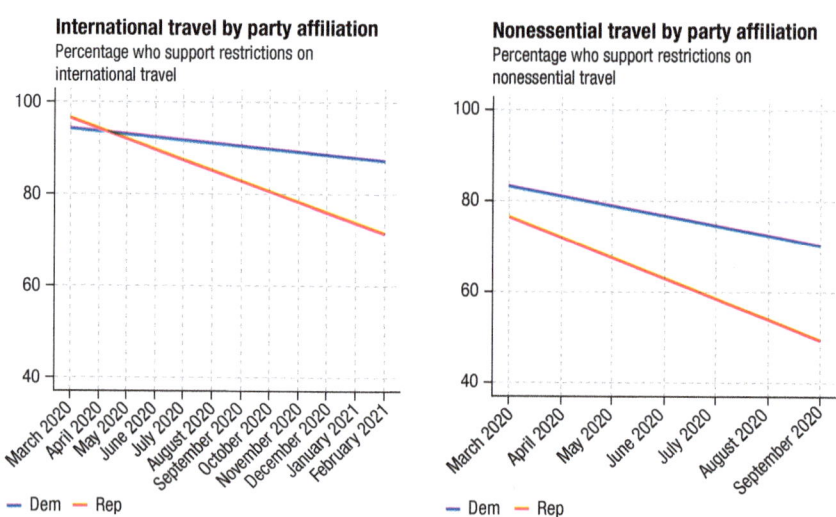

Figure 6.11. Support for travel restrictions by party
Source: Pew Research Center, 2021.

both parties, approval of such policies would steadily decline—by September 2020, 70 percent of Democrats and 49 percent of Republicans continued to support restrictions on nonessential travel.[25]

Restrictions on Group Gatherings

In March 2020, 82 percent of Republicans and 92 percent of Democrats supported policies restricting the public from gathering in large groups.[26] In September of that year, the percentage of Republicans and Democrats who expressed approval for canceling large gatherings decreased to 58 percent and 81 percent, respectively.[27] By February 2021, the percentage of Republicans who supported such policies decreased even further, to 56 percent, while the percent of Democrats increased to 93 percent. As was the case with attitudes toward travel restrictions, the partisan gap widened considerably over time.

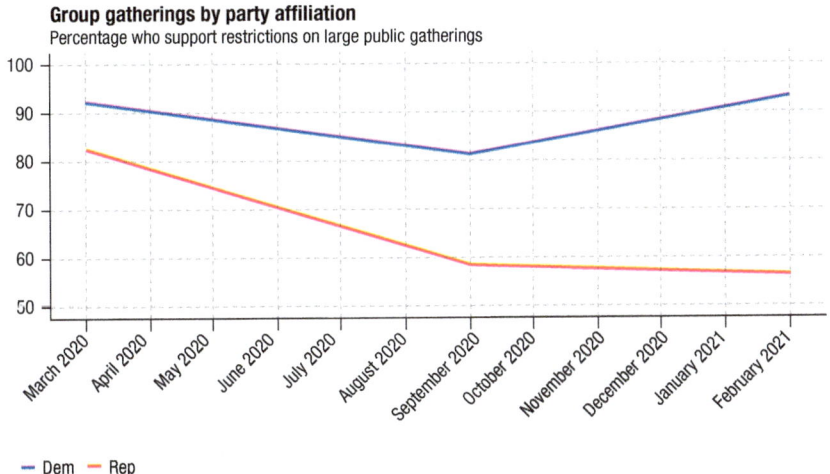

Figure 6.12. Support for group gathering restrictions by party

Sources: Pew Research Center, 2021; John Sides, Chris Tausanovitch, and Lynn Vavreck, "The Politics of COVID-19: Partisan Polarization about the Pandemic Has Increased, but Support for Health Care Reform Hasn't Moved at All," *Harvard Data Science Review*, November 30, 2020.

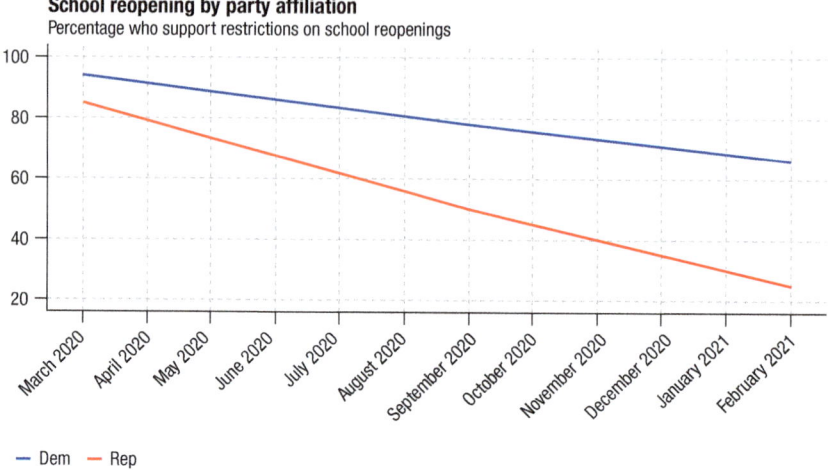

Figure 6.13. Support for K–12 school reopening restrictions by party
Sources: Pew Research Center, 2021; Sides, Tausanovitch, and Vavreck, "The Politics of COVID-19."

Restrictions on School Reopenings

In the early stages of the pandemic, 94 percent of Democrats and 85 percent of Republicans supported closing K–12 schools.[28] In September 2020, 78 percent of Democrats and 50 percent of Republicans expressed support for closing schools and universities.[29] By February 2021, 66 percent of Democrats and 25 percent of Republicans expressed support for closing K–12 schools in favor of a remote/virtual teaching arrangement.

Restrictions on Business Reopenings

Although 91 percent of Democrats supported limiting restaurants to carryout in March 2020, only 78 percent of Republicans did so (a difference of 13 percentage points).[30] In February 2021, among Democrats, 74 percent supported limiting restaurants to takeout only; meanwhile, only 23 percent of Republicans held similar beliefs during this same period.

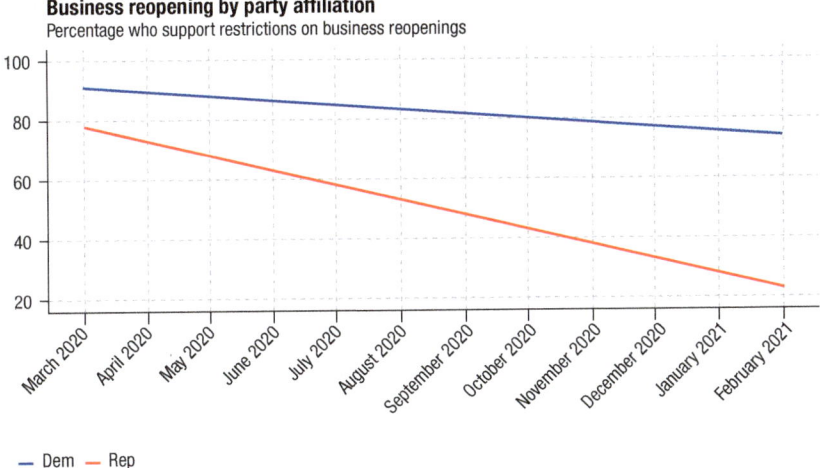

Figure 6.14. Support for business reopening restrictions by party
Sources: Pew Research Center, 2021; Sides, Tausanovitch, and Vavreck, "The Politics of COVID-19."

Support for Health Care Reform?

With the prominence of COVID-19 in the national discourse and its broader contextualization within conversations over public health, one might expect the pandemic to have affected public attitudes toward health care reform more generally. Indeed, given the extent to which the public now views the pandemic and efforts to combat COVID through a partisan lens, it seems intuitively plausible that this heightened role of party affiliation will spill over into other health/COVID-adjacent domains. Surprisingly, COVID does not appear to have substantially shifted the public's preferences with regard to domestic health care reform.

Rather, public attitudes toward health care reform appear to have hardly moved at all. In July 2019, 53 percent of the public supported a government-operated health insurance for all, 63 percent supported subsidizing health insurance for those less well-off, and 50 percent supported Medicare for All. By October 2020, support for these three policies would shift to 51, 64, and 48 percent, respectively.[31] Sides,

Tausanovitch, and Vavreck speculate that this is largely due to the absence of broader messaging (from elites or otherwise) that links the pandemic to state or national health policies.

Partisan and Gender Differences in COVID Attitudes

Although trends in COVID-related public opinion are well documented, the underlying factors driving these dynamics are less understood. Here, two particularly notable dynamics are those relating to partisan and gender-specific differences.

One possible explanation for this observed divergence between Democrats and Republicans emphasizes the role of partisan cue taking. As noted earlier, scholars have long documented the manner in which elites' political positioning informs public opinion and policy attitudes.[32] In the absence of policy information or in the presence of inconsistent information, persons may draw more heavily on other available heuristics, including elite cues and party affiliation, to assist them in formulating political opinions. When elites are united in their policy beliefs and cues to the public, individuals will adopt that given opinion. However, when elites remain divided, individuals will more heavily weigh the opinion expressed by members of their own party.[33]

With respect to COVID restrictions specifically and the pandemic more generally, elite messaging has been relatively mixed. Whereas Democratic leaders have remained strongly united in terms of messaging (emphasizing the importance of stay-at-home orders and social distancing measures, among others), Republican elites have been considerably more divided on the proper course of action. Against this political backdrop of elite division, we should expect the public to adopt attitudes toward COVID restrictions partly on the basis of their pre-existing political affiliation. And indeed, this is what we observe empirically: more Democrats than Republicans support COVID-related restrictions and believe the pandemic to pose a significant health threat to both themselves and the national public.

Interestingly, however, it may be precisely Republican elites' mixed messaging that has played an important role in shifting public opinion and behavior regarding COVID. Former president Trump as well as other prominent Republican elites, including Florida governor Ron DeSantis and Texas governor Greg Abbott, adopted increasingly dismissive attitudes toward COVID as the pandemic wore on, often trivializing the severity of the illness or the efficacy of proposed public health measures. In this context where certain Republican elites have already saturated the political space with particular antirestriction or anti-vaccination cues, other elites of the same political affiliation who contradict this party line may be treated more "seriously" by those of the opposite political persuasion. Put differently, when Republican officials "contradict" the broader messaging pushed by other national Republican elites and express, say, provaccination views, this precise divergence between the former and the latter may render it more likely for Democrat-identifying or weakly Republican-identifying individuals to respond by adjusting their views or behavior. Indeed, following a similar logic, Grossman et al. found that Democratic-leaning counties in Republican-governed states were particularly responsive to calls for more proactive COVID prevention from Republican governors.[34]

Also notable is that public attitudes differ not only across political parties but also within the parties themselves. Here, one viable explanation also seems to point toward partisan cue taking. Among Republicans who received their pandemic-related news primarily from the Trump administration, individuals were less likely to express support for COVID restrictions or to view the pandemic as an economic or public health threat.

The other prominent feature that is observable with respect to COVID-related public opinion is the persistent gender gap between male and female respondents. One possible explanation highlights gender differences with regard to perceptions and understandings of risk or risk taking. The risk-aversion literature suggests that women tend to be more cautious than men across a variety of different domains, including professional settings, financial decision making, and life-threatening situations.³⁵ Experimental evidence from the political psychology literature suggests that women also tend to take a more holistic approach toward risk taking, in the sense that they will account for not only the risk any given situation poses to themselves but also the risk that accumulates for individuals in their general proximity. In other words, they will consider the risk that accrues to themselves as well as to their parents, friends, and children. Other research has demonstrated that, relative to men, women have a greater tendency to anticipate and thus avoid negative outcomes.³⁶

Here, women's tendencies toward more holistic risk assessments and anticipation of negative outcomes suggest that they should be more supportive of restrictive COVID policies than their male counterparts. If holistic decision making involves aggregating the accumulated risk to themselves, their family, and those in their community, we should expect women to attach greater risk than men to a contagious disease such as COVID; this, then, should translate into greater relative support for policies designed to mitigate COVID risk.

However, this does not appear to be the case empirically. As evidenced above, men tend to be more supportive than women of COVID-related restrictions across a variety of policy types, from vaccine passports to across-the-board vaccination mandates. While it is unclear why this gender gap persists, one possible explanation may relate to the particular *type* of policy (e.g., vaccines) about which respondents were asked.

It is important to recognize that the lower percentage of women (relative to men) who support vaccine-related policies should not be taken to imply that smaller proportions of women are concerned about COVID or intend to take the pandemic "seriously." Rather, present research suggests the opposite. More women than men express concern over COVID (with 54 percent indicating that they were "somewhat worried" or "very worried" that they will contract COVID, compared to 42 percent of men). When asked how persons who do not exhibit COVID symptoms should respond to the pandemic, 28 percent of women indicated that they should "lead their normal lives as much as possible and avoid interruptions to work and business." In contrast,

40 percent of men believed this to be the best approach. Finally, when presented with a hypothetical situation in which government restrictions were lifted and "people were able to decide for themselves about being out in public," a lower percentage of women relative to men indicated that they would return to their normal day-to-day activities "right now" (24 percent versus 37 percent, respectively).[37] These preferences against a return to normalcy are especially notable "given that women seem to be carrying a disproportionately greater share of the COVID-19-related care-giving load at home, such as child care and remote schooling."[38]

These patterns suggest that women view COVID to be a greater threat than men do, which aligns with previous research into the gendered dynamics of risk perception. And yet, we observe a distinct gender gap with respect to support for proof-of-vaccination laws and vaccination mandates, which women are less likely to support than are their male counterparts. One partial explanation might be that this observed dynamic is particular to vaccine-related or vaccine-adjacent policies and *not* to COVID policies more broadly. As a group, women exhibit high rates of compliance with general COVID policies. Women are more likely than men to engage in preventive health behaviors intended to prevent the spread of COVID; women report, for instance, greater compliance with social distancing measures, stay-at-home orders, and other hygiene recommendations.[39]

Yet, just as women are less likely to support vaccine mandates and passports, women are also less likely to report that they will "definitely" or "probably" get the COVID vaccine if one was available to them today. Here, the gender gap appears to have widened across time, with 67 percent of men and 54 percent of women in November 2020 indicating that they would get vaccinated (in comparison to 76 and 69 percent, respectively, in May 2020).[40] Studies that specifically examine COVID vaccine acceptance frequently highlight gender as an important factor: men are, again, more likely to report a willingness to get vaccinated than women are.[41] For the COVID vaccine specifically, women are more likely than men to delay or altogether reject the vaccine. While men and women were equally likely to justify their hesitancy by invoking religious or philosophical commitments, women were more likely to state that they believe the vaccine to be too new, they are concerned about negative side effects, and they have preexisting conditions that make the vaccine undesirable from a health point of view.[42]

The extent to which the gender divide persists with respect to the COVID vaccine is surprising, especially given relatively mixed findings in the vaccine hesitancy literature on the role of gender in determining vaccination uptake. Women were less likely to express intentions to receive H1N1 vaccinations.[43] Nonetheless, some studies have found that women are more likely to vaccinate against the flu.[44] However, others suggest the exact opposite.[45]

State Variation: The Case of California

Perhaps unsurprisingly, the attitudinal dynamics described above do not necessarily travel across individual states. This may be especially true for states on the far ends of the "restrictiveness" distribution, that is, those that have adopted either more lax or more aggressive approaches toward managing the pandemic. California in particular has taken an especially aggressive approach toward COVID-19, whether that is with respect to the more cautious timeline by which it reopened businesses or the implementation of vaccine requirements for indoor dining in highly populated areas.

Overall, Governor Gavin Newsom and other officials have mounted a particularly strong response in reaction to the pandemic. In March 2020, California became the first state in the country to implement a stay-at-home order. Following a highly cautious county-by-county reopening in May, California implemented a statewide mask mandate and renewed social distancing restrictions in June after local governments had lifted their masking requirements. In November, amid a surge in COVID infections, Governor Newsom implemented a limited stay-at-home order that required nonessential businesses across forty-one counties to close operations. Once the number of reported COVID cases exceeded one million by the end of November, California expanded its limited stay-at-home order to additional counties. By June 2021, in response to declining infection rates, California moved to fully reopen its economy. In August of that year, the California Departments of Public Health and Technology launched the optional Digital COVID-19 Vaccine Record portal, which allows state residents to upload a digital copy of their vaccination record. Since then, counties and cities across the state have implemented their own coronavirus restrictions, including vaccine passports or verification of negative COVID tests.

We might expect California's more cautious approach to spill over onto public attitudes or for state officials to adopt policies that are reflective of more cautious public sentiments. And perhaps unsurprisingly, the California public is consistently at the higher end in terms of support for vaccine mandates and other vaccine requirements. In April 2021, approximately 70 percent of the state population stated that they "somewhat approve" or "strongly approve" of an across-the-board vaccine requirement. Moreover, 77 percent supported a vaccine requirement for airline travel, while 67 percent and 75 percent supported mandatory vaccination for students attending K–12 schools and universities, respectively.[46]

Interestingly, the percentage of Californians who expressed support for certain state- and national-level COVID restrictions appeared to decrease over time. In June/July 2021, the percentage of California respondents who supported a mandatory vaccine requirement remained the same, at 70 percent. Yet, the percentage who supported a COVID vaccine requirement for air travel decreased by approximately 4 percentage points, to 73 percent. Meanwhile, the percentage of respondents who support COVID vaccine requirements within the school and university contexts decreased by 1 and 6 percentage points (to 66 percent and 70 percent), respectively.[47]

Along similar lines, Californians' behaviors outside the home have also changed as the pandemic has continued and vaccines have become more readily available. Since March 2021, more respondents were likely to report that they went to a café/bar/restaurant, went to the gym, or have gone to work. Around this time, there was also a doubling of the percentage of persons who report they have been in an indoor space with someone outside of their household. These behavior trends mirror changes in the extent to which California residents decreased adherence to public health recommendations. Since January 2021, fewer respondents were likely to report that they wore a face mask while outside their home, frequently washed their hands, avoided public and/or crowded spaces, and avoided contact with other people outside of their household.[48] It is unclear, however, whether these behavioral changes are driven by decreased concern over COVID as a function of more widespread vaccines and testing, some form of quarantine/COVID fatigue, or other factors.

Conclusion

In an unprecedented scientific achievement, researchers successfully developed vaccines against COVID-19 within the span of one year. Yet, the success of a vaccine is determined not only by how effectively it builds immunity in the population or how efficiently governments are able to roll out vaccination programs. Rather, it also depends on public "readiness," that is, the extent to which the public is prepared to get vaccinated once the vaccine becomes available to them.

More generally, for public health or immunization campaigns to be successful, policy makers must effectively communicate to the public the importance of policy compliance, which, in part, helps secure individual "readiness." Polling during the coronavirus pandemic has made clear that, after a brief period of generalized consensus, significant divisions across the public settled in. Among those subgroups who view measures that are designed to reduce the spread of COVID with skepticism, the reasons underlying their hesitancy often differ, thus suggesting that any form of "one size fits all" public health campaign is unlikely to be effective or may even engender backlash. With this in mind, future research may wish to examine how to construct tailored, targeted strategies for more effective public health and science communication.

Notes

1. Centers for Disease Control and Prevention 2022, "CDC COVID Data Tracker," February 2, 2022, https://covid.cdc.gov/covid-data-tracker/#datatracker-home.
2. Pew Research Center, "US Public Sees Multiple Threats from the Coronavirus – and Concerns Are Growing," March 18, 2020, https://www.pewresearch.org/politics/2020/03/18/u-s-public-sees-multiple-threats-from-the-coronavirus-and-concerns-are-growing/.
3. Pew Research, "US Public Sees Multiple Threats."
4. Pew Research.
5. Pew Research.
6. Pew Research.
7. Ariel Fridman, Rachel Gershon, and Ayelet Gneezy, "COVID-19 and Vaccine Hesitancy: A Longitudinal Study," *PLOS One* 16, no. 4 (2021): e0250123.
8. Fridman, Gershon, and Gneezy, "COVID-19 and Vaccine Hesitancy."
9. Pew Research Center, "Majority in U.S. Says Public Health Benefits of COVID-19 Restrictions Worth the Costs, Even as Large Shares Also See Downsides," September 15, 2021, https://www.pewresearch.org/science/2021/09/15/majority-in-u-s-says-public-health-benefits-of-covid-19-restrictions-worth-the-costs-even-as-large-shares-also-see-downsides/.
10. Fridman, Gershon, and Gneezy, "COVID-19 and Vaccine Hesitancy."
11. Pew Research, "US Public Sees Multiple Threats."
12. Pew Research.
13. Pew Research.
14. Pew Research.
15. Matthew Baum, Matthew D. Simonson, Hanyu Chwe, Roy Perlis, Jon Green, Katherine Ognyanova, David Lazer, et al., "The COVID States Project #53: Public Support for Vaccine Passports," May 14, 2021, https://doi.org/10.31219/osf.io/5zkuv.
16. Baum et al., "COVID States Project #53."
17. Emily A. Largent, Govind Persad, Samantha Sangenito, Aaron Glickman, Connor Boyle, and Ezekiel J. Emanuel, "US Public Attitudes toward COVID-19 Vaccine Mandates," *JAMA Network Open* 3, no. 12 (2020): e2033324-e2033324.
18. Baum et al., "COVID States Project #53."
19. Baum et al.

20. Largent et al., "US Public Attitudes."
21. Baum et al., "COVID States Project #53."
22. Baum et al.
23. Megan Brenan, "Roundup of Gallup COVID-19 Coverage," *Gallup*, November 16, 2021, https://news.gallup.com/opinion/gallup/308126/roundup-gallup-covid-coverage.aspx.
24. Pew Research Center, "Despite Wide Partisan Gaps in Views of Many Aspects of the Pandemic, Some Common Ground Exists," March 24, 2021.
25. John Sides, Chris Tausanovitch, and Lynn Vavreck, "The Politics of COVID-19: Partisan Polarization about the Pandemic Has Increased, but Support for Health Care Reform Hasn't Moved at All," *Harvard Data Science Review*, November 30, 2020.
26. Pew Research, "Despite Wide Partisan Gaps."
27. Sides, Tausanovitch, and Vavreck, "Politics of COVID-19."
28. Pew Research, "Despite Wide Partisan Gaps."
29. Sides, Tausanovitch, and Vavreck, "Politics of COVID-19."
30. Pew Research, "Despite Wide Partisan Gaps."
31. Chris Tausanovitch and Lynn Vavreck, *The Democracy Fund + UCLA Nationscape Project*, data from the weeks of July 19, 2019–October 15, 2020, Los Angeles.
32. Alan I. Abramowitz, "The Impact of a Presidential Debate on Voter Rationality," *American Journal of Political Science* (1978): 680–90; Bernard R. Berelson, Paul F. Lazarsfeld, and William N. McPhee, *Voting: A Study of Opinion Formation in a Presidential Campaign* (Chicago: University of Chicago Press, 1954); Angus Campbell, Philip E. Converse, Warren E. Miller, and Donald E. Stokes, *The American Voter* (New York: John Wiley & Sons, 1960); Thomas M. Carsey and Geoffrey C. Layman, "Changing Sides or Changing Minds? Party Identification and Policy Preferences in the American Electorate," *American Journal of Political Science* 50, no. 2 (March 2006), 464–77; Christopher Achen and Larry Bartels, "Democracy for Realists: Holding Up a Mirror to the Electorate," *IPPR Progressive Review* 22, no. 4 (2016), 269–75.
33. John R. Zaller, *The Nature and Origins of Mass Opinion* (New York: Cambridge University Press, 1992).
34. Guy Grossman, Soojong Kim, Jonah M. Rexer, and Harsha Thirumurthy, "Political Partisanship Influences Behavioral Responses to Governors' Recommendations for COVID-19 Prevention in the United States," *Proceedings of the National Academy of Sciences* 117, no. 39 (2020): 24144–53.
35. Paul Slovic, "Trust, Emotion, Sex, Politics, and Science: Surveying the Risk-Assessment Battlefield," *Risk Analysis* 19, no. 4 (August 1999): 689–701; Jocelyn A. Hollander, "Vulnerability and Dangerousness: The Construction of Gender through Conversation about Violence," *Gender and Society* 15, no. 1

(February 2001): 83–109; Sylvia Maxfield, Mary Shapiro, Vipin Gupta, and Susan Hass, "Gender and Risk: Women, Risk Taking and Risk Aversion," *Gender in Management: An International Journal* 25, no. 7 (October 2010): 586–604.

36. Maria E. Grabe and Rasha Kamhawi, "Hard Wired for Negative News? Gender Differences in Processing Broadcast News," *Communication Research* 33, no. 5 (2006), 346–69; Stuart N. Soroka, *Negativity in Democratic Politics: Causes and Consequences* (New York: Cambridge University Press, 2014).

37. Deborah J. Brooks and Lydia Saad, "Double Whammy: Why the Underrepresentation of Women among Workplace and Political Decision Makers Matters in Pandemic Times," *Politics & Gender* (August 18, 2020): 1–13.

38. Brooks and Saad, "Double Whammy."

39. Irmak O. Okten, Anton Gollwitzer, and Gabriele Oettingen, "Gender Differences in Preventing the Spread of Coronavirus," June 2020, https://doi.org/10.31234/osf.io/ch4jy.

40. Pew Research, "US Public Sees Multiple Threats."

41. Sadie Bell, Richard Clarke, Sandra Mounier-Jack, Jemma L. Walker, and Pauline Paterson, "Parents' and Guardians' Views on the Acceptability of a Future COVID-19 Vaccine: A Multi-Methods Study in England," *Vaccine* 38, no. 49 (November 2020): 7789–98; Sebastian Neumann-Böhme, Nirosha Elsem Varghese, Iryna Sabat, Pedro Pita Barros, Werner Brouwer, Job van Exel, Jonas Schreyögg, and Tom Stargardt, "Once We Have It, Will We Use It? A European Survey on Willingness to Be Vaccinated against COVID-19," *European Journal of Health Economics* 21, no. 7 (September 2020): 977–82; Paul L. Reiter, Michael L. Pennell, and Mira L. Katz, "Acceptability of a COVID-19 Vaccine among Adults in the United States: How Many People Would Get Vaccinated?" *Vaccine* 38, no. 42 (2020): 6500–6507; Jeanine P. D. Guidry, Linnea I. Laestadius, Emily K. Vraga, Carrie A. Miller, Paul B. Perrin, Candace W. Burton, Mark Ryan, Bernard F. Fuemmeler, and Kellie E. Carlyle, "Willingness to Get the COVID-19 Vaccine with and without Emergency Use Authorization," *American Journal of Infection Control* 49, no. 2 (2021): 137–42; Jeffrey V. Lazarus, Scott C. Ratzan, Adam Palayew, Lawrence O. Gostin, Heidi J. Larson, Kenneth Rabin, Spencer Kimball, and Ayman El-Mohandes, "A Global Survey of Potential Acceptance of a COVID-19 Vaccine," *Nature Medicine* 27, no. 2 (2021): 225–28.

42. "Gender Differences in Covid-19 Vaccine Hesitancy," interview with Margot Bellon, Clayman Institute for Gender Research, Stanford University, September 15, 2021, https://gender.stanford.edu/news-publications/gender-news/gender-differences-covid-19-vaccine-hesitancy.

43. Jaffar A. Al-Tawfiq, "Willingness of Health Care Workers of Various Nationalities to Accept H1N1 (2009) Pandemic Influenza A Vaccination," *Annals of Saudi Medicine* 32, no. 1 (January–February 2012): 64–67; Gianluigi Ferrante, Sandro Baldissera, Pirous Fateh Moghadam, Giuliano Carrozzi, Massimo

Oddone Trinito, and Stefania Salmaso, "Surveillance of Perceptions, Knowledge, Attitudes and Behaviors of the Italian Adult Population (18–69 Years) During the 2009–2010 A/H1N1 Influenza Pandemic," *European Journal of Epidemiology* 26, no. 3 (April 2011): 211–19; Ingrid Gilles, Adrian Bangerter, Alain Clémence, Eva G. T. Green, Franciska Krings, Christian Staerklé, and Pascal Wagner-Egger, "Trust in Medical Organizations Predicts Pandemic (H1N1) 2009 Vaccination Behavior and Perceived Efficacy of Protection Measures in the Swiss Public," *European Journal of Epidemiology* 26, no. 3 (2011): 203–10; Céline Pulcini, Sophie Massin, Odile Launay, and Pierre Verger, "Factors Associated with Vaccination for Hepatitis B, Pertussis, Seasonal and Pandemic Influenza among French General Practitioners: A 2010 Survey," *Vaccine* 31, no. 37 (2013): 3943–49.

44. Elizabeth M. La, Laurel Trantham, Samantha K. Kurosky, Dawn Odom, Emmanuel Aris, and Cosmina Hogea, "An Analysis of Factors Associated with Influenza, Pneumoccocal, Tdap, and Herpes Zoster Vaccine Uptake in the US Adult Population and Corresponding Inter-state Variability," *Human Vaccines & Immunotherapeutics* 14, no. 2 (2018): 430–41; Varun Vaidya, Gautam Partha, and Monita Karmakar, "Gender Differences in Utilization of Preventive Care Services in the United States," *Journal of Women's Health* 21, no. 2 (2012): 140–45.

45. Pulcini et al., "Factors Associated with Vaccination"; Michael M. Endrich, Patricia R. Blank, and Thomas D. Szucs, "Influenza Vaccination Uptake and Socioeconomic Determinants in 11 European Countries," *Vaccine* 27, no. 30 (2009): 4018–24.

46. Jennifer Lin, James Druckman, Matthew Baum, David Lazer, Roy Perlis, Mauricio Santillana, Katherine Ognyanova, et al., "The COVID States Project #51: Trajectory of Health-Related Behaviors in California," OSF Preprints, May 13, 2021, https://doi.org/10.31219/osf.io/bas8w.

47. Lin et al., "COVID States Project #51."

48. Lin et al.

Chapter 7

Court Evaluation of COVID-19 State Emergency Orders
Upholding Fundamental Rights during Times of Crisis

Victoria Ochoa

There is no doubt that the COVID-19 pandemic has disrupted the lives of millions across the country. Despite the pandemic's national reach, the government responses that most directly impact people's day-to-day lives have largely been local. Throughout the spring of 2020, governors in every state declared an emergency under state emergency management statutes.[1] Enacted years before the pandemic (as detailed in chapter 2), these statutes granted governors the authority to unliterally amend or suspend existing laws or put forth new orders to stem the spread of COVID. These orders—limiting gatherings, closing nonessential businesses, requiring masks, and restricting interstate travel—have reignited civic debate over the government's ability to inconvenience daily life for the public good. In the courts, they have ignited debate over the proper standard of review of state regulation put forth during a public health emergency.

Through police powers, states have authority to safeguard public health and safety. State police powers are vast, and courts impose few, yet important, parameters on how they can be exercised. Most fundamentally, state action must comply with federal law and the US Constitution. However, since individual liberties are not absolute, exercises of state police power can limit constitutionally protected rights. Historically, courts granted states great deference and upheld state regulations that infringed on civil liberties so long as they bore a real and substantial relation to public safety and were not unreasonable and arbitrary.[2]

However, following the advent of modern constitutional review in the mid-twentieth century, state exercises of police power that infringed on fundamental rights in areas outside of public health were subject to "strict scrutiny." Under this more exacting review, state governments must provide a compelling interest to contravene fundamental rights, and their actions must be narrowly tailored to address this interest.

Yet, when reviewing various state responses to COVID-19, some courts have refrained from invoking strict scrutiny review and instead applied *Jacobson v. Massachusetts*, a 116-year-old case that famously articulated the breadth of state police power to regulate health. *Jacobson* stood for the proposition that police powers are broad enough to enable a state to require that individuals get vaccinated, a holding that has been used over the last 116 years to uphold compulsory vaccination laws. Developing in isolation from strict scrutiny review, this case law expanded to apply to individual quarantine orders imposed on travelers returning to the United States or prostitutes police officers reasonably suspected of having venereal disease. Now, during the COVID pandemic, *Jacobson* has frequently been applied as a framework for constitutional review, resurrecting the underdeveloped and deferential review of state regulation that courts imposed over one hundred years ago.

More generally, COVID case law reveals a struggle within the courts as they attempt to reconcile the dictates of strict scrutiny with the need for deference to state public health judgments during emergencies. Though the Supreme Court has stepped in to provide some clarity on how to evaluate claims that states' pandemic responses violate the First Amendment's free exercise clause, uncertainties remain. This chapter discusses court applications of *Jacobson* and advances the view that strict scrutiny should apply to public health regulation, put forth during an emergency or otherwise, that abridges fundamental rights. The first section provides an overview of state police powers and the evolving standards of review that courts have used when reviewing state regulation throughout history. The second section recounts how courts struggled to identify the correct standard of review in the context of COVID measures during the first year of the pandemic between March 2020 and April 9, 2021. Section three delves into the limited court review of state emergency powers during nonhealth emergencies, and the fourth section argues that strict scrutiny should apply to any state regulation, during emergencies or otherwise, that infringes on fundamental rights. Since this chapter evaluates judicial review of COVID state emergency orders between March 2020 and April 9, 2021, it will evaluate and discuss fundamental rights as they existed before the recent *Dobbs v. Jackson Health* decision, which further defined fundamental rights and held that abortion was not a fundamental right. Similarly, this chapter does not apply or engage *Kennedy v. Bremerton School District* when discussing court evaluation of whether COVID orders were neutral and generally applicable as this June 2022 case was decided after April 9, 2021.

Overview of State Police Powers

Under the Tenth Amendment, the powers not delegated to the federal government by the Constitution nor prohibited by it to the states, are reserved to the states.[3] Known colloquially as police powers, these inherent powers grant states "great latitude . . . to [protect] . . . the lives, limbs . . . comfort, and quiet of all persons."[4] As the COVID-19 pandemic has illustrated, police powers also enable states to enact "health laws of every description."[5]

Though vast, police power is constrained by state and federal constitutions. States, for example, cannot deny any person equal protection of the laws nor can they abridge constitutional rights under the *guise* of a police power regulation.[6] By virtue of the supremacy clause, state action authorized under police powers must bow when in conflict with federal law or the US Constitution.[7] Yet, a legitimate police power regulation is not automatically invalid because it incidentally infringes on a constitutional right. Many exercises of police power necessarily affect constitutionally protected rights. Individual liberties, after all, are rarely absolute.[8]

Prior to modern constitutional review, state regulations were generally held to be valid so long as they bore a real and substantial relation to the public health, safety, morals, or general welfare and were not unreasonable and arbitrary.[9] Under this deferential standard, courts rarely struck down state action. There were few exceptions. Courts did strike down overly broad statutes and invalidated statutes or ordinances that demonstrated clear racial animus, finding them unreasonable.[10] In *Jew Ho*, for example, a California court famously found that a city ordinance sealing off the Chinese sector of San Francisco was unjust and unreasonable because the community had not demonstrated a propensity for having or spreading the bubonic plague.[11]

Supreme Court deference to police power regulation began to shift in 1938, when Justice Stone famously introduced the possibility that rights guaranteed by the Bill of Rights should receive "more searching judicial inquiry" in footnote 4 of *United States v. Carolene Products Co.*[12] Three years later, the court made its first mention of strict scrutiny in *Skinner v. Oklahoma*, a case invalidating the forced sterilization of criminals as an equal protection violation.[13] Soon after, in *Korematsu v. United States*, a case evaluating the constitutionality of Japanese American internment, the Supreme Court once again discussed strict scrutiny, holding that heightened scrutiny is appropriate for classifications based on race and national origin.[14]

Though the court first limited the use of heightened scrutiny to equal protection claims, vibrant debate on speech regulation in the 1950s reignited discussion of strict scrutiny.[15] First Amendment case law from this period reflects a split among justices calling for strong judicial deference to legislative regulation of speech and those adopting the belief that First Amendment guarantees were absolute.[16] By the early 1960s, a new body of First Amendment case law emerged, formalizing strict scrutiny review as a standard requiring statutes that infringed on key rights to be justified by a compelling government interest and be narrowly tailored to achieve that interest.[17] By the end of the decade, strict scrutiny review applied to many equal protection claims, First Amendment claims, and other infringements of fundamental rights.[18] Though the Supreme Court has never defined with significant precision what constitutes a fundamental right,[19] they are generally conceived as rights "deeply rooted in [the] Nation's history and tradition."[20] Today, rights that receive the protection of strict scrutiny review are contained in four amendments—the First Amendment, the Second Amendment, the Fifth Amendment's due process clause, and the Fourteenth Amendment's equal protection clause.[21]

In the 1970s, several varieties of intermediate-scrutiny review emerged, requiring courts to evaluate whether a challenged law furthers an important government interest by means substantially related to that interest.[22] Today, sex-based discrimination,[23] restrictions based on illegitimacy,[24] and First Amendment restrictions that target content-neutral speech[25] are subject to intermediate scrutiny. Prior to *Dobbs* and during the period between March 2020 and April 9, 2021, restrictions on the constitutional right to an abortion triggered an "undue burden standard," which asked whether a state regulation places a "substantial obstacle in the path of a woman seeking an abortion."[26] Outside of these areas of heightened scrutiny (strict or intermediate), claims of constitutional violations are subject to rational basis review, which simply asks whether a government regulation is rationally related to a government interest.[27]

In keeping with these changes, courts generally shifted to using strict scrutiny when reviewing exercises of the state police power that infringe on fundamental rights. In 1972, the Supreme Court famously considered the constitutionality of Wisconsin's compulsory high school education law in *Wisconsin v. Yoder* and began to articulate the prongs of strict scrutiny analysis within the free exercise context. The court acknowledged that the state's interest to advance education was highly ranked, but "not totally free from a balancing process when it impinges on fundamental rights and interests."[28] If Wisconsin was going to compel school attendance beyond the eighth grade, an act in conflict with the religious beliefs of Amish plaintiffs, the court reasoned it must have an interest of "sufficient magnitude to override the interest claiming protection under the Free Exercise clause."[29] Admitting that Wisconsin failed to "show with more particularity how its admittedly strong interest in compulsory education would be adversely affected by granting an exemption to the Amish," the court held that the First and Fourteenth Amendments prevented Wisconsin from compelling Amish residents to send their children to school until age sixteen.[30] When reviewing

Indiana's denial of employment benefits to a man who quit his job for religious purposes less than ten years later, the Supreme Court cited *Yoder* to find that a government must justify an inroad on religious liberty by demonstrating it is the least restrictive means of furthering a compelling interest, which must be "of the highest order."[31] Courts have similarly applied strict scrutiny in evaluating a wide range of state regulations—addressing zoning,[32] speech,[33] religion,[34] and marriage[35]—that infringed on fundamental rights.

One notable exception to this framework stems from *Employment Division, Department of Human Resources of Oregon v. Smith*, a religious liberty case in which the Supreme Court ruled that two Native American employees in Oregon could be denied unemployment benefits after being fired for smoking peyote as part of their religious practice.[36] Decided after *Yoder*, *Smith* holds that the right of free exercise does not excuse an individual from complying with a "neutral law of general applicability" that proscribes or prohibits conduct that contradicts their religious beliefs.[37] The Supreme Court distinguished its decision from *Yoder* and other decisions barring the application of neutral, generally applicable laws to religiously motivated actors by stating that Smith's claim did not involve another constitutional protection—such as the right to free speech or to parent—in conjunction with the free exercise clause.[38] As we will see later in the chapter, the seemingly straightforward test articulated in *Smith* has proven remarkably difficult to apply, creating room for uncertainty and competing standards of review.

State Police Powers and COVID-19

Despite the import of strict scrutiny analysis to police power regulations, courts that have reviewed state emergency measures during COVID-19 have not consistently applied strict scrutiny when faced with allegations of fundamental rights violations. Instead, some courts have turned to the 116-year-old *Jacobson v. Massachusetts* case to guide their analysis.

In *Jacobson*, a man challenged a mandatory vaccination law that imposed a fine for noncompliance but exempted children who could provide a physician's note verifying they were unfit for vaccination.[39] Jacobson claimed that the Cambridge law violated his Fourteenth Amendment substantive due process and equal protection rights and was therefore unconstitutional.[40] The Supreme Court disagreed. According to the court, states and localities can impose restrictions on constitutional rights as "the liberty secured by the Constitution . . . does not import an absolute right . . . to be, at all times and in every circumstance, wholly freed from restraint."[41] The court clarified that restrictions placed on rights through police power authority can be unlawful only when they are applied in "an arbitrary, unreasonable manner, or may go beyond what was reasonably required for the safety of the public."[42] Further, courts can intervene only when restrictions pose a "plain, palpable invasion of rights secured by the fundamental law."[43] In this instance, smallpox's prevalence in Cambridge necessitated the law, and the exemption for children was neither arbitrary nor an equal protection violation because "the statute is applicable to all in like condition" and was based on "obvious reason[ing]" that regulations for adults may not always be safely applied to children.[44]

The standard articulated in *Jacobson* is extremely deferential. As scholars have observed, it approximates rational basis review, the lowest standard within the modern tiers of constitutional analysis. Though the Supreme Court's notion of what constituted "reasonable" government action was perhaps more expansive 116 years ago, the ways courts have balanced civil liberties when reviewing quarantine orders in more recent times suggests that *Jacobson* still requires governments to conduct the functional equivalent of rational basis review during health emergencies.[45]

Today, courts have again turned to *Jacobson* to analyze the hundreds of executive orders governors have issued in response to the COVID pandemic. Beginning with *In re Abbott*, when the Fifth Circuit declared *Jacobson* to be "the controlling Supreme Court precedent that squarely governs judicial review of rights-challenges to emergency public health measures," some courts have held that "*Jacobson* instructs that all constitutional rights may be reasonably restricted to combat a public health emergency."[46] Under this standard, a state, "when faced with a society-threatening epidemic . . . may implement emergency measures that curtail constitutional rights so long as the measures have at least some 'real or substantial relation' to the public health crisis and are not 'beyond all question, a plain, palpable invasion of rights secured by the fundamental law.'"[47] Holding that the state needed greater deference to respond to a "society-threatening epidemic," the Fifth Circuit advanced the view that modern constitutional analysis must be suspended during public health emergencies.[48] At the height of the pandemic between March 2020 and April 2021, courts throughout the country applied *Jacobson* exclusively to at least twenty-six COVID orders that implicate abortion rights, religious freedom, and a variety of other constitutional rights.

Abortion Claims

Between the start of the COVID pandemic and the spring of 2021, courts applied *Jacobson* in three cases involving restrictions on abortion access, holding that it was the appropriate standard during a public health emergency. One was *Abbott*, discussed above. Following *Abbott*, the Eighth Circuit applied the *Jacobson* framework to a COVID executive order prohibiting nonessential procedures like abortion, finding that the lower court's application of *Casey v. Planned Parenthood* was inconsistent with Jacobson and constituted an abuse of discretion.[49] When Arkansas later put forth an executive order requiring women to have a negative COVID test forty-eight hours before an abortion, the Eastern District of Arkansas also upheld the order.[50]

However, in four other cases, courts analyzed abortion-related executive orders under both the traditional undue burden standard and *Jacobson*, without explicitly stating which was the appropriate standard. In *South Wind Women's Center*, for example, an Oklahoma district court held that a COVID abortion restriction was simultaneously "unreasonable, arbitrary, and oppressive" under *Jacobson* and posed an undue burden under *Casey*.[51] In all of these instances, courts arrived at the same conclusions about the constitutionality of these orders under both standards. Yet, courts varied in what that conclusion was. Only in *Pre-Term Cleveland* did a court fully grant an abortion provider's motion for preliminary injunction, blocking the state from enforcing the order against physicians "making case-by-case determinations that a surgical abortion is essential."[52] In the remaining three cases, courts upheld the executive orders in part.[53]

Despite issuing opaque opinions on which standard was most appropriate during the pandemic, some courts, like the Sixth Circuit, rejected the "notion that COVID-19 . . . somehow demoted *Roe* and *Casey* to second class rights, enforceable against only the most extreme and outlandish violations."[54] The Sixth Circuit found this notion to be "incompatible not only with *Jacobson*, but also with American constitutional law writ large."[55] Decisions like these advance an alternative approach to judicial review during public health emergencies, suggesting that the "Supreme Court's civil liberties jurisprudence can be reconciled with *Jacobson*'s broad language."[56] However, they also highlight the struggle of lower courts to have it both ways: to apply heightened scrutiny review without abandoning *Jacobson* outright and, in turn, to grant state officials great deference to address the pandemic while also scrutinizing how their actions impact individual liberties. With a limited understanding of how to balance both state deference and individual rights, courts have struggled to resolve this tension with a range of decisions that only underscore *Jacobson*'s malleability as a standard.

Free Exercise Claims

Between March 2020 and April 2021, places of worship brought at least forty-eight First Amendment free exercise challenges to COVID executive orders placing constraints on indoor and outdoor gatherings. Court evaluation of these claims was contentious and where the struggle over whether to apply either *Jacobson* or strict scrutiny review was greatest. But since strict scrutiny does not apply to neutral laws of general applicability even when they infringe on religious liberty, the decision of what standard to apply often hinged on whether judges perceived that the COVID executive orders disfavored religion—in other words, whether they treated religious institutions less favorably than comparable secular establishments.

This conflict initially came to a head in *South Bay I*, a Supreme Court decision that upheld an order issued by the governor of California limiting attendance at places of worship to 25 percent of a building's capacity or one hundred attendees. There was no majority opinion, but in his concurrence, Justice Roberts asserted that the restrictions "appear consistent with the Free Exercise Clause of the First Amendment" because "similar or more severe restrictions apply to comparable secular gatherings, including lectures, concerts, movie showings, spectator sports, and theatrical performances, where large groups of people gather in close proximity for extended periods of time," and the order gave preferential treatment "only [to] dissimilar activities, such as operating grocery stores, banks, and laundromats, in which people neither congregate in large groups nor remain in close proximity for extended periods."[57] He cited *Jacobson* for the principle that the court must grant deference to public officials in areas "fraught with medical and scientific uncertainties."[58] In his dissent, Justice Kavanaugh, faced with the same facts, reached the opposite conclusion about the nature of California's guidelines. He found that they "discriminate against places of worship and in favor of comparable secular businesses," which, in his view, included "factories, offices, supermarkets, restaurants, retail stores, pharmacies, shopping malls, pet grooming shops, bookstores, florists, hair salons, and cannabis dispensaries." He thus would have applied strict scrutiny to strike down the order.

From May 2020, when *South Bay I* was decided, until October 2020, most lower courts applied rational basis review and/or *Jacobson* to religious exercise challenges to COVID orders, so long as they were part of a larger effort to regulate similar public spaces.[59]

Two months after South Bay I, in *Calvary Chapel Dayton Valley*, the Supreme Court denied a church's application for injunctive relief from an executive order that subjected religious houses of worship to a capacity of fifty people.[60] While the per curium opinion did not offer reasoning, Justice Kavanaugh's dissent foreshadowed how judges would "disagree about how to characterize a law [that implicates religion]" or "what it means for a law to be neutral toward religion."[61] He identified four categories of laws that implicate religion and argued that without sufficient justification, the last category—laws that divide organizations into favored and disfavored categories—cannot stand if they place religious organizations in the disfavored category and presumably treat secular organizations more favorably.[62] He concluded that the executive order in question discriminated against religious organizations because it allowed certain business establishments, including casinos and bowling alleys, to operate at 50 percent capacity. In the case of some casinos, the 50 percent rule would translate to thousands of people.

After the Supreme Court's composition shifted in October 2020, the court—and lower courts following its lead—began to subscribe to Justice Kavanaugh's reasoning to find that many COVID orders were not generally applicable, resulting in an application of strict scrutiny. Debate continued to center on the seemingly factual question of whether various COVID orders were neutral with respect to religious practice, with the justices often reaching opposite conclusions when faced with the same facts—but the justices, and therefore the prevailing conclusions, had changed.

This turning point is best illustrated through the Supreme Court's decision in *Roman Catholic Diocese of Brooklyn v. Cuomo*, reversing lower court decisions in New York that upheld the state's COVID restrictions.[63] In New York, the governor classified areas as "red," "orange," or "yellow" zones. In red zones, nonessential gatherings were canceled, and nonessential businesses were closed.[64] Religious services were subject to a capacity limit of 25 percent of maximum occupancy or ten people, whichever was fewer.[65] In orange zones, nonessential gatherings were limited to ten people and certain nonessential businesses, like gyms and nail salons, remained closed. Religious services were subject to a maximum capacity limit of the lesser of 33 percent of maximum occupancy or twenty-five people, whichever was fewer.[66] In yellow zones, nonessential gatherings were limited to twenty-five people, and religious services were subject to a capacity limit of 50 percent of maximum occupancy.[67] In multiple instances, lower courts initially applied rational basis review and relied upon *Jacobson* to uphold these capacity restrictions, finding that they treated religious gatherings "as well or better than comparable gatherings."[68]

When the Supreme Court reviewed these restrictions in November 2020, it found that they were not neutral or generally applicable, since religious services were subject to stricter capacity restrictions than businesses designated as "essential," which in New York included acupuncture facilities, garages, and campgrounds, as well as laundromats and liquor stores.[69] Accordingly, the court applied strict scrutiny to enjoin these restrictions.[70] Acknowledging the lack of public health expertise in the judiciary, the court stated the "Constitution [could not] be put away and forgotten" during a pandemic and called for a "serious examination" of drastic measures.[71]

In dissenting opinions, Justices Breyer, Sotomayor, and Kagan disputed the conclusion that the order disfavored religious institutions. They noted that medical experts had testified that the conditions in houses of worship posed a much greater risk of COVID transmission than the conditions in the essential businesses that were exempted from the order. In other words, although some secular institutions were treated more favorably, those institutions were not comparable. In words that carried echoes of *Jacobson*, Justice Sotomayor warned, "Justices of this court play a deadly game in second guessing the expert judgment of health officials about the environments in which a contagious disease, now infecting a million Americans each week, spreads most easily."[72]

While the court's majority applied strict scrutiny to a free exercise claim in *Roman Catholic*, the case did not clarify whether strict scrutiny was the appropriate standard to apply to *all* fundamental rights violations during a public health emergency, nor did it fully delineate *Jacobson*'s role when reviewing COVID executive orders.[73] In his concurring opinion, for instance, Justice Gorsuch distinguished *Jacobson* as "a decision [that] involved an entirely different mode of analysis, an entirely different right, and an entirely different kind of restriction" that hardly "supports cutting the Constitution loose during a pandemic."[74] Equating the court's review in *Jacobson* to rational basis review, he argued that this was the correct standard because *Jacobson* did not involve "a claim of fundamental right." He dismissed any notion of an analogy between the substantive due process right to "bodily integrity" claimed by *Jacobson* and the First Amendment right claimed by the religious institutions in New York: "Even if judges may impose emergency restrictions on rights that some of them have found hiding in the Constitution's penumbras, it does not follow that the same fate should befall the textually explicit right to religious exercise."[75]

Justice Gorsuch's distinction of *Jacobson* only obfuscates how courts should review public health regulations during an emergency or otherwise. His opinion and the majority opinion fail to clarify whether strict scrutiny applies to textually explicit fundamental rights other than free exercise (although Justice Kavanaugh's concurrence hinted that it would apply to claims involving "racial discrimination" and "free speech") and whether any and all implicit fundamental rights must yield during emergencies. Justice Gorsuch also muddies the waters by suggesting a temporal aspect to the applicability of *Jacobson*, or at least its underlying principles. Noting Chief Justice Roberts's willingness in *South Bay I* to defer to the judgement of public health officials at the start of a pandemic that was then new and poorly understood,[76] he argues that several months later, this "rationale . . . expired according to its own terms."[77] This introduction of a temporal limitation on courts' deference to the legislative branch in matters of public health undercuts the approach courts have taken to public health regulation over the last 116 years.

A couple months later, in *South Bay II*, the Supreme Court prevented California from enforcing an outright prohibition on indoor worship services pending disposition of the petition for a writ of certiorari.[78] The court declined, however, to enjoin California from imposing a 25 percent capacity limitation on indoor worship or prohibiting chanting or singing at these services. Though the majority opinion did not provide a rationale for its decision and avoided addressing strict scrutiny or questions about the appropriate role of *Jacobson*, the concurring and dissenting opinions fully engaged these issues.

In agreeing that an outright ban on indoor worship reflects an "insufficient appreciation . . . of the interests at stake," Chief Justice Roberts again stated that broad deference to government officials has limits and that the judiciary also has the obligation to protect people's rights.[79] In a statement, joined by Justices Thomas and Alito, Justice Gorsuch upheld the need for strict scrutiny review and reiterated that "it has never been enough for the State to insist on deference or demand that individual rights give way to collective interests."[80] In her dissent, Justice Kagan argued that California treated attendance at religious services the same as comparable secular activities, such as going to political meetings, lectures, movies, plays, concerts, restaurants, wineries, or bars. She chided the majority for its insistence that "science-based policy yield to judicial edict," noting that the court would be insulated from responsibility for any suffering that might occur from its overturning of COVID restrictions.[81]

Finally, in *Tandon v. Newsom*, the Supreme Court applied strict scrutiny to California's restrictions on private gatherings, finding that the state treated comparable secular activities more favorably than at-home religious exercise—with Justices Breyer, Sotomayor, and Kagan once again disagreeing with the majority about which secular activities should be considered comparable.[82] Neither the majority opinion nor the dissent discussed *Jacobson*.

The silence of majority opinions in *Roman Catholic*, *South Bay II*, and *Tandon* on *Jacobson* and on whether strict scrutiny applies to fundamental rights beyond religious exercise in the state emergency context, still leaves some uncertainties for lower courts. Post–*Roman Catholic*, lower courts have tended to apply strict scrutiny when evaluating free exercise claims without addressing *Jacobson*.[83] One such case explicitly interpreted *Roman Catholic* and *Tandon* to mean that courts must reject *Jacobson* and apply strict scrutiny to free exercise, free speech, and assembly and association claims to state uses of emergency power during the pandemic when they are not neutral and generally applicable.[84] However, as will be explored in the next section, court evaluation of other constitutional rights after *Roman Catholic* indicates that *Jacobson* might not be entirely dead as a standard of review. In the absence of a clear Supreme Court holding how *Jacobson* or strict scrutiny review should apply to rights beyond free exercise of religion during a public health emergency, lower courts may continue to apply *Jacobson* in a variety of conflicting ways.

Moreover, even within the context of free exercise claims, the Supreme Court's case law has not truly resolved the question of which standard to apply. The legal debate over whether to apply *Jacobson* or strict scrutiny has simply shifted to a factual debate over whether a given order is neutral and generally applicable. Judges' conclusions on the latter question seem to track their desire to exhibit or avoid deference to public health officials during the pandemic—raising the specter that a surprisingly malleable fact-based inquiry into what constitutes a "comparable" secular activity has become an indirect way for judges to apply the legal standard of their choice during the pandemic.

Constitutional Challenges Brought by Business Owners

Business owners have also brought numerous challenges to COVID orders, illuminating the range of First, Fifth, and Fourteenth Amendment rights implicated during the pandemic. Many of these challenges involved claims alleging Fourteenth Amendment equal protection, Fifth Amendment due process, and First Amendment free speech and free assembly fundamental rights violations.

These challenges implicate a range of standards of review. The standard for First Amendment free speech and assembly claims depends on whether restrictions are content neutral. While content-based restrictions are subject to strict scrutiny, content-neutral "time, place, and manner" regulations are permitted "so long as they are designed to serve a substantial governmental interest and do not unreasonably limit alternative avenues of communication."[85] Successful free speech claims also require speech,[86] a hurdle that many businesses could not demonstrate.[87] The Fourteenth Amendment's equal protection clause provides the strongest protection against discriminatory laws when they create or result in suspect or quasi-suspect classifications, like race and gender.[88] If so, courts subject the discriminatory law to strict or intermediate scrutiny. When a law does not create or result in these classifications, courts scrutinize the law under rational basis review only.[89]

Between March 2020 and April 9, 2021, business brought at least forty-three cases challenging governors' COVID executive orders.[90] Courts exclusively applied *Jacobson* at least six times, upholding executive orders in every instance.[91] In four of these instances, courts applied *Jacobson* despite business owners alleging Fifth Amendment due process, First Amendment free speech, or Fourteenth Amendment equal protection fundamental rights violations.[92] In *Columbus Ale House v. Cuomo* and *4 Aces Enterprises, LLC v. Edwards*, lower courts explicitly stated that Fifth Amendment substantive due process guarantees did not grant bar and restaurant owners a fundamental right to run a business.[93] In the remaining two cases, courts did not find a valid equal protection claim, because their allegations were insufficient.[94] Notably, all of these cases were decided before *Roman Catholic* articulated guidance on how to evaluate challenges to COVID measures that affect fundamental rights.

In at least seventeen instances, courts applied both *Jacobson* and modern tiers of constitutional review to claims alleging First Amendment free speech, free exercise, free assembly, or Fourteenth Amendment equal protection fundamental rights violations.[95] In almost all of these cases, courts subjected the executive orders to rational basis review—a standard that itself closely approximates *Jacobson*—because business owners did not have a fundamental right to operate their business, did not constitute a protected class, or were subject to neutral and generally applicable laws. Notably, however, in *Hopkins Hawley LLC*, a case decided after *Roman Catholic* in which a business owner alleged a First Amendment free assembly violation, the Southern District of New York concluded that *Jacobson*'s deferential standard of review was still applicable because the Supreme Court had not explicitly overturned the case and because the case at hand did not involve a free exercise claim.⁹⁶ Though unpublished, *Hopkins Hawley* signaled how lower courts could interpret heightened scrutiny to apply only to First Amendment free exercise claims during the pandemic and for *Jacobson* to "provide a workable framework" for all other rights violations.⁹⁷

Similarly, courts exclusively applied rational basis review (without mentioning *Jacobson*) in at least ten of the business cases decided between March 2020 and April 9, 2021, upholding executive orders in all of these instances.⁹⁸

Lastly, there was one case, *Bayley's Campground*, which applied strict scrutiny to an executive order that burdened the fundamental right to travel.⁹⁹ Few courts have rebuked *Jacobson*—generally and as the appropriate standard during the pandemic—as strongly as Judge Lance Walker did in that case:

> [T]he permissive *Jacobson* rule floats about in the air as a rubber stamp for all but the most absurd and egregious restrictions on constitutional liberties, free from the inconvenience of meaningful judicial review. This may help explain why the Supreme Court established the [modern] tiers of scrutiny in the course of the 100 years since *Jacobson* was decided. Although *Jacobson* reflects that, when one weighs competing interests in the balance, the presence of a major public health crises is a very heavy weight indeed and scientific uncertainties about the best response will afford the state some additional leeway to err on the side of caution, it does not provide the standard of review for this case. Civil libertarians may question whether it ought to provide the standard of review in any case. But perhaps that depends on whose ox is being gored.¹⁰⁰

In highlighting some of the inadequacies of *Jacobson* and the subjectivity with which it could have been (and likely was) applied during the COVID pandemic, Judge Walker challenges courts' rationale for applying *Jacobson*. While the Supreme Court did not explicitly overturn *Jacobson* or clarify its application to rights beyond free exercise claims, it did use COVID litigation to advance a seismic shift in religious freedom jurisprudence. Whether the court will insist on heightened constitutional scrutiny when evaluating other fundamental rights implicated during uses of state emergency power—during health and other emergencies—remains to be seen. As Judge Walker recognized, perhaps that too depends on whose ox is being gored.

State Police Powers and Nonhealth Emergencies

In emergencies other than those involving public health, courts have also occasionally abandoned analysis under the modern tiers of constitutional review and instead applied a reasonableness standard similar to rational basis review. As previously mentioned, governors can declare emergencies through emergency management statutes, accessing vast emergency powers. Most frequently invoked following natural disasters like hurricanes and floods—but also available to address instances of civil unrest—these powers are typically authorized under emergency management statutes that give governors the authority to unilaterally impose curfews, stay-at-home orders, and other safety measures.

Courts have never explicitly stated the standard that applies to judicial review of state emergency powers, but their rulings have suggested some parameters. The Supreme Court famously reviewed emergency state police powers in *Home Building and Loan Association v. Blasdell* when it upheld a Minnesota law providing temporary relief for mortgagors unable to make payments during the Great Depression.[101] Observing that "emergency does not create power," the Supreme Court made clear that an emergency is merely a justification for a state to use existing power—albeit more broadly and flexibly than might be appropriate in nonemergency situations.

Though state orders in response to non-public-health emergencies are promulgated similarly, if not identically, to COVID orders, they have not generated nearly as much case law. Compared to the indefinite duration of the pandemic, hurricanes, floods, and instances of civil unrest are brief, and the emergency orders put forth to address them have imminent expiration dates, minimizing the likelihood they will be challenged in court. Most legal scholarship on state emergency powers focuses on government responses to natural disasters, and analysis of state emergency responses beyond this context is even more limited.[102] Yet, two patterns emerge. First, when reviewing state emergency responses to recent natural disasters that infringe on fundamental rights, courts have applied a deferential standard that resembles *Jacobson*. Second, when courts have reviewed state emergency responses to mass protests that infringe on First Amendment speech rights, they have applied heightened scrutiny.

Upon reviewing a range of cases, including those that allege fundamental rights violations, scholars like Michael Cook have described the review of modern emergency responses to natural disasters as a two-pronged process–reasonableness test.[103] Under the process prong, courts first ask whether the government has the authority to use the powers it seeks to employ; under the reasonableness prong, whether an emergency actually exists and whether the action is pretextual or done in bad faith.[104] If the court finds the government does not have authority to use state emergency police powers, it will not reach the reasonableness prong. When scrutinizing emergency police power under the reasonableness prong, courts grant substantial deference to a state's determination that an emergency exists, rarely declaring that an emergency does not actually exist. Like *Jacobson*, this standard of review is undeniably deferential, enables "politically unaccountable branches . . . to make poor choices," and reduces the sole issue before the court to "whether these poor choices had an ulterior motivation that went beyond addressing the motive."[105]

During Hurricane Andrew, the governor of Florida issued an executive order that declared a state of emergency and explicitly allowed Miami and Miami-Dade County officials to impose curfews until December 12, 1992, a few months after the hurricane struck on August 24.[106] The Miami-Dade county manager imposed a curfew until November 16, and residents challenged the measures for impinging on their rights of travel, expression, association, and free exercise of religion.[107] The Eleventh Circuit upheld the lower court's decision, finding that the county official had explicit authority from the legislature to issue the curfew and affirming that "governing authorities must be granted the proper deference and wide latitude necessary for dealing with [an] emergency."[108] The court articulated the contours of the process–reasonableness test, stating that "the scope of review 'is limited to a determination whether the [executive's] actions were taken in good faith and whether there is a factual basis for the decision.'"[109] Similarly, during Hurricane Hugo, the governor of the US Virgin Islands enforced a curfew a man later challenged for violating his First Amendment rights to association, religion, and speech, as well as his right to interstate travel.[110] The District Court for the Virgin Islands upheld the curfew, finding that it "clearly [fell] within the Governor's emergency powers and [was] reasonably necessary to preserve order."[111]

By contrast, court review of emergency responses to riots and protests has evolved over time, moving from a reasonableness standard to heightened scrutiny. In 1971, in *United States v. Chalk*,[112] the mayor of Asheville, North Carolina, declared a state of emergency and imposed a curfew following "a battle between police officers and black students."[113] Officers placed two men under arrest for violating the curfew and soon after discovered a shotgun in their car.[114] The men were convicted of possession of a firearm and subsequently challenged the emergency order to suppress evidence, alleging that it broadly swept into constitutionally protected activity. Acknowledging that the curfew had an incidental effect on speech, the court still reasoned that a "declaration of a state of emergency and the restrictions imposed pursuant to it must appear to be reasonably necessary for the preservation of order."[115] A few years later, in *ACLU of West Tennessee v. Chandler*, the district court cited *Chalk* to uphold a Memphis curfew imposed after a civil emergency declaration.[116] Acknowledging that the curfew infringed on First Amendment rights, the court still held that the restrictions were necessary to maintain order.[117] However, the court went a step further, determining that the curfew had been imposed in the "least restrictive manner necessary to preserve order," effectively applying a prong of strict scrutiny review.[118] Decades later, in *Menotti v. City of Seattle*, the Ninth Circuit reviewed the constitutionality of an emergency order that imposed a curfew on a portion of Seattle following mass protests of the 1999 WTO Conference.[119] In upholding the order's restrictions on speech, the court did not apply a deferential reasonableness standard, but instead applied traditional First Amendment case law to find that the order was a facially valid time, place, and manner restriction.[120]

Clearly, there are inconsistencies in how or whether courts rely on modern tiers of constitutional review to evaluate curfews following natural disasters and curfews following protests or civil unrest. Like court review of COVID orders, courts may arrive at the same outcome, but the confusion over *which* emergencies and which rights trigger strict scrutiny diminishes the idea that fundamental rights are deserving of the highest scrutiny regardless of context.

Applying Strict Scrutiny to All Uses of State Emergency Police Powers That Infringe on Fundamental Rights

During both health and nonhealth emergencies, some courts have declined to apply strict scrutiny when evaluating infringements on fundamental rights. Whatever merit this approach might have in dealing with a prototypical emergency scenario that is fleeting in nature and addressed through highly targeted interventions, the duration of the COVID pandemic has challenged notions that emergencies are brief, state responses are limited, and there is little harm in suspending strict scrutiny for the entirety of an emergency.

The pandemic's nature illustrates why courts should not suspend strict scrutiny when reviewing state emergency police power. The pandemic's indefiniteness and the virus's insidiousness increase opportunities for inconsistencies and abuse. State pandemic responses must regulate mundane aspects of daily life, and courts must remain vigilant.

Jacobson is an inadequate standard to scrutinize and decipher state motives and actions. Like the process–reasonableness standard, *Jacobson* simply checks whether the state actor has authority to put forth an order and whether it is reasonably necessary. *Jacobson* and other forms of reasonableness review deny courts the opportunity to balance fundamental rights with state interests when these rights arguably face their greatest threat.

When nearly every aspect of public life is affected by COVID, governors have immense authority to not only advance public health but to advance thinly veiled political agendas if they so choose. Under *Jacobson*, a governor who has long sought ways to limit abortion can use the pandemic to justify unilaterally banning these procedures through state police powers while preventing COVID-stricken counties from enforcing local stay-at-home orders.[121] Governors can also prioritize business activities that contribute to the state's economic well-being—and thus to the governors' reelection prospects—over religious practices that don't carry the same incidental benefit. But as *Blaisdell* recognized, "limitations of the power of the states were determined in light of emergency, and they are not altered by emergency."[122] Allowing governors to put forth abortion bans or religious restrictions that a court would likely not uphold in the absence of an emergency through deferential standards alters limitations on state power during emergencies and prevents courts from thoroughly scrutinizing state action.

As the country looks beyond COVID, some state governors are increasing their reliance on state emergency powers to address emergencies beyond the pandemic. In Texas[123] and Arizona,[124] Governors Abbott and Ducey have declared state emergencies to circumvent federal policy on immigration and border security. Texas's emergency declaration criminalizes the movement of immigrants on private property and authorizes the governor to suspend any state statute or administrative rule regarding contracting or procurement, paving the way for Texas to purchase equipment to build barriers and pay for additional law enforcement without legislative oversight. President Trump deployed national emergency powers to build a border wall and now both governors, taking a page from his playbook, will likely continue construction using state emergency powers.[125] Governors Ducey's and Abbott's use of state emergency powers to enforce federal immigration policy in communities of color suggests that these broad powers—removed from legislative oversight and frequently subject to less exacting judicial review—will be a way for opposition parties to impose restrictive immigration policies when more progressive policy makers take hold of the federal executive and state legislative branches.

Such developments underscore why courts should apply strict scrutiny to all emergency uses of state police power when they infringe on fundamental rights. This does not mean courts should show no deference to the expertise of state public health officials. Even when applying strict scrutiny, courts will need to make factual determinations on matters such as which activities create which risks. It is entirely appropriate for courts to place heavy reliance on the experts' assessment on these factual matters. But that deference should take place within the context of assessing whether the government's interest is compelling and whether its actions are narrowly tailored to advancing that interest. Scholars have routinely called for strict scrutiny review of state responses to emergencies[126] and vaccination mandates,[127] noting that safeguarding the public during natural disasters, economic crises, security threats, or public health emergencies would surely be a compelling interest that government regulations could narrowly tailor policy around.

Applying the modern standards of constitutional review that emerged after *Jacobson* complies with the principles articulated in *Blaisdell* and allows courts to better scrutinize state action and require specific justification for regulation. As legal scholars like Wiley and Vladeck have argued, strict scrutiny allows for courts to take extraordinary circumstances into consideration, properly balance how states may need to address emergencies, and still require greater scrutiny and analysis of how civil liberties are implicated.[128] Embracing this standard would not compromise a state's ability to respond to an emergency, and explicitly applying it in emergency circumstances would finally allow for consistent protection of fundamental rights.

Conclusion

The future is rife with potential emergencies. Climate change threatens to bring more natural disasters. Deep racial and political divides, if left unaddressed, could yield greater civil unrest and more emergency declarations. The challenges of today indicate that questions about how a court must review emergency police powers will not subside.

Our courts must be prepared to safeguard our civil liberties accordingly. The application of *Jacobson* has led to needless inconsistencies in the courts, and the use of the process–reasonableness prong during other state-level emergencies, though infrequently invoked, may not account for future indefinite or politically motivated emergencies. Courts need to treat fundamental rights consistently during ordinary and emergency periods, extending to them the highest level of protection in order to prevent their erosion during times of crisis.

Notes

Appendix 2, which contains the database compiled for this chapter, may be found at https://www.hoover.org/research/who-governs-emergency-powers-time-covid.

1. "Status of State COVID-19 Emergency Orders," National Governors Association (December 3, 2020), https://www.nga.org/wp-content/uploads/2020/12/Status-of-State-COVID-19-Emergency-Orders_Last-December29.xlsx.

2. *See* Graves v. Minnesota, 272 U.S. 425, 428 (1926) (upholding a Minnesota statute requiring dentists to hold a diploma from a dental school of good standing since it was not an "[a]rbitrary or unreasonable attempt to exercise . . . [state police power authority]"); Watson v. State of Maryland, 218 U.S. 173, 178 (1910) (finding that a Maryland medical regulation excluding certain individuals from licensing requirements was within the power of the state as the regulation as was not "[s]o unreasonable and extravagant as to interfere with property and personal rights of citizens, unnecessarily and arbitrarily"); Jacobson v. Commonwealth of Massachusetts, 197 U.S. 11, 26 (1905).

3. U.S. Const. amend. X.

4. Metropolitan Life Ins. Co. v. Massachusetts, 471 U.S. 724, 756 (1985).

5. *Jacobson*, 197 U.S. at 25 (citing Gibbons v. Ogden, 22 U.S. 1, 203–4 (1824). *See also* Compagnie Francaise de Navigation a Vapeur v. La. State Bd. of Health, 186 U.S. 380, 387 (1902) (stating it is "[b]eyond question" for states to enact laws "[f]or the safety and protection of their inhabitants").

6. *See* Nat'l Fed'n of Indep. Bus. v. Sebelius, 567 U.S. 519, 535–36 (2012) ("The Constitution may restrict state governments—as it does, for example, by forbidding them to deny any person the equal protection of the laws."); Panhandle E. Pipe Line Co. v. State Highway Comm'n of Kansas, 294 U.S. 613, 619 (1935) ("A claim that action is being taken under the police power of the state cannot justify disregard of constitutional inhibitions."); *Gibbons*, 22 U.S. at 210 ("But the framers of our constitution foresaw this state of things, and provided for it, by declaring the supremacy not only of itself, but of the laws made in pursuance of it.").

7. Bibb v. Navajo Freight Lines, Inc., 359 U.S. 520, 529 (1959) ("Local regulations which would pass muster under the Due Process Clause might nonetheless fail to survive other challenges to constitutionality that bring the Supremacy Clause into play."); *Day-Brite Lighting Inc. v. State of Mo.*, 342 U.S. 421, 423 (1952) ("[S]tate legislatures . . . are entitled to their own standard of the public welfare . . . so long as specific constitutional prohibitions are not violated and so long as conflicts with valid and controlling federal laws are avoided.").

8. *Jacobson*, 197 U.S. 11, 26 (1905).

9. *See Graves*, 272 U.S. at 428; *Watson*, 218 U.S. at 178; *Jacobson*, 197 U.S. at 26.

10. *See* Hannibal & St. J. R. Co. v. Husen, 95 U. S. 465, 471–473 (1877) (finding a Missouri law prohibiting the driving of *any* Texas, Mexican, or Indian cattle during a specific time period went beyond the necessary measures to stave off a disease); *In re Smith*, 146 N.Y. 68, 40 N.E. 497 (1895) (holding that a blanket quarantine of individuals who refused vaccination to be overbroad when there was no reason to believe these individuals had been infected or exposed to the disease in question).

11. Jew Ho v. Williamson, 103 F.10 (C.C.D. Cal. 1900).

12. United States v. Carolene Prod. Co., 304 U.S. 144, 153 n. 4 (1938).

13. Skinner v. Oklahoma, 316 U.S. 533, 541 (1942).

14. Korematsu v. United States, 323 U.S. 214, 216 (1944).

15. Stephen A. Siegel, "The Origin of the Compelling State Interest Test and Strict Scrutiny," *American Journal of Legal History* 48 (2006): 355–56.

16. Richard H. Fallon Jr., "Strict Judicial Scrutiny," *UCLA Law Review* 54 (June 2007): 1267–1337, at 1289–91.

17. *Id.*

18. *Id.* at 1293.

19. Adam Winkler, "Fundamentally Wrong about Fundamental Rights," *Constitutional Commentary* 23 (2006): 227–39, at 228.

20. Moore v. City of E. Cleveland, 431 U.S. 494, 537 (1977) (Stewart, J., dissenting).

21. Winkler, *supra* note 19, at 228.

22. *Id.*

23. *See* Craig v. Boren, 429 U.S. 190, 199 (1976).

24. *See* Matthews v. Lucas, 427 U.S. 495 (1976).

25. *See* City of Renton v. Playtime Theatres, Inc., 475 U.S. 41 (1986) (applying intermediate scrutiny to a zoning ordinance prohibiting adult theaters from locating within one thousand feet of any residential zone, single- or multiple-family dwelling, church, park, or school).

26. Planned Parenthood of Southeastern Pennsylvania v. Casey, 505 U.S. 833, 877 (1992).

27. Fallon, *supra* note 16, at 193.

28. Wisconsin v. Yoder, 406 U.S. 205, 214-215 (1972).

29. *Yoder*, 406 U.S. at 214.

30. *Id.* at 236.

31. Thomas v. Rev. Bd. of Indiana Emp. Sec. Div., 450 U.S. 707, 718 (1981) (finding that the government's interest to avoid widespread unemployment and detailed probing into a job applicant's religious beliefs were not sufficiently compelling to deny Thomas unemployment benefits).

32. *See* City of Highland Park v. Train, 519 F.2d 681, 696 (7th Cir. 1975) ("Unless it is based upon a suspect classification or impinges on a fundamental right . . . zoning legislation may be held unconstitutional only if it is shown to bear no possible relationship to the State's interest in securing the health, safety, morals or general welfare of the public and is, therefore, manifestly unreasonable and arbitrary.") (citation omitted).

33. *See* Threesome Entm't v. Strittmather, 4 F. Supp. 2d 710, 717 (N.D. Ohio 1998) ("If the Ordinance is aimed specifically at curbing Harris's speech, as Harris contends, then the Ordinance may be upheld only if it furthers a vital governmental interest by the least restrictive means.").

34. *See* Espinosa v. Rusk, 634 F.2d 477, 482 (10th Cir. 1980), *aff'd*, 456 U.S. 951 (1982) ("Regulation which burdens the free exercise of religion and poses a threat of entanglement between the affairs of Church and State must be justified by a compelling state interest and there must not exist less restrictive and entangling alternative.").

35. *See* Potter v. Murray City, 585 F. Supp. 1126, 1137–38 (D. Utah 1984), *aff'd as modified*, 760 F.2d 1065 (10th Cir. 1985) ("When a statute in exercise of the police power impinges upon fundamental rights, the court examining the statute must employ a strict scrutiny test requiring a compelling state interest and a showing that no less restrictive alternatives are reasonably available.").

36. Emp. Div., Dep't of Hum. Res. of Oregon v. Smith, 494 U.S. 872, 874, (1990).

37. *Smith*, 494 U.S. at 879.
38. *Id.* at 881.
39. *Jacobson*, 197 U.S. at 12.
40. *Id.* at 14.
41. *Id.* at 26.
42. *Id.* at 28.
43. *Id.* at 31.
44. *Id.* at 28, 30.
45. Lindsay F. Wiley and Stephen I. Vladeck, "Coronavirus, Civil Liberties, and the Courts: The Case against 'Suspending' Judicial Review," *Harvard Law Review Forum* 133, no. 9 (July 2020): 179–98, at 193–94.
46. In re Abbott, 954 F.3d 772, 786 (5th Cir. 2020).
47. *Abbott*, 954 F.3d at 784–85 (quoting *Jacobson*, 197 U.S. at 31, 38).
48. *Id.* at 783.
49. In re Rutledge, 956 F.3d 1018 (8th Cir. 2020).
50. Little Rock Family Planning Servs. v. Rutledge, No. 4:20-CV-00470 BSM, 2020 WL 2240105 (E.D. Ark. May 7, 2020) (finding that the order bore a substantial relation to the COVID-19 health crisis and was not a plain and palpable invasion of a woman's right to elective abortion).
51. S. Wind Women's Ctr. LLC v. Stitt, No. CIV-20-277-G, 2020 WL 1677094, at *2 (W.D. Okla. Apr. 6, 2020), *appeal dismissed*, 808 F. App'x 677 (10th Cir. 2020).
52. Preterm-Cleveland v. Attorney Gen. of Ohio, 456 F. Supp. 3d 917, 939 (S.D. Ohio 2020).
53. *See* Adams & Boyle, P.C. v. Slatery, 956 F.3d 913 (6th Cir. 2020) (blocking a ban on nonessential procedures from being enforced against individuals who would face delayed, costlier, and lengthier abortions); Robinson v. Attorney Gen., 957 F.3d 1171 (11th Cir. 2020) (prohibiting a ban on nonessential procedures from being enforced against individuals who would face a delayed abortion); *S. Wind Women's* 2020 WL 1677094, at *6 (prohibiting a ban on medication abortion and the ban on nonessential procedures from being enforced on ban to any patient who would lose her right to lawfully obtain an abortion in Oklahoma).
54. *Adams & Boyle*, 956 F.3d at 925, 927.
55. *Id.*
56. Wiley and Vladeck, *supra* note 45, at 192.
57. S. Bay United Pentecostal Church v. Newsom, 140 S. Ct. 1613 (2020).
58. S. Bay United Pentecostal Church v. Newsom, 140 S. Ct. 1613 (2020).
59. Roman Catholic Diocese of Brooklyn v. Cuomo, 495 F. Supp. 3d 118, 127 (E.D.N.Y. Oct. 16, 2020).
60. Calvary Chapel Dayton Valley v. Sisolak, 140 S. Ct. 2603 (2020).
61. Calvary Chapel Dayton Valley v. Sisolak, 140 S. Ct. 2603 (2020) (Kavanaugh, B., dissenting).

62. *Id.*
63. *See* Roman Catholic Diocese of Brooklyn v. Cuomo, No. 20-CV-4844 (NGG)(CLP), 2020 WL 5994954 (E.D.N.Y. Oct. 9, 2020) (upholding an order limiting places of worship to a capacity limit of 25 percent of maximum occupancy or ten people, whichever is fewer).
64. Roman Cath. Diocese, 495 F. Supp. 3d at 122.
65. *Id.*
66. *Id.*
67. Id.
68. Roman Cath. Diocese of Brooklyn, New York v. Cuomo, 495 F. Supp. 3d 118, 131 (E.D.N.Y.), *rev'd and remanded sub nom.* Agudath Israel of Am. v. Cuomo, 983 F.3d 620 (2d Cir. 2020).
69. Roman Cath. Diocese of Brooklyn v. Cuomo, 141 S. Ct. 63, 66 (2020).
70. *Id.*
71. *Id.*
72. *Id.* at 79
73. *Id.* at 67.
74. *Id.* at 70.
75. *Id.* at 71.
76. *Id.* at 70.
77. *Id.*
78. S. Bay United Pentecostal Church v. Newsom, 141 S. Ct. 716 (2021).
79. S. Bay, 141 S. Ct. at 717 (Roberts, J., concurring).
80. *Id.* at 718.
81. *Id.* at 722 (Kagan, E., dissenting).
82. Tandon v. Newsom, 141 S. Ct. 1294, 1298 (2021).
83. *See* Pleasant View Baptist Church v. Beshear, 838 F. App'x 936 (6th Cir. 2020); Denver Bible Church v. Becerra, No. 120CV02362DDDNRN, 2021 WL 1220758 (D. Colo. Mar. 28, 2021); Bond v. Brown, No. 6:20-CV-01656-AA, 2021 WL 1237114 (D. Or. Apr. 2, 2021).
84. Abundant Life Baptist Church of Lee's Summit v. Jackson Cty, No. 4:20-00367-CV-RK, 2021 WL 1970666 (W.D. Mo. May 17, 2021).
85. *See* Ward v. Rock Against Racism, 491 U.S. 781, 791 (1989); City of Renton v. Playtime Theatres, Inc., 475 U.S. 41, 46–47 (1986).
86. *See* Texas v. Johnson, 491 U.S. 397, 404 (1989).
87. *See* Belle Garden Est., LLC v. Northam, No. 7:21CV00135, 2021 WL 1156855, at *4 (W.D. Va. Mar. 26, 2021).
88. *See* McLaughlin v. Florida, 379 U.S. 184, 192 (1964); Frontiero v. Richardson, 411 U.S. 677, 686 (1973).
89. City of Cleburne v. Cleburne Living Ctr., 473 U.S. 432, 440 (1985).
90. Open Our Oregon v. Brown, No. 6:20-CV-773-MC, 2020 WL 2542861 (D. Or. May 19, 2020); Best Supplement Guide, LLC v. Newsom, No.

220CV00965JAMCKD, 2020 WL 2615022 (E.D. Cal. May 22, 2020); Prof'l Beauty Fed'n of California v. Newsom, No. 2:20-CV-04275-RGK-AS, 2020 WL 3056126 (C.D. Cal. June 8, 2020); Slidewaters LLC v. Washington Dep't of Labor & Indus., No. 2:20-CV-0210-TOR, 2020 WL 3130295 (E.D. Wash. June 12, 2020); Slidewaters LLC v. Washington Dep't of Labor, No. 2:20-CV-0210-TOR, 2020 WL 3979661 (E.D. Wash. July 14, 2020); 4 Aces Enterprises, LLC v. Edwards, No. CV 20-2150, 2020 WL 4747660 (E.D. La. Aug. 17, 2020); 910 E Main LLC v. Edwards, No. 6:20-CV-00965, 2020 WL 4929256 (W.D. La. Aug. 21, 2020); Luke's Catering Serv., LLC v. Cuomo, No. 20-CV-1086S, 2020 WL 5425008 (W.D.N.Y. Sept. 10, 2020); Bimber's Delwood, Inc. v. James, No. 20-CV-1043S, 2020 WL 6158612 (W.D.N.Y. Oct. 21, 2020); Columbus Ale House v. Cuomo, No. 20-CV-4291 (BMC), 2020 WL 6507326 (E.D.N.Y. Nov. 5, 2020); Antietam Battlefield KOA v. Hogan, No. CV CCB-20-1130, 2020 WL 6777590 (D. Md. Nov. 18, 2020); ARJN #3 v. Cooper, 2021 WL 409927 (M.D. Tenn. Feb. 5, 2021); Stewart v. Justice, 2021 WL 472937 (S.D. W. Va. Feb. 9, 2021); Amato v. Elicker, No. 3:20-CV-464 (MPS), 2020 WL 2542788 (D. Conn. May 19, 2020); Antietam Battlefield KOA v. Hogan, No. CV CCB-20-1130, 2020 WL 2556496 (D. Md. May 20, 2020); Benner v. Wolf, No. 20-CV-775, 2020 WL 2564920 (M.D. Pa. May 21, 2020); McCarthy v. Cuomo, No. 20-CV-2124 (ARR), 2020 WL 3286530 (E.D.N.Y. June 18, 2020); Tigges v. Northam, No. 3:20-CV-410, 2020 WL 4197610 (E.D. Va. July 21, 2020); Vill. of Orland Park v. Pritzker, No. 20-CV-03528, 2020 WL 4430577 (N.D. Ill. Aug. 1, 2020); Savage v. Mills, No. 1:20-CV-00165-LEW, 2020 WL 4572314 (D. Me. Aug. 7, 2020); Alsop v. Desantis, No. 8:20-CV-1052-T-23SPF, 2020 WL 4927592 (M.D. Fla. Aug. 21, 2020); BILL & TED'S RIVIERA, INC. & PARTITION STREET PROJECT, LLC, on behalf of themselves & all other similarly situated individuals, Plaintiffs, v. ANDREW M. CUOMO, LETITIA JAMES, GREELEY T. FORD, EMPIRE STATE DEVELOPMENT CORPORATION & NEW YORK STATE LIQUOR AUTHORITY, Defendants, No. 120CV1001FJSTWD, 2020 WL 6043991 (N.D.N.Y. Oct. 13, 2020); Big Tyme Investments v. Edwards, 985 F.3d 456 (5th Cir. 2021); Culinary Studios v. Newsom, 2021 WL 427115 (E.D. Cal. Feb. 8, 2021); Kelley O'Neill's Inc. v. Ige, 2021 WL 767851 (D. Haw. Feb. 26, 2021); Our Wicked Lady LLC v. Cuomo, 2021 WL 915033 (S.D.N.Y. Mar. 9, 2021); Calm Ventures LLC v. Newsom, 2021 WL 1502657 (C.D. Ca. Mar. 25, 2021); Hopkins Hawley LLC v. Cuomo, 2021 WL 465437 (S.D.N.Y. Feb. 9, 2021); McCafferty v. Wolf, 2021 WL 1340002 (W.D. Pa. Apr. 9, 2021); Cummings v. DeSantis, No. 220CV351FTM38NPM, 2020 WL 2512805 (M.D. Fla. May 15, 2020); Commcan, Inc., and Others v. Charlie Baker, In His Official Capacity as Governor Of The Commonwealth Of Massachusetts, No. 2084CV00808-BLS2, 2020 WL 1903822 (Mass. Super. Apr. 16, 2020); Hartman v. Acton, No. 2:20-CV-1952, 2020 WL 1932896 (S.D. Ohio Apr. 21, 2020); Bayley's Campground Inc. v. Mills, No. 2:20-CV-00176-LEW, 2020 WL 2791797 (D. Me. May 29,

2020), reconsideration denied, No. 2:20-CV-00176-LEW, 2020 WL 3037252 (D. Me. June 5, 2020); Talleywhacker, Inc. v. Cooper, No. 5:20-CV-218-FL, 2020 WL 3051207 (E.D.N.C. June 8, 2020); League of Independent Fitness Facilities And Trainers, Inc., et al., Plaintiffs-Appellees, v. Governor Gretchen Whitmer, et al., Defendants-Appellants, No. 20-1581, 2020 WL 3468281 (6th Cir. 2020); Xponential Fitness v. Arizona, No. CV-20-01310-PHX-DJH, 2020 WL 3971908 (D. Ariz. July 14, 2020); Auracle Homes, LLC v. Lamont, No. 3:20-CV-00829 (VAB), 2020 WL 4558682 (D. Conn. Aug. 7, 2020); Lebanon Valley Auto Racing Corp. v. Cuomo, No. 120CV0804LEKTWD, 2020 WL 4596921 (N.D.N.Y. Aug. 11, 2020); Mesa Golfland, Ltd., Plaintiff, v. Douglas A. Ducey, Defendant, No. CV-20-01616-PHX-JJT, 2020 WL 5632141 (D. Ariz. Sept. 21, 2020); Michigan Rest. & Lodging Ass'n v. Gordon, No. 1:20-CV-1104, 2020 WL 6866649 (W.D. Mich. Nov. 20, 2020); Bayley's Campground Inc. v. Mills, 985 F.3d 153 (1st Cir. 2021); Nowlin v. Pritzker, 2021 WL 669333 (C.D. Ill. 2021); Belle Garden Estate, LLC v. Northam, 2021 WL 1156855 (W.D. Va. Mar. 26, 2021); Hopkins Hawley LLC v. Cuomo, No. 20-CV-10932 (PAC), 2021 WL 1894277 (S.D.N.Y. May 11, 2021); Peinhopf v. Leon Guerrero, No. CV 20-00029, 2021 WL 2417150 (D. Guam June 14, 2021); Mission Fitness Ctr., LLC v. Newsom, No. 220CV09824CASKSX, 2021 WL 1856552 (C.D. Cal. May 10, 2021).

91. *See* Slidewaters LLC v. Washington Dep't of Labor, No. 2:20-CV-0210-TOR, 2020 WL 3979661 (E.D. Wash. July 14, 2020) (upholding order disallowing employees to perform work where a business activity is prohibited by an emergency proclamation); Slidewaters LLC v. Washington Dep't of Labor & Indus., No. 2:20-CV-0210-TOR, 2020 WL 3130295 (E.D. Wash. June 12, 2020) (upholding order disallowing employees to perform work where a business activity is prohibited by an emergency proclamation).

92. Columbus Ale House v. Cuomo, No. 20-CV-4291 (BMC), 2020 WL 6507326 (E.D.N.Y. Nov. 5, 2020) (upholding order prohibiting service after midnight at New York food establishments); Bimber's Delwood, Inc. v. James, No. 20-CV-1043S, 2020 WL 6158612 (W.D.N.Y. Oct. 21, 2020) (upholding provisions of reopening plan requiring indoor dining to comply with strict social distancing restrictions); Luke's Catering Serv., LLC v. Cuomo, No. 20-CV-1086S, 2020 WL 5425008 (W.D.N.Y. Sept. 10, 2020) (upholding an executive order limiting gatherings to fifty people); 4 Aces Enterprises, LLC v. Edwards, No. CV 20-2150, 2020 WL 4747660 (E.D. La. Aug. 17, 2020) (upholding orders banning on-site consumption of food and drink at bars).

93. Columbus Ale House, 495 F. Supp. 3d 88, 93; 4 Aces Enterprises, No. CV 20-2150, 2020 WL 4747660 at 325-326., *aff'd sub nom.* Big Tyme Invs., LLC v. Edwards, No. 20-30526, 2021 WL 118628 (5th Cir. 2021).

94. Bimber's Delwood, 496 F. Supp. 3d 760, 785 (W.D.N.Y. 2020); Luke's Catering Serv. LLC, 485 F. Supp. 3d 369, 382 (W.D.N.Y. 2020).

95. Big Tyme Invs., LLC v. Edwards, No. 20-30526, 2021 WL 118628 (5th Cir. 2021) (applying *Jacobson* and rational basis to an equal protection claim; McCafferty v. Wolf, No. 2:20-CV-02008-CCW, 2021 WL 1340002 (W.D. Pa. Apr. 9, 2021) (applying rational basis and *Jacobson* to an equal protection claim); Calm Ventures LLC v. Newsom, No. CV2011501JFWPVCX, 2021 WL 1502657 (C.D. Cal. Mar. 25, 2021) (applying *Jacobson* and rational basis to a substantive due process claim since the right to pursue one's profession is not a fundamental right); Our Wicked Lady LLC v. Cuomo, No. 21CV0165 (DLC), 2021 WL 915033 (S.D.N.Y. Mar. 9, 2021) (upholding an order limiting dining and fitness classes by applying *Jacobson* and rational basis review to a Fourteenth Amendment due process claim); Kelley O'Neil's Inc. v. Ige, No. CV 20-00449 LEK-RT, 2021 WL 767851 (D. Haw. Feb. 26, 2021) (applying *Jacobson* and rational basis review to an equal protection claim); Hopkins Hawley LLC v. Cuomo, No. 20-CV-10932 (PAC), 2021 WL 465437 (S.D.N.Y. Feb. 9, 2021) (upholding an order limiting dining by applying *Jacobson* to First Amendment claim); Stewart v. Just., No. CV 3:20-0611, 2021 WL 472937 (S.D. W. Va. Feb. 9, 2021) (upholding a West Virginia mask order); Antietam Battlefield KOA v. Hogan, No. CV CCB-20-1130, 2020 WL 6777590 (D. Md. Nov. 18, 2020) (upholding order limiting gatherings to ten people and requiring nonessential businesses to stay closed); Bill & Ted's Riviera, Inc. v. Cuomo, No. 120CV1001FJSTWD, 2020 WL 6043991 (N.D.N.Y. Oct. 13, 2020) (applying *Jacobson* and rational basis review to uphold order allowing gatherings of fifty or fewer individuals for any lawful purpose or reason, so long as any such gatherings occurring indoors did not exceed 50 percent of the maximum occupancy for a particular indoor area); Alsop v. Desantis, No. 8:20-CV-1052-T-23SPF, 2020 WL 4927592 (M.D. Fla. Aug. 21, 2020) (citing *Jacobson* to state how governors have broad latitude to put forth orders during the pandemic and applying rational basis review to Alsop's equal protection claim); 910 E Main LLC v. Edwards, No. 6:20-CV-00965, 2020 WL 4929256 (W.D. La. Aug. 21, 2020) (upholding orders banning on-site consumption at bars, restricting indoor and outdoor crowd sizes to fifty, and mandating mask requirements for the public); Vill. of Orland Park v. Pritzker, No. 20-CV-03528, 2020 WL 4430577 (N.D. Ill. Aug. 1, 2020) (applying *Jacobson* and rational basis review to uphold order limiting gatherings to fifty people); Tigges v. Northam, No. 3:20-CV-410, 2020 WL 4197610 (E.D. Va. July 21, 2020) (applying *Jacobson* and rational basis review to a free exercise claim and intermediate scrutiny to a free assembly claim to uphold a COVID order); McCarthy v. Cuomo, No. 20-CV-2124 (ARR), 2020 WL 3286530 (E.D.N.Y. June 18, 2020) (applying *Jacobson* and rational basis review to Fourteenth Amendment equal protection and First Amendment speech and assembly claims); Talleywhacker, Inc. v. Cooper, No. 5:20-CV-218-FL, 2020 WL 3051207 (E.D.N.C. June 8, 2020) (applying *Jacobson* and rational basis to Talleywhacker's First Amendment free speech and Fourteenth Amendment equal protection claim); Prof'l Beauty Fed'n of California v. Newsom, No. 2:

20-CV-04275-RGK-AS, 2020 WL 3056126 (C.D. Cal. June 8, 2020) (upholding order requiring nonessential businesses to close); Amato v. Elicker, No. 3:20-CV-464 (MPS), 2020 WL 2542788 (D. Conn. May 19, 2020) (applying *Jacobson* and rational basis review to uphold order requiring nonessential businesses to close).

96. Hopkins Hawley LLC v. Cuomo, No. 20-CV-10932 (PAC), 2021 WL 465437, at *5 (S.D.N.Y. Feb. 9, 2021).

97. *Id.* at 5.

98. ARJN #3 v. Cooper, No. 3:20-CV-00808, 2021 WL 409927 (M.D. Tenn. Feb. 5, 2021) (applying rational basis review to an equal protection claim in light of the holding in *Roman Catholic*); League of Independent Fitness Facilities and Trainers, Inc. v. Whitmer, No. 20-1581, 2020 WL 3468281 (6th Cir. 2020) (upholding order prohibiting fitness facilities from opening by applying rational basis to equal protection claim); Belle Garden Est., LLC v. Northam, No. 7:21CV00135, 2021 WL 1156855 (W.D. Va. Mar. 26, 2021) (applying rational basis to free assembly and equal protection claims); Culinary Studios, Inc. v. Newsom, No. 1:20-CV-1340 AWI EPG, 2021 WL 427115 (E.D. Cal. Feb. 8, 2021) (applying rational basis review to plaintiff's equal protection claim); Michigan Rest. & Lodging Ass'n v. Gordon, No. 1:20-CV-1104, 2020 WL 6866649 (W.D. Mich. Nov. 20, 2020) (applying rational basis review to uphold order closing Michigan bars and restaurants for indoor, in-person services for three weeks); Mesa Golfland v. Ducey, No. CV-20-01616-PHX-JJT, 2020 WL 5632141 (D. Ariz. Sept. 21, 2020) (applying rational basis to an as-applied challenge to upholding order); Lebanon Valley Auto Racing Corp. v. Cuomo, No. 120CV0804LEKTWD, 2020 WL 4596921 (N.D.N.Y. Aug. 11, 2020) (applying traditional tiers of constitutional review to find that plaintiffs failed to state a selective enforcement equal protection claim); Xponential Fitness v. Arizona, No. CV-20-01310-PHX-DJH, 2020 WL 3971908 (D. Ariz. July 14, 2020) (applying rational basis to equal protection claim to uphold order requiring gyms to close); Benner v. Wolf, No. 20-CV-775, 2020 WL 2564920 (M.D. Pa. May 21, 2020) (applying rational basis review to Benner's free speech claim); Hartman v. Acton, No. 2:20-CV-1952, 2020 WL 1932896 (S.D. Ohio Apr. 21, 2020) (upholding order requiring non-life- sustaining businesses to close).

99. Bayley's Campground Inc. v. Mills, 463 F. Supp. 3d 22, 33–35 (D. Me. 2020), *reconsideration denied*, No. 2:20-CV-00176-LEW, 2020 WL 3037252 (D. Me. June 5, 2020), and *aff'd*, No. 20-1559, 2021 WL 164973 (1st Cir. 2021)

100. Bayley's Campground, No. 2:20-CV-00176-LEW, at *8.

101. Home Bldg. & Loan Ass'n v. Blaisdell, 290 U.S. 398, 444–45 (1934).

102. Karen J. Pita Loor, "When Protest Is the Disaster: Constitutional Implications of State and Local Emergency Power," *Seattle University Law Review* 43, no. 1 (2019): 1–70.

103. Michael Cook, "Get Out Now or Risk Being Taken Out by Force: Judicial Review of State Government Emergency Power following a Natural Disaster," *Case Western Reserve Law Review* 57, no. 1 (Fall 2006): 265, 269.

104. *Id.*
105. *Id.* at 270.
106. Smith v. Avino, 91 F.3d 105, 108 (11th Cir. 1996), *abrogated by Steel Co. v. Citizens for a Better Env't*, 523 U.S. 83 (1998).
107. Smith v. Avino, 866 F. Supp. 1399, 1402 (S.D. Fla. 1994), *aff'd*, 91 F.3d 105 (11th Cir. 1996).
108. *Smith*, 91 F.3d at 109.
109. *Smith*, 91 F.3d at 109 (citing United States v. Chalk, 441 F.2d at 1281).
110. Moorhead v. Farrelly, 24 V.I. 329, 331 (D.V.I. 1989).
111. Moorhead v. Farrelly, 24 V.I. 318, 324–25 (D.V.I. 1989).
112. U.S. v. Chalk, 441 F.2d 1277, 1278 (4th Cir. 1971).
113. Chalk, 441 F.2d at 1278.
114. *Id.* at 1279.
115. *Id.* at 1281.
116. Am. Civil Liberties Union of W. Tennessee, Inc. v. Chandler, 458 F. Supp. 456, 461 (W.D. Tenn. 1978).
117. *Id.*
118. *Id.*
119. Menotti v. City of Seattle, 409 F.3d 1113, 1125 (9th Cir. 2005).
120. *Menotti*, 409 F.3d at 1129–1130.
121. *See* In re Abbott, 954 F.3d 772 (5th Cir. 2020); *See also* Sarah R. Champagne, "Hidalgo County Judge Tries Slowing Coronavirus, but Gov. Greg Abbott Has Limited His Options," *Texas Tribune*, July 20, 2020; Jolie McCullough and Julián Aguilar, "El Paso Is Fighting the Coronavirus and State Resistance as Officials Desperately Try to Keep Up with Sick and Dying Texans," *Texas Tribune*, November 18, 2020.
122. *Blaisdell*, 290 U.S. at 440.
123. Texas Border Proclamation of Emergency, May 31, 2021, https://gov.texas.gov/uploads/files/press/DISASTER_border_security_IMAGE_05-31-2021.pdf.
124. 2021 Border Crisis Arizona Declaration of Emergency, April 20, 2021, https://azgovernor.gov/sites/default/files/declaration_of_emergency.pdf.
125. Letter from Texas Governor Greg Abbott to Bryan Collier, Executive Director, Texas Department of Corrections, June 16, 2021, https://gov.texas.gov/uploads/files/press/O-CollierBryan202106162544.pdf.
126. *See generally* Mitchell F. Crusto, "State of Emergency: An Emergency Constitution Revisited," *Loyola Law Review* 61 (2015): 471–523.
127. Ben Horowitz, "A Shot in the Arm: What a Modern Approach to Jacobson v. Massachusetts Means for Mandatory Vaccinations during a Public Health Emergency," *American University Law Review* 60, no. 6 (August 2011): 1715–50, 1730.
128. Wiley, *supra* note 45.

Chapter 8

Legislative Opposition to the Exercise of State Emergency Powers

Cameron DeHart and Morris P. Fiorina

On March 4, 2020, California governor Gavin Newsom declared a state of emergency to meet the developing COVID-19 pandemic. Within a week Pennsylvania, New York, and Michigan followed with their own declarations. Ultimately all the nation's governors issued executive orders that invoked the emergency powers authorized by their state constitutions and the implementing statutes discussed in chapter 2. Business shutdowns, stay-at-home orders, and other restrictions quickly followed. Probably most of the governors and state legislators had little experience with such extensive orders, and in the case of the legislators probably only vague ideas of what emergency powers their state governors legitimately could exercise. In the modern era, the typical invocation of emergency powers has been in response to natural disasters of various sorts—wildfires, hurricanes, floods, and earthquakes. In such circumstances, getting first responders and various forms of aid to the affected communities is the priority. Such emergencies typically are short-lived, although recovery efforts may continue over a longer period of time. Longer emergencies, such as California's continuing water emergency, generally do not affect the day-to-day lives of people.[1]

At first, Americans largely supported actions taken under the state declarations. Initial expectations were that the emergency restrictions would be short-lived, just long enough to "flatten the curve," although as Ochoa details in chapter 7, court suits centered on religious liberties were filed soon after restrictions on movements and meetings went into effect.

But as the shutdowns lengthened and the various other restrictions were imposed, lifted, then imposed again, public opinion became less supportive overall and more divided by party, as Wang describes in chapter 6.

By the spring of 2021, the exercise of emergency powers in many states had become sufficiently controversial that legislatures began to attempt to limit some of the statutory powers described in the preceding chapter. At the time of this writing (November 2021) more than three hundred bills introduced in forty-five state legislatures have sought to restrict the emergency powers of governors in various ways, some as mild as specifying legislative oversight and consultation, others by imposing significant curbs on gubernatorial powers. In addition, resolutions, initiatives, and court suits have addressed the emergency powers of the states where legislation was not a realistic option because of interinstitutional conflict. Many of these conflicts pitted Republican legislatures and conservative interest groups against Democratic governors, but there are noteworthy examples of intraparty conflict as well.

Efforts to modify state powers are continuing as we write, so this chapter simply provides a brief snapshot of some of the efforts to amend powers described in chapter 2. (The database in the online appendix incorporates these changes and will be updated as new revisions and amendments occur.) In addition, we highlight some new conflicts arising from federalism that are wending their way through the courts as we write.

Duration and Extension

The most common subject of legislative action centered on the duration of state declarations of emergency and the renewal of such declarations.[2] How long could shutdowns and other restrictions be imposed, how many times could they be extended, and who should have a say in these decisions? Although in some states constitutional provisions and statutes were silent on this subject (for example, fourteen states featured no time limits on emergency declarations and another three did not allow declarations to be renewed), even black letter laws were challenged and in some cases modified as the pandemic went on.

As far as we have been able to ascertain, Kansas led the way in June 2020 by (1) requiring the governor to end "emergency proclamations" within fifteen days unless the legislature voted to extend them; (2) limiting the number of days the governor could close businesses; and (3) requiring new gubernatorial orders to secure approval from two-thirds of the members of the state finance council. Democratic governor Laura Kelly signed the bill passed by the Republican legislature. (As in many other states the Kansas legislature sits only part of the year—three months generally; hence, the delegation of gubernatorial oversight and approval to other—continuing—bodies in some states.)

Political warfare erupted in Michigan, where intense partisan conflict combined with interbranch disputes. In the first four months of the pandemic, Governor Gretchen Whitmer took aggressive action and issued well over one hundred executive orders, although many were short-term or later rescinded.[3] Since the Democratic governor could veto any legislation passed by the Republican legislature, the latter turned to the courts. The Michigan Senate sued Governor Whitmer, and in October 2020 the state supreme court ruled that the 1945 Emergency Powers of Governor Act was an unconstitutional delegation of legislative power to the executive.[4] To put the court decision on firmer ground, the legislature repealed the 1945 law in July 2021 in response to a citizen petition.[5] Governor Whitmer was unable to veto the repeal because a quirk in the Michigan constitution allows the legislature to enact a citizen petition without the signature of the governor or a statewide vote of approval.

After the fall–winter COVID holiday surge, Kentucky acted in February 2021. The legislature limited the governor's executive orders to thirty days' duration unless extended by the legislature and required approval from the state attorney general if the governor proposed to suspend any statutes. The Republican legislature passed the legislation over the veto of Democratic governor Andy Beshear. After some court suits, the Kentucky Supreme Court affirmed the legislation. In March

Arkansas limited "disaster emergencies" to sixty days and gave the Legislative Council the power to block extensions beyond sixty days. Kansas acted again to further limit gubernatorial powers by empowering an eight-member Legislative Coordinating Council to override executive orders. In addition, the Kansas legislation allowed "anyone burdened by an executive order, school board policy, or county health directive" to file suit.[6] Courts must hold a hearing within seventy-two hours to determine if the order is narrowly tailored.

At the height of the initial COVID surge in New York, the Democratic legislature had given extraordinary emergency powers to Democratic governor Andrew Cuomo—something of a national hero at the time.[7] Among other things by executive order, Cuomo could mandate masks and impose quarantines. The governor used his powers aggressively, issuing some four hundred executive orders. A year later, with Cuomo in deep political difficulty, the legislature voted to revoke the new powers, allowing them to remain in effect for thirty days, but requiring any new orders to have legislative approval.[8]

Also in March 2021 the Republican-controlled Ohio General Assembly passed a bill requiring the governor to renew executive orders every sixty days (previously, emergency orders were open ended except in the case of a public health emergency due to an "adulterated consumer product," which is limited to sixty days unless renewed by the governor).[9] Moreover, any executive order that the governor issued could be canceled by the legislature after thirty days. Other provisions (to be discussed below) limited the powers of local health officials. Republican governor Mike DeWine vetoed the legislation, but his Republican copartisans in the legislature overrode his veto.

In neighboring Pennsylvania, the situation was similar to that in Michigan—a Democratic governor facing a Republican legislature. Earlier the legislature had passed seven bills that reopened some businesses and set clear standards for COVID mitigation. Governor Tom Wolf vetoed all seven.[10] Unlike in Michigan, the state supreme court had a majority of Democratic appointees that had upheld previous challenges to Governor Wolf's actions. Hence the Pennsylvania

General Assembly took the route of constitutional amendment, placing two proposed amendments before the electorate. The first would limit the duration of a "disaster declaration" to twenty-one days (previously ninety) and required a joint resolution of the General Assembly to extend such a declaration. The second proposed amendment would empower the legislature to end an emergency by a joint resolution that the governor cannot veto. In the May primary elections, both amendments passed by 54 percent to 46 percent. To go into effect, the General Assembly must pass the identical propositions in the next session, and the electorate must approve them again.

In April Indiana reprised the earlier Ohio developments. The Republican House and Senate overrode Republican governor Eric Holcomb's veto. The legislation empowered the General Assembly to call itself into a forty-day special session in which it could terminate emergency orders. The case is in the courts as we write.

Although the number of cases is small, as we look across the current examples, the patterns of conflict within state governments seem fairly clear. Conflict over the exercise of emergency powers is most likely in states that have Republican legislative majorities and a Democratic governor.[11] The executive attempts to impose more stringent restrictions than the legislature prefers. The constituencies of the two parties provide a ready explanation even before appealing to partisan differences in mass public opinion (chapter 6). Business groups were by and large opposed to restrictions and made their case to Republican legislators. In contrast, Democratic groups like public sector workers were not as affected financially by lockdowns and other orders, for the most part. Democratic governors ran little political risk in aggressively implementing their powers. Where Republicans controlled both the executive and legislative branches in their states, governors either exercised their powers sparingly or cooperated with legislatures in limiting them, as in the case of Kansas. In a few cases, such as Indiana and Ohio, Republicans fought among themselves, again with executives favoring more stringent COVID restrictions. Only a few states, such as Massachusetts and Maryland, have Republican governors and Democratic legislatures, and in these states the governors behaved similarly to Democrats, resulting in little conflict.

Specific Exceptions

Limitations aimed at specific actions or at creating specific exceptions or carve-outs are a second area of legislative action to limit the exercise of emergency powers. For example, the Ohio legislation passed over the governor's veto and restricted the power of local health officials to order quarantines or self-isolation without a medical diagnosis of infection. Lawmakers in some states, such as New Hampshire, designated churches and other religious organizations as "essential" under the state emergency laws, thus shielding them from future restrictions during an emergency.[12]

To Strengthen Emergency Powers?

In the overwhelming number of cases, action to address state emergency powers meant curbs or restrictions. But after the start of the pandemic, there were a few attempts to *strengthen* state powers. As noted above, in March 2020 the New York legislature bestowed enhanced emergency powers on Governor Cuomo, only to take them back a year later. In Illinois, private schools and many schools in smaller cities opened for in-person learning during the year, but Chicago schools and those in some other large metropolitan areas did not. Acting on behalf of one of the two large teachers' unions, legislative supporters introduced a bill that would have required all districts to follow the dictates of the State Board of Education.[13] This meant that the state could require all schools to close regardless of local conditions. In addition, home schools and private schools would have to meet all safety and other requirements set by the state (they already must follow local department of health guidelines, of course). According to media commentators, the union believed that it was easier to influence one large state agency than to have to deal with numerous smaller ones. In addition, the legislation would give the state control over home and private schools, something the union desired. Interestingly, the State Board of Education opposed the bill, which passed the Illinois House but died in the Senate.

Conflicts between Governmental Levels

There have been a number of attempts by Democratic and other liberal groups to stop Republican governors from utilizing emergency orders to prevent other government entities from acting. In Florida, Governor Ron DeSantis consistently declined to issue a statewide mask mandate, and in March 2021 he issued an executive order prohibiting any government unit or private business from requiring vaccine passports or other documentation as a condition of service.[14] DeSantis ordered all schools to reopen for fall 2021 instruction, and when schools promulgated mask mandates, the governor issued an executive order prohibiting such mandates and threatening to withhold state funds to any school district that did not comply.[15] A series of court suits followed.[16]

In Texas, Governor Greg Abbott issued an executive order in August 2021 that (1) prohibited any government entity from promulgating a vaccine mandate; (2) prohibited any state or local government entity from enforcing a vaccine requirement; and (3) prohibited any public or private entity that received state funding of any kind from enforcing a vaccine mandate as a condition of service or attendance.[17] The Texas legislature failed to codify the governor's ban, however, after opposition from Texas businesses left the proposal short of the necessary votes in the upper chamber.[18]

Other states joined Florida and Texas in enacting bans on mask and vaccine mandates, attracting the attention of the Biden administration, as well as state and local courts. The US Department of Education announced in August 2021 a civil rights investigation into five states with bans on local mask mandates: Iowa, Oklahoma, South Carolina,

Tennessee, and Utah.[19] State and federal courts blocked or temporarily halted mask mandates in at least three of these states. In September, a federal district judge struck down South Carolina's mask mandate ban as a violation of the Americans with Disabilities Act, and a federal appeals court upheld the ruling a month later.[20] Two similar rulings in Tennessee blocked that state's governor from enacting a mask mandate ban through an executive order. The state legislature responded by including the ban in legislation that passed in late October.[21] An Oklahoma judge put that state's mask mandate ban on hold, but allowed parents to seek exemptions for their children from their local school districts.[22]

A law passed by the Arkansas legislature, prohibiting local school districts from enforcing mask requirements, was halted by a county court in September. The state supreme court upheld the injunction and prevented the state from enforcing the ban. In November, Arizona's supreme court upheld a lower court's ruling that the legislature had illegally enacted its ban on mask mandates via an amendment to the budget, a violation of the state's constitution.[23]

Several states have prohibited state and local government officials from requiring proof of vaccination from members of the public. According to the National Academy for State Health Policy, twenty-one states had some form of a ban on vaccine mandates as of October 2021.[24] The Kaiser Family Foundation lists thirteen states with prohibitions on vaccine mandates.[25]

Governors in Arizona, Georgia, Florida, Oklahoma, and Texas enacted their bans on vaccine mandates through executive orders directed to state and local agencies. Other states, including Arkansas, Indiana, Montana, New Hampshire, North Dakota, Tennessee, and Utah, passed legislation to enact similar policies. In Montana, for example, Republican governor Greg Gianforte signed a bill passed by the state's legislature to ban employers and governments from discriminating against job seekers based on their vaccination status.[26] As of November 2021, Texas and Montana were the only states that prohibited employers from requiring proof of vaccination.

County Sheriffs Refusing to Enforce State Orders

In states where the governor, state legislature, or public health officials did implement mask and vaccine mandates, there was some resistance from the local government officials tasked with enforcing these mandates, especially county sheriffs. In all states except Alaska, Hawaii, Connecticut, and Rhode Island, the county sheriffs play an important role in enforcing state and local laws within their jurisdictions. In most counties, the sheriff's office is not only responsible for executing the law and policies of their state, including issuing citations and making arrests, but often they also administer the local jail(s) and provide security for county courthouses and other public property. In many rural counties, the sheriff's office is the primary law enforcement agency, whereas sheriffs in many urban counties serve the unincorporated areas beyond the patrol of municipal police departments.

Although sheriffs operate as an appendage of the state government wherever they are found, they enjoy a degree of independence from the governor, the state legislature, and even the county government, by virtue of their being elected independently by the voters. Sheriffs' offices may be, in a legal sense, agents of the state, but the state government can rarely dictate how a sheriff ought to do his or her job. For example, sheriffs in many states enjoy broad discretion over the hiring and firing of employees, the day-to-day operation of their offices, and setting policies about the priority assigned to enforcing different laws. Sheriffs exercise this discretion in view of the county's voters, who have the power to reward or punish the sheriff at the next election.

During the coronavirus pandemic, a number of sheriffs across the country announced that they would not enforce emergency measures such as stay-at-home orders and curfews, social distancing and maximum occupancy rules, and mandates for mask wearing and vaccination.[27] Some of these sheriffs voiced concerns about the feasibility of enforcing these policies, while others highlighted the risks to their reputation if they were seen enforcing unpopular rules against the public.

Other sheriffs argued that emergency orders were an overreach of power by the state government, echoing similar claims made by so-called constitutional sheriffs who claim their office has greater authority than the state or federal governments.[28] The constitutional sheriffs, many of whom have refused to enforce other state laws in the past (such as gun control laws), feel they are empowered to resist unlawful orders because they are directly elected by the voters in their counties.[29] Some in the movement have ties to militia groups and other right-wing movements.[30] Although research on the extent of the constitutional sheriff movement is ongoing, we have identified such sheriffs asserting their authority to resist emergency orders and mandates in several states, including Arizona, Arkansas, Florida, Maine, Michigan, Nevada, Oregon, and Washington.[31] It is important to note, however, that not all sheriffs who resist emergency orders are members of this extreme movement.

In California, sheriffs from four major counties refused to enforce Governor Gavin Newsom's fall 2020 curfew, which required Californians to stay home between 10:00 p.m. and 5:00 a.m. ahead of the Thanksgiving season.[32] Sheriffs in Los Angeles, Sacramento, Orange, and Fresno Counties announced they would not commit deputies to enforcing emergency measures at local businesses, opting instead to focus on an "education-first approach" and voluntary compliance.[33] None of the four California sheriffs, representing nearly half of the state's population, claim membership in the constitutional sheriff movement. Opposition to Governor Newsom's emergency orders was fierce across the state, including in Southern California, the Central Valley, and the rural north of the state. Sheriffs in Butte, El Dorado, Fresno, Glenn, Kings, Merced, Placer, Shasta, Solano, Stanislaus, Sutter, and Tulare Counties also refused to enforce the governor's pandemic orders, at least at some point in 2020.[34] The Riverside County sheriff, for example, vowed that his deputies would "not be blackmailed, bullied or used as muscle" to enact the stay-at-home order.[35] The sheriff in San Diego County next door, however, committed half a dozen deputies to assist local health officials in enforcing the policies.

As the pandemic progressed beyond the initial two-week "wait and see" period, state and local officials continued to issue emergency orders to abate the virus's spread. Mask mandates were one such emergency measure implemented in a majority of states: thirty-nine states had a mask mandate at some point in 2020.[36] Sheriffs in several states quickly announced that their departments would not enforce mandates for wearing masks in indoor settings, citing a common refrain that voluntary compliance would be a more effective use of police resources.[37] In other cases, sheriffs demurred, saying either that they lacked clear authority to enforce such orders for mask wearing (with some sheriffs suggesting this authority rested with local health officials) or that they opposed the use of state power to force compliance with health orders. For example, the sheriff of Butler County in Ohio, Richard Jones, announced he would not be "the mask police."[38] Even in Republican-led states, some sheriffs refused to enforce mask mandates and other orders issued by Republican governors (for example, Texas).[39]

The sheriff of Los Angeles County, Alex Villanueva, has been a vocal critic of Governor Gavin Newsom and local health officials, announcing to the public on multiple occasions that he would not enforce stay-at-home orders, curfews, mask mandates, or vaccine mandates for his employees. As of October 2021, Sheriff Villanueva refused to enforce a new indoor mask mandate issued by the county's public health department.[40]

As vaccine mandates were rolled out at the federal, state, and local levels in 2021, some sheriffs' offices announced that they would not require their employees (including deputies) to be vaccinated. As of November, Los Angeles County's sheriff Villanueva refused to enforce a vaccine mandate directed at police officers and other public employees, citing concerns that noncompliant deputies would leave the department. Villanueva told reporters for the *Los Angeles Times*, "The collective risk [of losing sheriff's deputies] does not justify this type of an intrusion [the mandate]."[41] Sheriffs in other states, including Pinal County in Arizona, Spokane County in Washington, and Knox County in Tennessee, have announced their opposition to vaccine mandates.[42]

According to sheriff researcher Jessica Pishko, sheriffs have stated similar opposition to vaccine mandates in Arkansas, Iowa, Missouri, Oklahoma, Oregon, and Texas.[43] As of this writing, it is unclear whether the vaccine mandates in place by November 2021 had led to a mass exodus of law enforcement workers.[44] The South Carolina Sheriffs' Association, an industry group that represents sheriffs across the Palmetto State, issued a blanket statement that deputies there could not and would not enforce President Biden's vaccine mandate.[45]

The Biden Administration Vaccine Mandate

Finally, although this book addresses state emergency powers, we note one federal example. In September 2021, President Biden announced a federal vaccine mandate covering all federal employees and employees of businesses that employed more than one hundred people. According to the terms of his executive order, either vaccination or weekly testing was required. In refusing to issue nationwide instructions in 2019–2020, the Trump administration contended that the federal government lacked constitutional authority; it was the responsibility of states to exercise the emergency powers authorized by their constitutions and statutes. The Biden administration contended that the Occupational Safety and Health Administration (OSHA) had the authority to enforce the mandate under a 1970 law that permitted the agency to suspend its lengthy rule-approval process and issue an emergency temporary standard, or ETS. Within a few days of the president's announcement, twenty-four states had announced their plans to bring suit.[46] Several district courts issued temporary stays against enforcement of the federal mandate, and another federal court issued a nationwide injunction against enforcement of the mandate.[47]

In early January 2022 the US Supreme Court blocked the federal mandate, ruling that OSHA lacked the statutory authority to issue the ETS, although in a separate case the Court let stand a mandate applied to health care workers in facilities that received federal funds.[48] OSHA then withdrew the ETS, although not foreclosing the possibility of acting in other ways consistent with its statutory authority.

The preceding survey of efforts to restrict the use of state emergency powers suggests two trends, one procedural, the other substantive. First, many citizens and their representatives in legislatures and other bodies have concluded that state laws concentrate too much power in the hands of governors and public health authorities: nearly all efforts to modify state emergency powers focus on restricting their use or expanding the group of people or bodies authorized to employ them. Second, as the pandemic continues, the pendulum seems to be moving away from an exclusive focus on protecting the community from COVID infections and toward a more inclusive focus on protecting other values such as individual liberties as well. In the early days of the pandemic, public support for restrictions on individual liberties was largely unquestioned, but as experience with the restrictions and their associated effects accumulated, the public became more skeptical.[49] In short, fundamental questions of representation in decision making, and accountability for determining the trade-offs involved in decision making have increasingly come to the fore. That is the subject of our concluding chapter.

Notes

Appendix 1, which contains the database compiled for this chapter, may be found at https://www.hoover.org/research/who-governs-emergency-powers-time-covid.

1. At least not yet. Continuing drought in the American Southwest may impinge on the lives of people living in major metropolitan areas and already has seriously affected farming in these states.

2. This section relies heavily on the excellent summaries prepared by Ballotpedia. In particular, "Changes to State Emergency Power Laws in Response to the Coronavirus (COVID-19) Pandemic, 2020–2022," https://ballotpedia.org/Changes_to_state_emergency_power_laws_in_response_to_the_coronavirus_(COVID-19)_pandemic,_2020-2022 (accessed March 1, 2022).

3. Derick Hutchinson, "Here Are All 140 Executive Orders Issued by Michigan Gov. Whitmer during COVID-19 Pandemic," *Click on Detroit*, June 3, 2020 (updated July 2, 2020).

4. Jason Slotkin, "Michigan Supreme Court Rules against Governor's Emergency Powers," NPR, October 3, 2020.

5. Sergio Martínez-Beltrán, "Michigan Lawmakers Repeal Whitmer Powers Months after Court Overturned Them," *Bridge Michigan*, July 21, 2021.

6. SB 40 (Kan. 2021).

7. Karen DeWitt, "With COVID-19 Waning, Cuomo Retains Emergency Powers," WXXI News, June 17, 2021.

8. Bill Chappell, "New York Legislature Strips Cuomo of Extraordinary Emergency Powers, with a Caveat," NPR, March 5, 2021.

9. Ohio Rev. Code § 3715.74 (2020).

10. Jennifer Stefano, "Pennsylvania Lawmakers Aim to Keep Tom Wolf at Bay," *Wall Street Journal*, March 26, 2021.

11. Some of the proposed limits by Republican legislators appeared to be drawn from the model Emergency Power Limitation Act, written by the conservative American Legislative Exchange Council (January 8, 2021). Others were home-grown reflections of state and local conditions. https://www.alec.org/model-policy/emergency-power-limitation-act.

12. Holly Ramer, "Churches Deemed Essential in Future States of Emergency," *AP News*, August 11, 2021.

13. Amy Korte, "Illinois Teachers Unions Push Bill for New Health Rules on All In-Person Schooling," *Illinois Policy*, April 29, 2021.

14. "State of Florida, Office of the Governor, Executive Order Number 21-81," https://www.flgov.com/wp-content/uploads/2021/04/EO-21-81.pdf.

15. Office of Governor Ron DeSantis, "Governor DeSantis Issues an Executive Order Ensuring Parents' Freedom to Choose," news release, July 30, 2021, https://www.flgov.com/2021/07/30/governor-desantis-issues-an-executive-order-ensuring-parents-freedom-to-choose.

16. Jon Brodkon, "Florida Order Requiring All Schools to Reopen Was Illegal, Judge Rules," *Ars Technica*, August 25, 2020; Adriana Gomez Licon and Mike Schneider, "Florida Mayors Defy Governor with Their Own Mask, Vaccine Mandates," Associated Press, July 29, 2021.

17. Office of the Texas Governor, "Governor Abbott Issues Executive Order 39 Prohibiting Vaccine Mandates in Texas," August 25, 2021, https://gov.texas.gov/news/post/governor-abb-iss-execut-order-39-prohibiting-vaccine-mandates-in-texas.

18. Mitchell Ferman and James Barragan, "Texas Bill to Block COVID-19 Vaccine Mandates for Employers Failed in Legislature after Business Groups Rallied against It," *Texas Tribune*, October 18, 2021.

19. US Department of Education, "Department of Education's Office for Civil Rights Opens Investigations in Five States Regarding Prohibitions of Universal Indoor Masking," news release, August 30, 2021.

20. Meg Kinnard, "Court Keeps South Carolina School Mask Mandate Ban on Hold," Associated Press, October 5, 2021.

21. Ashley Sharp, "'People Are Ready for Freedom and Liberty': Tenn. Lawmakers Pass Restrictions on Mask, Vaccine Mandates," WJHL News, November 1, 2021.

22. Ken Miller, "Oklahoma School Mask Mandate Ban Blocked, Exemptions a Must," Associated Press, September 1, 2021.

23. Associated Press, "Arizona High Court Upholds Ruling Blocking School Mask Bans," *US News & World Report*, November 2, 2021.

24. The twenty-one states cited by NASHP are Alabama, Alaska, Arizona, Arkansas, Florida, Georgia, Idaho, Indiana, Iowa, Kansas, Mississippi, Missouri, Montana, North Dakota, Oklahoma, Tennessee, Texas, South Carolina, South Dakota, Utah, and Wyoming. Ed Browne, "The US States Where Covid Vaccine Mandates Are Banned and Allowed," *Newsweek*, October 20, 2021.

25. The thirteen states cited by KFF are Alabama, Arizona, Arkansas, Florida, Georgia, Idaho, Michigan, Montana, New Hampshire, South Dakota, Tennessee, Texas, and Utah. Kaiser Family Foundation, "State COVID-19 Data and Policy Actions," December 14, 2021, https://www.kff.org/report-section/state-COVID-19-data-and-policy-actions-policy-actions.

26. KQED, "Montana Private Hospitals Could Lose Funding Due to State Ban on Vaccine Mandates," NPR, October 31, 2021.

27. Maurice Chammah, "The Rise of the Anti-Lockdown Sheriffs," Marshall Project, May 18, 2020.

28. Jason Wilson, "US Sheriffs Rebel against State Mask Orders Even as COVID-19 Spreads," *Guardian* (US edition), July 31, 2020.

29. Zoe Nemerever, "Why 'Constitutionalist Sheriffs' Won't Enforce Coronavirus Restrictions," *Washington Post*, April 23, 2020; Kimberly Kindy, "Boosted by the Pandemic, 'Constitutional Sheriffs' Are a Political Force," *Washington Post*, November 2, 2021.

30. Luke Mogelson, "The Militias against Masks," *New Yorker*, August 17, 2020.

31. See, respectively: Jessica Pishko, "He Calls Himself the 'American Sheriff.' Whose Law Is He Following?" *Politico*, October 15, 2021; Mark Gregory, "Sheriff: Won't Cite Mask-Rule Violators," *Arkansas Democrat Gazette*, July 20, 2020; Alessandro Marazzi Sassoon, "'Constitutional Sheriff' Wayne Ivey Says He's a Patriot. Others See Something More Menacing," *Florida Today*, July 22, 2021; Dan Neumann, "Franklin Co. Sheriff Touts Award from Far-Right Group Promoting Defiance of State, Federal Laws," *Beacon* (Maine), October 8, 2020; Ted Roelofs, "Michigan's 'Constitutional Sheriffs' Vow to Keep Voters Safe at Polls," *Bridge Michigan*, October 14, 2020; Associated Press, "Rural Nevada Counties Join Constitutional Sheriff's Group," *US News*, June 22, 2021; Hillary Borrud, "Oregon 'Constitutional Sheriffs' Seize on Mask Mandates to Attack State Government's Authority," *Oregonian*, August 27, 2021; Martin Kaste, "When Sheriffs Won't Enforce the Law," NPR, February 21, 2019.

32. Jerusalem Demsas, "Southern California Sheriffs Are Refusing to Enforce Stay-at-Home Orders," *Vox*, December 10, 2020.

33. Aila Slisco, "Some California Sheriffs Won't Enforce Newsom Curfew, LA to Focus on 'Voluntary Compliance,'" *Newsweek*, November 20, 2020.

34. Alanea Cremen, "13 Law Enforcement Agencies That Refuse to Enforce California's New Curfew and Why," ABC-10, November 20, 2020; Austin Herbaugh, "COVID Curfew: Northstate Agencies Say They Won't Enforce Newsom's Order," KRCR, November 20, 2020.

35. Richard Allyn, "Which Southern California Sheriffs Are Defying New Stay-at-Home Order?" CBS-8, December 7, 2020.

36. Ballotpedia, "State-Level Mask Requirements in Response to the Coronavirus (COVID-19) Pandemic, 2020–2022," https://ballotpedia.org/State-level_mask_requirements_in_response_to_the_coronavirus_(COVID-19)_pandemic,_2020-2022 (accessed March 1, 2022).

37. Tom Knight, "Why Law Enforcement Isn't Enforcing Mask Mandates," *The Hill*, July 30, 2020.

38. Hannah Sparling, "Butler County Sheriff Richard Jones Says He Won't Enforce Mask Mandate," *Cincinnati.com*, July 7, 2020.

39. Sophie Lewis, "Growing Number of Texas Sheriffs Refuse to Enforce Governor's Mask Requirement," CBS News, July 8, 2020.

40. Sophie Kasakove, "Los Angeles County's Sheriff Declines to Enforce the Mask Mandate About to Resume," *New York Times*, July 17, 2021.

41. Alene Tchekmedyian, Kevin Rector, and Richard Winton, "As Villaneuva Blasts Vaccine Mandate, Sheriff's Department Falls Further Behind LAPD in Shots," *Los Angeles Times*, November 3, 2021.

42. Kelly Ann Krueger, "'I Will Not Comply with This Unconstitutional Order' Knox Co. Sheriff writes to President Biden," WVLT, October 25, 2021.

43. Jessica Pishko, "Not Anti-Vax, but Pro-Freedom (for Some)," *Posse Comitatus* (newsletter), September 21, 2021, https://sheriffs.substack.com/p/not-anti-vax-but-pro-freedom-for.

44. Jessica Pishko, "How Law Enforcement Tried to Capitalize on Vaccine Mandates and Failed," *Slate*, November 5, 2021.

45. Marcus Flowers, "S.C. Sheriff's Association Says Officers Cannot Enforce President Biden's Vaccine Mandate," *MSN*, September 18, 2021.

46. Paul Wiseman, "Small Agency, Big Job: Biden Tasks OSHA with Vaccine Mandate," Associated Press, September 16, 2021.

47. Dareh Gregorian, "Judge Issues Nationwide Injunction against Biden's Vaccine Mandate for Federal Contractors," NBC News, December 7, 2021.

48. Adam Liptak, "Supreme Court Blocks Biden's Virus Mandate for Large Employers," *New York Times*, January 13, 2022.

49. Nate Cohn, "Americans Are Frustrated with the Pandemic: These Polls Show How Much," *New York Times*, February 8, 2022.

Chapter 9

COVID Restrictions and Democratic Governance

Morris P. Fiorina

As discussed in chapter 6, when news of the coming COVID-19 pandemic first broke, public opinion strongly supported government restrictions on citizens' movements and activities. Public health officials asserted that however economically costly or personally inconvenient, such actions were necessary to prevent a runaway epidemic that would overwhelm the health care system—the overriding necessity was to "flatten the curve." At first, large majorities of Americans "trusted the science" and the scientists. Many citizens followed public health recommendations such as social distancing, mask wearing, and staying home even in areas where restrictions were not ordered or before they were ordered, a fact that has made estimating the efficacy of the various measures difficult.[1] But although public concern about the coronavirus remained steady and high, support for travel limitations, restrictions on social gatherings, school closures, and other measures gradually declined, especially during the first four months of the pandemic in the spring and early summer of 2020.[2] Moreover, with the exception of mask wearing, people's reports of actually following CDC recommendations dropped significantly over the same time period.[3] The decline was greater for Republicans as the pandemic became increasingly politicized, but support among Democrats and Independents fell too, as questions about both the science and the experts gradually increased.

Fair and Efficacious Restrictions?

Commentators often attributed declining support for government restrictions to "COVID fatigue," suggesting that Americans were becoming increasingly frustrated by remote working and learning, the absence of social interaction, limitations on their everyday activities, and living in a state of continual stress.[4] Parenthetically, my suspicion is that the latter deserves more attention relative to the more tangible behavioral restrictions than it has received—the public health establishment seemed determined to find the dark lining in every silver cloud.[5] At least that is what the national media reported.[6] But COVID fatigue is a label, not an explanation. It was not simply a psychological state of mind; arguably it had a rational basis in reality. As the economic, mental health, educational, and other costs mounted, Americans became increasingly skeptical. Were the widely imposed restrictions with their attendant costs truly efficacious? If so, were they worth the costs? And were they fair? To be sure, in a large demographically and geographically heterogeneous country, working under conditions of great uncertainty, it would be miraculous if even the most competent and public-spirited health authorities could promulgate regulations that would be universally regarded as both fair and effective. In the absence of such miracles, it was not surprising that some people began to view public health orders as unfair and unnecessary, in a word, arbitrary. Such perceptions had myriad sources.

One controversy emerged very soon after the first shutdowns. "Essential" businesses could and should remain open, but what was an essential business? Grocery stores certainly were essential, but were liquor stores? Public health authorities in every state but Pennsylvania thought so.[7] Businesses classified as inessential naturally were aggrieved about their designation. And although not businesses, many churches and their congregations did not consider themselves inessential. Because big-box stores like Walmart and Costco sell groceries, they remained open while mom-and-pop stores that sold some of the same products (e.g., clothing) were classified as inessential and required to close. Some people restricted to their homes decided to plant vegetable gardens. They could buy plants and supplies in big-box stores but local garden centers initially were closed in some areas. As such clear inequities accumulated, many jurisdictions imposed restrictions on the products that big-box stores could sell, but there is no question that such large stores prospered during the pandemic, while the same cannot be said for small businesses.[8] The restrictions were particularly damaging for minority-owned small businesses.[9]

Some observers suggested that rather than classify businesses and activities as essential or inessential, COVID restrictions should address whether businesses could be operated safely. Perhaps a spacious hair salon or barbershop could rearrange a reduced number of chairs in a socially distant configuration and operate safely. Similarly, a sizable restaurant could operate safely with a reduced number of tables. A large old cathedral might allow a small number of congregants to socially distance and worship safely. While the suggestion seems sensible at first glance, in practice it would likely require physical inspections of each business—a practical impossibility—to determine which could operate safely. Moreover, businesses that did not make the cut would be angry about their competitors who did.

Finally, given the prevailing low levels of trust in government, it is not surprising that some Americans wondered whether politics affected the content of the shutdown orders. Indeed, there is some evidence of political influence in deciding which businesses and industries were included in essential business declarations. One study estimated that a business sector whose members had made a campaign contribution to the state governor in the preceding election was 10 percent more likely to be classified as essential in the first state essential declaration than one that had not.[10]

A second source of popular disaffection arose from what many viewed as overly broad restrictions. For example, during the spring 2020 surge, California governor Gavin Newsom ordered the closure of public parks, beaches, and playgrounds.[11] Coupled with restrictions on travel, the governor's order put much of the California population nearly under house arrest. Given that available information increasingly indicated that the risk of COVID transmission was much lower outside than inside, the restrictions seemed not only heavy-handed, but also counterproductive in that they would spur people to recreate inside, where the risk of virus transmission was higher. As the pandemic went on, some courts began to ask for evidence that health restrictions under challenge were in fact supported by evidence.[12] A Los Angeles court blocked a county ban on outdoor dining, writing that the ban "is an abuse of the [Health] Department's emergency powers, [and] is not grounded in science, evidence, or logic."[13] During the 2020 holiday surge the State of California once again ordered playgrounds closed only to rescind the order after backlash from health experts, politicians, and parents.[14]

A third source of dissatisfaction arose from the decentralized governmental structure of the US. Given any amount of geographic or social/demographic heterogeneity, no COVID restriction can possibly fit all parts of a polity equally well. A regulation perfectly appropriate for Paris or London may be far too stringent for a small village in Brittany or Wales. The decentralized institutional structure of the United States multiplied such geographical complications many times over. Early in the pandemic Governor Whitmer of Michigan issued a controversial stay-at-home order prohibiting Michigan residents from visiting their vacation homes.[15] The problem was that some residents of other states continued to visit *their* vacation homes in Michigan. Lake Tahoe ski resorts on the California side of the state border generally operated under greater restrictions than those on the Nevada side of the border.[16] At times, Sonoma County wineries were subject to more restrictions than Napa County wineries only a short distance away.[17] In many cases like these, local conditions seemed virtually identical, but emergency orders binding the larger units in which localities were included created significant disparities in who was allowed to do what.

Close to home, Stanford University found itself on the more restricted side of such jurisdictional differences. Stanford's eight thousand acres span two counties and four smaller cities and towns, but the university officially lies in Santa Clara County, which took a highly restrictive stance on all things COVID-related. In contrast, neighboring San Mateo County adopted a notably more lenient approach. The result was significantly different enforcement of restrictions on businesses and institutions only a few blocks apart.[18] Sports were especially affected. To hold practices, the Stanford football team had to board buses and travel to a high school field seven miles away in San Mateo County.[19] The net health benefits of the arrangement were not obvious. The university's men's and women's basketball teams spent two months living and playing on the road until Santa Clara County allowed them to return to campus to practice and play.[20] Stanford was not alone. The San Francisco Forty Niners were forced to decamp to Arizona for the final month of their season.[21] And the San Jose State football program created a stir by defying the county's order and flying to Las Vegas for their first bowl game in five years.[22]

Santa Clara County's strict COVID regimen created conflicts even within county jurisdictions. In the late spring of 2020 drive-by celebrations of birthdays and graduations became common. While the county was under a stay-at-home order, friends and relatives of those to be celebrated would organize car caravans to drive by the honoree's house, honking car horns in celebration. Sometimes local first responders even joined the caravans with official vehicles operating their sirens and flashing their lights. These feel-good occasions received considerable attention on local TV. In response the county public health director issued a stern rebuke of county residents and directed local police departments to enforce the stay-at-home order.[23] This directive elicited an exasperated response from the San Jose police chief, who complained to the media that his department was dealing with serious criminals being released with no bail and the health department expected his officers to crack down on people in their cars who were honking their horns.[24] Similarly, San Jose mayor Sam Liccardo complained that although "I understand that we are not their bosses," there needed to be more communication and explanation from county health officials.[25]

Santa Clara County's next-door neighbor adopted a more liberal stance. As the winter holiday surge began, the San Mateo County health officer found it advisable to explain to county residents why he was not following other counties, particularly neighboring Santa Clara, in imposing a new stay-at-home order. Explaining that he was focusing on the broader picture, not just COVID case rates, he wrote:

> The State has already put significant restrictions on businesses and the public space in San Mateo County. I am aware of no data that some of the business activities on which even greater restrictions are being put into place with this new order are the major drivers of transmission. In fact, I think these greater restrictions are likely to drive more activity indoors, a much riskier endeavor. While I don't have scientific evidence to support this, I also believe these greater restrictions will result in more job loss, more hunger, more despair and desperation (the structure of our economy is, for the most part, if you don't work, you don't eat or have a roof over your head), and more death from causes other than COVID. And I wonder, are these premature deaths any less worrisome than COVID deaths?
>
> ... I don't see us (governmental public health) looking at data other than case rates and positivity rates and hospital rates in order to make balanced decisions. When you only look at one thing, you only see one thing.[26]

Follow the Science, Except When . . .

At the beginning of the pandemic, trust in public officials and the public health experts who advised them was high. Dr. Anthony Fauci, for example, achieved near rock-star status.[27] But politics quickly intruded into the COVID conversation. Partisan commentators linked each positive or negative state trend in case frequency or hospitalizations to how the Democratic or Republican governor had handled or mishandled the situation despite little evidence that either party's officials performed better or worse by standard metrics.[28] Policy advocates selectively pointed to the experiences of other countries to support their recommendations for actions the United States should undertake or refrain from undertaking.[29] As the prospect of an effective vaccine increased, interest groups began jockeying for preferred placement of their members.[30] Not surprisingly, ordinary people increasingly realized that not all of their fellow citizens were equally committed to "following the science." This realization took off with a vengeance in the winter of 2021 when settled science proved no match for political power. Opening the schools was the arena in which science and politics clashed, to the detriment of the former.

In late March 2020 all US public schools shut down. By late May all states but Idaho and Wyoming had announced that schools would remain closed for the remainder of the academic year.[31] By autumn, however, the data showed that children rarely contracted serious cases of COVID and schools were not significant sources of community transmission.[32] Schools all over Europe opened (although some later closed temporarily during the holiday surge).[33] In the United States hundreds of private schools and charter schools opened, as did many public schools in smaller jurisdictions. Even in the face of mounting evidence of learning loss and mental health problems, especially among poorer children and ethnic minorities, however, schools remained closed in many big city public school systems where the teachers' unions were strongest. As the weeks passed, even liberal commentators called for schools to reopen.[34] In early December, with a third of the school year already lost, the *San Francisco Chronicle* called for the reopening of the schools.[35] In January Chicago narrowly averted a teachers' strike before a deal to reopen was reached.[36] In Los Angeles, the unions not only refused to return to in-person teaching but demanded policy concessions such as defunding the police and Medicare for All, whose relationship to education was, at a minimum, unclear.[37] Reflecting the growing frustration, one Southern California journalist wrote that the unions would not allow their members to return to the classroom "until COVID-19 is entirely gone, or all living beings in the Milky Way galaxy have been vaccinated, or the Rapture. Whichever comes first."[38]

Of course, some teachers with underlying health conditions had legitimate concerns about returning to the classroom, and some parents were indeed fearful of allowing their children to return to in-class learning, but for many people familiar with the science about COVID transmission, continued union recalcitrance was unacceptable.[39] By the time spring 2021 arrived, protests became increasingly common.[40] And with the school year dwindling away, a bipartisan group of governors pressured the unions and educational bureaucracy to open the schools.[41] In California, the situation contributed to a drive to recall Governor Newsom, and more generally, to an outbreak of "recall fever" in the words of the *Los Angeles Times*.[42]

The Deeper Questions

As noted in the preface to this volume, although the chapters focus mainly on the exercise of emergency powers during the COVID pandemic, the larger purpose is to raise several more general questions about emergency powers and democratic governance—questions that deserve serious consideration before the arrival of the next public health emergency requires another exercise of such powers. These questions are fundamental ones involving representation and accountability, which are essential components of representative democracy. Put most simply, in a democracy, citizens choose public officials to represent them and hold these officials accountable for their actions. The mechanism for selecting officials and holding them to account is free elections. The presumption is that whether motivated by public spirit or electoral ambition, public officials will do their best to represent the interests of their constituents.[43] The exercise of emergency powers during the pandemic clearly infringes on these democratic prerequisites, raising serious questions about the *legitimacy* of actions taken under emergency powers. In the years ahead, those committed to democratic governance should think about ways to keep such infringements to a minimum.

Accountability

On March 16, 2020, six *unelected* county public health officials and the health officer of Berkeley issued stay-at-home orders for the Bay Area jurisdictions that employed them. Appointed health officials in other jurisdictions around the country followed suit. Regardless of their efficacy, and however well-intended, these are problematic developments. To whom are such officials accountable? Across the country some are directly appointed by mayors or other elected officials, but many of them are appointed by a higher unelected official, such as a county executive or city manager.[44] Some have civil service status. Many are in a literal sense unaccountable to the publics whom they regulate, or at best, accountable only at a far remove.

Of course, bureaucratic discretion is a normal feature of public administration, but issuance of executive orders by local health officials differs from normal administration in which state or federal agencies issue specific regulations to implement a general law. In normal administration, appointed officials implement laws that have been passed by elected legislatures and signed into law by elected executives. When public health officials issue emergency orders, however, they are unilaterally *suspending* democratically adopted laws, regulations, and liberties. Skeptics may object that this is a distinction without a difference because, as chapter 2 details, state constitutions and statutes have delegated broad authority to public officials to act under emergency conditions. The constitutionality of such broad delegations of power increasingly is a matter of controversy in legal circles, however, and as Ochoa discusses in chapter 7, in some cases overly broad delegations have been overturned by the courts.[45] The same concerns arise here. More on this below.

A newspaper story on the first anniversary of the San Francisco Bay Area shutdown order reported:

> In a year framed by near-impossible choices in the coronavirus pandemic—between saving lives and causing widespread economic and

social devastation—the decision to issue the first shelter-in-place order in the United States and shut down the Bay Area ended up being one of the easiest, said Dr. Sara Cody.

It didn't feel that way on the gray and cold morning of March 16, when the order was announced. Cody, the Santa Clara County health officer, and her peers from six other Bay Area health jurisdictions, had barely slept. They'd spent the entire day before, a Sunday, crafting the health order, and the county lawyers had stayed up all night fine-tuning the language.

"We barely had time for the ink to dry before we ran downstairs and gave the press conference," Cody said in a recent interview.

The announcement came at noon. Just before, she recalled, she was in a conference room with the other health officers—from Alameda, Marin, Contra Costa, San Francisco and San Mateo counties, and from the City of Berkeley. They sat around a table, quietly exhausted, Cody said, "and we looked at each other, like, 'Are we really going to do it?'"[46]

Not a word here about democratically elected officials, only lawyers and appointed health officers asking "are we really going to do it?" Not until three days later did Governor Newsom weigh in with a statewide order. Dr. Cody later noted that "this really unilateral decision making is really a breathtaking departure from normal public health practice because normal public health practice is all about stakeholder engagement and shared decision making."[47] She added that local elected officials could not have acted as quickly or as boldly as the public health officers did.[48]

Clearly, democratic legitimacy would be enhanced if emergency orders were issued only by elected executives—governors and mayors or elected representative bodies such as legislatures and boards of supervisors—*following* a declared emergency by those elected officials. On rare occasions conditions might be so dire that there is insufficient time to get approval from elected officials, but one can imagine only a few cases that might require such immediate action: perhaps if earthquake prediction models became so accurate that public health officials received notice that a major earthquake would occur in a matter of hours, or a utility notified them that a nuclear reactor was about to melt down. In such rare cases, a commitment to democratic decision making suggests that emergency orders issued by unelected officials should be short-term, in effect only for a matter of hours or days until reissued by appropriate elected officials. It seems doubtful that the threat of COVID-19 was so imminent that local health officials could not take a day to seek formal approval of their proposed regulations by elected governing bodies.

In legal circles there is a long-standing debate about the role of an unelected judiciary in a democracy.[49] In particular, how does judicial review—wherein unelected judges overturn a law passed by an elected legislature and signed by an elected executive—square with the democratic process? Such judicial activism raises the same kind of questions about democratic legitimacy that unelected health officers do: federal judges are unaccountable to popular majorities, except under extreme circumstances.[50] Ironically, then, some legal commentators believe that these same unelected judges could play a significant role in limiting the powers of unelected health officers, as well as of elected officials. As Ochoa discusses in chapter 7, courts have traditionally given wide latitude to the other branches when emergency powers are invoked. But over the years the courts have increased the weight they attach to civil liberties when public health orders impinge on those liberties.[51] And the COVID pandemic has stimulated additional thinking about the matter, with arguments that courts should be more skeptical of emergency actions, especially where civil liberties are concerned.[52] Lindsay Wiley and Stephen Vladeck warn:

> The more that courts coalesce around a standard in which governments are held to exceedingly modest burdens of justification for incursions into our civil liberties during emergencies, the more those same governments might be incentivized not only to use emergencies as pretexts for scaling back our rights, but also to find pretexts for triggering such emergencies in the first place.[53]

The notion that governments might trump up emergencies in order to trample our liberties might seem a bit far-fetched, but democratic theorists long have recognized that power corrupts, as the old saying goes.[54] In the statement referenced earlier, the San Mateo health officer wrote: "Just because one has the legal authority to do something, doesn't mean one has to use it, or that using it is the best course of action."[55] My impression is that during the pandemic relatively few health officers were so modest. No doubt the great majority of public health officials are motivated only by the desire to maximize the health and safety of their communities. But for a small minority the exercise of emergency powers may be addictive—difficult to give up to elected officials they see as less qualified to make decisions that affect public health. Moreover, as noted in the next section of this chapter, in their zeal to minimize the impact of COVID on the health and safety of their communities, they may lose sight of other important considerations.

Finally, even if emergency orders are issued only by elected officials, there remain the empirically intertwined questions of which elected officials, the duration of their public health orders, and the termination of those orders. As chapter 2 describes, in more than three-quarters of the states the governor has the power to declare an emergency; in the remaining states the legislature is involved to some degree. Given the plain meaning of "emergency," a primary role for the executive seems appropriate, but how long that primacy should last raises more questions, as the discussion in chapter 8 illustrates. In March 2021 the Ohio legislature passed legislation to limit the emergency powers of the governor.[56] Republican governor Mike DeWine vetoed the legislation, but the Republican legislature overrode his vetoes. The bills shifted considerable power from the executive back to the legislature. Under the new legislation the governor must renew the executive orders every sixty days, but the legislature can cancel any order after thirty days. The legislation also limited the authority of local health officials to quarantine citizens or to require them to self-isolate unless medically diagnosed and provided that Ohio citizens could sue as unconstitutional any health orders in their home county.

At about the same time, in neighboring Pennsylvania the Republican General Assembly approved two ballot measures that would limit the powers of Democratic governor Tom Wolf.[57] One would dramatically shorten the length of a disaster declaration from ninety days to twenty-one. The second would amend the state constitution to provide that the General Assembly by a simple majority could terminate or extend an emergency declaration, a resolution that would not be subject to gubernatorial veto. By the end of March 2001, more than three hundred proposals to limit gubernatorial powers had been introduced in the various states. Most were sponsored by Republican legislatures, but as in Ohio, some were aimed at Republican governors.[58]

Finally, I take note of the obvious rebuttal to the concerns raised in this section. Stepping back from a concern about democracy to the larger question of the democratic community's survival, might a lack of accountability sometimes be a good thing? Elected officials do not always want to be held accountable for their actions.[59] What if their very lack of accountability is what makes an unelected official willing to issue a draconian order that elected officials are too fearful to do? My belief is that most elected officials would prefer to act too quickly and too strongly rather than be held responsible for a health catastrophe, but I concede that it is an empirical question. Dr. Cody pointed out that her counterpart in New York City, who reports directly to the mayor, was unable to persuade him to issue a shelter-in-place order.[60] The possibility of a trade-off between accountability and the quality of policy decisions is a question that deserves serious examination.

Representation

No large-scale society operates under unanimity rules. Consequently, in real world democracies some interests win and some lose in normal policy making. But at a minimum, democracy demands that all significant interests have a chance to be heard—to have a seat at the table.[61] The experience of the COVID pandemic raises questions about whether that has been the case.

A prima facie question concerns the fact that a single public health official in some cases can assume near-dictatorial powers. One public health official can partially shut down the economy or suspend civil liberties in his or her jurisdiction. If elected, like mayors or governors, a single decision maker would be less of a problem, as just discussed—elected officials represent and are accountable to the constituencies that elected them. But public health officials are *selected*, not elected, and they are selected on the basis of their expertise, not because they represent the community. Concentrating such power in the hands of a single unelected official raises an immediate concern about the absence of representation.

A second problem of representation that arises from the experience of the pandemic is that the officials who promulgated emergency orders did not experience the costs of those orders. This is not a reference to the numerous reported cases in which public officials attended dinners, wedding receptions, and other social functions that were disallowed under existing regulations. Rather, no matter how stringent the policies that public health officials imposed, they continued to draw their salaries and accumulate their benefits. They suffered no personal cost from the shutdowns and other restrictions that damaged or destroyed the livelihoods of people who owned or worked in nonessential businesses. Probably their higher economic status allowed many of them to send their children to in-person schools more than was the case for the average citizen, or to engage paid help to make remote schooling easier. As a Harvard Medical School doctor dryly commented:

> Lockdowns have protected the laptop class of young low-risk journalists, scientists, teachers, politicians and lawyers, while throwing children, the working class and high-risk older people under the bus.[62]

Academic research documented the unequal economic and other costs associated with the pandemic.[63] The unequal impact of lockdowns and similar restrictions possibly contributed to the notable partisan difference in support for such policies noted in chapter 6. A higher proportion of Democrats than Republicans are public sector workers, with millions employed in education, government, and the nonprofit sector, parts of the economy generally less subject to pay cuts and layoffs—not to mention bankruptcies—than private sector workers.

Finally, former French prime minister Georges Clemenceau once said that "war is too important to be left to the generals." Much the same sentiment applies to the decisions by public health officials in pandemics. In the early days of the COVID pandemic, economics and business commentators argued that the public health benefits of shutdowns should be weighed against the likely economic costs. Civil libertarians raised the same concerns about trade-offs between shutdowns and civil liberties. My impression is that unlike the San Mateo County health officer quoted above, few public health officials gave more than lip service to the recognition of such trade-offs. Instead, most discounted them. As noted above, public health officials are chosen on the basis of expertise, not representativeness. Like all specialists, they exhibit a degree of tunnel vision, focusing on the variable their professional training emphasizes—public health in this case—and discounting much else. The Santa Clara County health officer remarked, "It's clear that public health officials have a singular focus and a duty and commitment to protect the public health; that's why we're in the field. I think it's immensely more complicated for elected officials."[64] Depending on your point of view, Dr. Cody is identifying a feature or a bug.

Dr. Fauci, who by most accounts performed admirably throughout the crisis, provided a striking illustration of the specialist perspective after a testy exchange with Jim Jordan (R-OH) at a congressional hearing, where Jordan charged that pandemic guidelines "trampled" on Americans' liberties. Fauci told CNN's Dana Bash, "This has *nothing* to do with liberties, Dana. We're talking about the fact that 560,000 people in our country have died. We're talking about [60,000] to 70,000 new infections per day. That's the issue. This is a public health issue. It's not a civil liberties issue" (my emphasis).[65] Probably most Americans would agree with Fauci that public health considerations often outweighed civil liberties infringements during the pandemic, but not that the latter are completely ignorable.

Public health officials were not alone in this regard. Some elected officials saw the issues raised by the pandemic similarly as one-sided as Fauci did. Democratic governors in blue states such as New York and California (chapter 3) tended to issue more stringent restrictions than Republican governors in red states such as Florida and Texas (chapter 4) did. New York governor Andrew Cuomo famously commented that "if everything we do saves just one life, I'll be happy."[66] No one really believes that, of course; if they did, they would lobby for five-mile-per-hour speed limits so almost no one would die in car accidents. Again, as the San Mateo County health officer quoted earlier commented on his profession's focus on infection rates, "When you only look at one thing, you only see one thing."[67] Regardless of whether they are issued by elected or appointed officials, the issuance and maintenance of emergency orders would have greater legitimacy if done by collective bodies more representative of the community, bodies that include health officers, but also others—economists, business leaders, educators, psychologists, clergy, and politicos who would articulate other interests held by community members. Indeed, according to the Santa Clara County health officer, "This unilateral decision making is really a breathtaking departure from normal public health practice because normal public health practice is all about stakeholder engagement and shared decision making.... So, this was quite different."[68] Perhaps after the initial response to the emergency there should be a greater emphasis on returning to the more normal public health practice where a "more holistic" approach is adopted.[69]

In his remarks, Governor Cuomo went on to comment that "no American is going to say accelerate the economy at the cost of human life. Because no American is going to say how much a life is worth."[70] Actually, of course, many Americans say just that virtually every day—personally and professionally. As a dissenting commentator on the political left observes:

In virtually every realm of public policy, Americans embrace policies which they know will kill people, sometimes large numbers of people. They do so not because they are psychopaths but because they are rational: they assess that those deaths that will inevitably result from the policies they support *are worth it* in exchange for the benefits those policies provide. This rational cost-benefit analysis, even when not expressed in such explicit or crude terms, is foundational to public policy debates—except when it comes to COVID, where it has been bizarrely declared off-limits.[71]

Program analysts evaluate the value of human lives when they do cost-benefit analyses of environmental, health and safety, and other regulations. Insurance companies and Medicare actuaries assign a value to human lives when they decide what drugs and procedures to cover. Courts decide how much lives are worth when they determine damages in lawsuits involving loss of lives. And speaking personally, as a reasonably healthy senior citizen, I may have some productive years left, but my life certainly is not worth anywhere near as much as the lives of my grandchildren, even less so if I had a serious illness or dementia. Treating all lives as equally valuable is a political decision, not a public health decision. In asserting that he would do anything to save one life, Governor Cuomo was attempting to camouflage a political decision as a public health decision.[72]

In responding to criticism that her department's response to the pandemic was too heavily focused on the pandemic itself and not on the other economic and social harms that accompanied it, Dr. Cody commented that it was a "fair criticism" to ask, "Why weren't we looking at health in a more holistic way?"[73] She went on to say,

> My challenge and the tension that I have felt over the last year and a half has been one feeling constrained, like as far as an order, I should really just think about communicable disease and I also know that all of these economic social (*sic*) harms translate to health harms. And it's like, I wished that I could take the economic and social harms and magically

convert them to some health harm scale, right? And then compare trade-offs. But that little formula, it doesn't exist, best I know.[74]

Unfortunately, Dr. Cody is correct. Such a scale does not exist. And lacking such a scale, the comparison of trade-offs is a matter of judgment, and in a democratic society, that judgment is a political one. The essence of political decision making is weighing benefits and costs—on whom they accrue, how much, when, and where. The case of emergency powers is more complex and consequential than day-to-day political decision making, but it cannot escape this basic fact. As such, the use of emergency powers should be studied and evaluated in the context of democratic governance, not set over and above it.

Notes

1. Dylan Scott, "California Mandated Masks. Florida Opened Its Restaurants. Did Any of It Matter?" *Vox*, June 3, 2021.

2. Wang, chapter 6. See also John Sides, Chris Tausanovitch, and Lynn Vavreck, "The Politics of COVID-19: Partisan Polarization about the Pandemic Has Increased, but Support for Health Care Reform Hasn't Moved at All," *Harvard Data Science Review*, November 30, 2020.

3. David Lazer, Mauricio Santillana, Roy H. Perlis, Alexi Quintana, Katherine Ognyanova, Jon Green, Matthew Baum et al., "The COVID States Project #26: Trajectory of COVID-19-Related Behaviors," OSF Preprints, February 2021.

4. "'COVID Fatigue' Is Hitting Hard. Fighting It Is Hard, Too, Says UC Davis Health Psychologist," UC Davis Health, July 7, 2020.

5. David Leonhardt, "Vaccine Alarmism," *New York Times*, February 19, 2021.

6. Bruce Sacerdote, Ranjan Sehgal, and Molly Cook, "Why Is All COVID-19 News Bad News?" National Bureau of Economic Research, November 2020.

7. Max Jordan, Nguemeni Tiako, and Kelsey C. Priest, "Yes, Liquor Stores Are Essential Businesses," *Scientific American*, April 7, 2020.

8. Teresa Rivas, "Mom and Pop Retailers Are Struggling during the Lockdowns. Big Box Giants Are Thriving," *Barron's*, May 22, 2020.

9. G. Cristina Mora and Eric Schickler, "Disparate Impact of Covid on CA Small Businesses: Minority Owners Most Negatively Impacted," UC Berkeley IGS Poll, October 4, 2021, https://escholarship.org/content/qt1jx6c3zw/qt1jx6c3zw.pdf.

10. Jesse M. Crosson and Srinivas C. Parinandi, "Essential or Expedient? COVID-19 and Business Closures in the US States," *Journal of Political Institutions and Political Economy* 2, no. 1 (2021): 81–102.

11. Hetty Chang and Robert Kovacik, "Governor Set to Close All Beaches and State Parks in California," NBC Los Angeles, April 29, 2020.

12. Jacob Sullum, "California Judge Blocks Enforcement of State and Local Bans on Restaurant Dining in San Diego County," *Reason*, December 18, 2020.

13. Christian Britschgi, "California Judge Says Los Angeles County's Outdoor Dining Ban Isn't 'Grounded in Science, Evidence, or Logic,'" *Reason*, December 10, 2020.

14. Amy Graf, "California Reverses Closure of Children's Playgrounds under New Order," *SFGate*, December 9, 2020.

15. Liz Skala, "Border Battles: Patchwork Rules Have Residents Questioning When to Cross State Lines," *The Blade*, April 18, 2020.

16. Dani Anguiano, "'Why Aren't They Home?' Lake Tahoe Struggles to Keep Winter Vacationers at Bay," *Guardian* (US edition), January 2, 2021.

17. Cheryl Sarfaty, "Where Wine Country Is with Coronavirus Reopening: Napa County Moves Up to 'Orange' Tier, Marin Close Behind," *North Bay Business Journal*, October 23, 2020.

18. Maggie Angst, "Why San Mateo County Businesses Are Far Less Likely to Get a COVID Fine Than Those in Santa Clara," *MSN*, March 28, 2021.

19. Robert Handa, "Stanford Football Team Holds Practice at Woodside High," NBC Bay Area, October 9, 2020.

20. Mechelle Voepel, "Inside Stanford Women's Basketball's Nine-Week Road Trip: Six States, 12 Flights and DIY Haircuts," ESPN, February 5, 2021.

21. Jeff Kerr, "49ers Will Play in Arizona for Remainder of 2020 Season after COVID-19 Restrictions Extended in Santa Clara," *CBS Sports*, December 18, 2020.

22. Henry Schulman, "Santa Clara County, San Jose State Remain at Odds over Pending Bowl Trip," *San Francisco Chronicle*, December 23, 2020.

23. Dan Thorn, "Santa Clara County Bans Car Parades Amid Pandemic," KRON-4 News, May 7, 2020.

24. Dustin Dorsey, "Coronavirus Impact: Santa Clara County Prohibits Drive-By Celebrations, Causing Confusion for Police, Community," ABC-7 News, May 7, 2020.

25. Eduardo Cuevas and Mauricio La Plante, "Santa Clara County Health Officials Criticized for Rollout of Latest Shelter-in-Place Order," *San Jose Spotlight*, June 8, 2020.

26. Scott Morrow, "December 7, 2020 Health Officer Statement," San Mateo County Health.

27. Ricki Lewis, "Dr. Fauci Evokes Memories of Past Rock Star Scientists," DNA Science (blog), *PLOS*, April 16, 2020.

28. German Lopez, "Everyone Failed on Covid-19," *Vox*, January 2, 2021; Lisa Lerer, "DeSantis Is Ascendant and Cuomo Is Faltering," *New York Times*, March 6, 2021.

29. Michael Hobbes, "'S**thole' Countries Have Handled the Coronavirus Better Than the United States," *Huffpost*, June 8, 2020.

30. Elaine S. Povich, "Interest Groups Lobby to Get Ahead in Vaccine Line," *Pew*, January 14, 2021.

31. Stacey Decker, Holly Peele, and Maya Riser-Kositsky, "The Coronavirus Spring: The Historic Closing of US Schools (A Timeline)," *Education Week*, July 1, 2020.

32. Anya Kamenetz, "Are the Risks of Reopening Schools Exaggerated?" NPR, October 21, 2020.

33. Anya Kamenetz, "Lessons from Europe, Where Cases Are Rising but Schools Are Open," NPR, November 13, 2020.

34. Nicholas Kristof, "When Trump Was Right and Many Democrats Wrong," *New York Times*, November 18, 2020.

35. "Editorial: California Should Be Ashamed of Its Shuttered Schools," *San Francisco Chronicle*, December 3, 2020.

36. Hannah Leone and Katherine Rosenberg-Douglas, "Chicago Public Schools Is Reopening after a Bitter Union Fight. Now the Hard Part Begins: Rebuilding Trust, and Making Good on Covid-19 Protection Vows," *Chicago Tribune*, February 11, 2021.

37. Bethany Blankley, "LA Teachers Union Says Public Schools Should Not Reopen Unless Demands Are Met," Center Square, July 13, 2020.

38. Joe Matthews, "Outsource School Reopenings to Amazon," *San Francisco Chronicle*, February 21, 2021.

39. Jonathan Chait, "Just Reopen the Schools Now," *New York Magazine*, March 16, 2021.

40. Christine Rosen, "Outraged Parents Take to the Streets over School Closures," *Commentary*, March 15, 2021.

41. Kate Taylor, "Fed Up with Remote Learning, Governors Make a Push to Reopen Schools," *New York Times*, April 3, 2021.

42. Jeremy B. White, "Too Little, Too Late? Schools Deal May Not Alter Newsom Recall Politics," *Politico*, March 4, 2021; Julia Wick, "Recall Fever Strikes California as Angry Voters Take on Politicians in Large Numbers," *Los Angeles Times*, June 11, 2021.

43. The political theory literature over several centuries ponders the nature of the "interests" to be represented. I will not enter this intellectual thicket here.

44. Institute of Medicine, *The Future of the Public's Health in the 21st Century* (Washington, DC: National Academies Press, 2003), chap. 5, https://www.nap.edu/read/10548/chapter/5.

45. Ballotpedia, "List of Court Cases Relevant to the Nondelegation Doctrine," https://ballotpedia.org/List_of_court_cases_relevant_to_the_nondelegation_doctrine (accessed March 1, 2022).

46. Erin Allday, "They Ordered the Bay Area to Shut Down. Then Came the Hard Part," *San Francisco Chronicle*, March 16, 2021.

47. Sara Cody, "Arrow Lecture on Ethics and Leadership," Stanford University, McCoy Family Center for Ethics in Society, June 24, 2021, at about the 20:25 minute mark: https://www.youtube.com/watch?v=GovcLTyqRAk.

48. Cody, "Arrow Lecture," at about the 22:40 mark.

49. Alexander Bickel, *The Least Dangerous Branch* (New York: Bobbs-Merrill, 1962); John Hart Ely, *Democracy and Distrust* (Cambridge, MA: Harvard University Press, 1980).

50. The debate centers mostly on the US Supreme Court because more than three-quarters of the American states elect some or all of their judges. https://ballotpedia.org/Judicial_election_methods_by_state (accessed March 1, 2022).

51. Wendy K. Mariner, George J. Annas, and Leonard H. Glantz, "*Jacobson v. Massachusetts*: It's Not Your Great-Grandfather's Public Health Law," *Government, Politics, and Law* 95 (2005): 581–90.

52. Surprisingly, the American Civil Liberties Union has moved in the opposite direction, strongly opposing vaccine mandates in the 2008 bird flu pandemic, but strongly supporting them in 2021. Glenn Greenwald, "The ACLU, Prior to COVID, Denounced Mandates and Coercive Measures to Fight Pandemics," (newsletter), September 7, 2021.

53. Lindsay F. Wiley and Stephen I. Vladeck, "Coronavirus, Civil Liberties, and the Courts: The Case against 'Suspending' Judicial Review," *Harvard Law Review Forum* 133, no. 9 (July 2020): 179–98.

54. Maybe not completely far-fetched. For example, there is some suspicion among California observers that Governor Jerry Brown kept a water emergency in place for more than three years in 2014–17 in order to skirt all the veto points that characterize normal policy making.

55. Morrow, "December 7, 2020 Health Officer Statement."

56. Jeremy Pelzer, "Ohio Lawmakers Override DeWine Veto, Pass Limits on Governor's Coronavirus Powers," *Cleveland.com*, March 24, 2021.

57. Jennifer Stefano, "Pennsylvania Lawmakers Aim to Keep Tom Wolf at Bay," *Wall Street Journal*, March 26, 2021.

58. Michael Wines, "State Lawmakers Take Aim at the Emergency Powers Governors Have Relied On in the Pandemic," *New York Times*, March 26, 2021.

59. Morris P. Fiorina, "Group Concentration and the Delegation of Legislative Authority," in *Regulatory Policy and the Social Sciences*, ed. Roger Noll (Berkeley: University of California Press, 1985), 175–97.

60. Cody, "Arrow Lecture," at about the 22:25 mark.

61. As the cynical observation goes, "If you don't have a seat at the table, you're on the menu."

62. John Tierney, "Death and Lockdowns," *City Journal*, March 21, 2021.

63. Brea L. Perry, Brian Aronson, and Bernice A. Pescosolido, "Pandemic Precarity: COVID-19 Is Exposing and Exacerbating Inequalities in the American Heartland," *Proceedings of the National Academy of Sciences* 118, no. 8 (February 2021).

64. Cody, "Arrow Lecture," at about the 26:00 mark.

65. Joseph Choi, "Fauci Says Comments Like Rep. Jim Jordan's Are 'Quite Frustrating,'" *The Hill*, April 18, 2021.

66. Lauren Sonnenberg, "New York Governor Cuomo Tells All Non-essential Workers to Stay Home," *Cheddar News*, March 20, 2020.

67. Morrow, "December 7, 2020 Health Officer Statement."

68. Cody, "Arrow Lecture," at the 20:30 mark.

69. Cody, "Arrow Lecture," at the 34:40 mark.

70. Governor Andrew Cuomo, press conference, March 24, 2020, https://www.facebook.com/GovernorAndrewCuomo/videos/674412803312108.

71. Glenn Greenwald, "The Bizarre Refusal to Apply Cost-Benefit Analysis to COVID Debates," (newsletter), August 25, 2021.

72. A fact that became all too obvious to many of his public health experts as time went on. J. David Goodman, Joseph Goldstein, and Jesse McKinley, "9 Top N.Y. Health Officials Have Quit as Cuomo Scorns Expertise," *New York Times*, February 1, 2021.

73. Cody, "Arrow Lecture," at the 34:30 mark.

74. Cody, "Arrow Lecture," at the 48:30 mark.

About the Contributors

Cameron DeHart is a political science lecturer at the University of California–Merced, where he teaches courses on American politics, state politics, and urban and rural politics. His research focuses on state and local politics in the United States, with a special interest in how institutions affect representation. He received a PhD in political science from Stanford University. A native of the Dayton, Ohio, area, Cameron received his BA from Ohio State University. He lives in Northern California with his girlfriend and their loving rescue dog.

Emily M. Farris is an associate professor of political science and a member of the core faculty of comparative race and ethnic studies at Texas Christian University. Her research in American politics focuses on local politics and explores questions of representation and participation with regard to gender and racial and ethnic identity. She received her MA and PhD from Brown University and her BA from Furman University. She is currently working on a book manuscript with Mirya R. Holman on the politics of sheriffs.

John Ferejohn is the Samuel Tilden Professor of Law at New York University. His primary areas of scholarly interest are political theory and the study of political institutions and behavior. His current research focuses on the US Congress; judicial institutions; law and legislation; constitutional adjudication in the United States, Europe, and the developing world; separation of powers; political campaigns and elections; water politics in California; and the philosophy of social science. Ferejohn earned his PhD at Stanford University and received an honorary doctorate from Yale University. He has written several books, including *Forged through Fire* (Liveright, 2016) and *A Republic of Statutes* (Yale University Press, 2010), and coedited others, including *Constitutional Culture and Democratic Rule* (Cambridge University Press, 2001) and *The New Federalism: Can the States Be Trusted?* (Hoover Institution Press, 1997).

Morris P. Fiorina is the Wendt Family Professor of Political Science at Stanford University and a senior fellow of the Hoover Institution. He has written widely on American politics, with special emphasis on the study of representation, public opinion, and elections. He has published numerous articles and written or edited thirteen books, including *Culture War? The Myth of a Polarized America* (with Samuel Abrams and Jeremy Pope; Pearson Longman, 2005), *Disconnect: The Breakdown of Representation in American Politics* (with Samuel Abrams; University of Oklahoma Press, 2009), and *Unstable Majorities* (Hoover Institution Press, 2017). Fiorina has served on the editorial boards of a dozen journals and from 1986 to 1990 chaired the Board of Overseers of the American National Election Studies.

Mirya R. Holman is an associate professor of political science at Tulane University, with joint appointments in environmental studies and Tulane Law School. She is an expert on gender and politics, local politics, and political behavior. She has published widely in these areas, including her book *Women in Politics in the American City* (Temple University Press and Project MUSE, 2014) and her coedited volume *Good Reasons to Run: Women and Political Candidacy* (Temple University Press, 2020). She is the author or coauthor of more than sixty articles published in leading outlets, including *American Political Science Review, Climatic Change, Journal of Politics, Perspectives on Politics, Political Behavior, Political Psychology*, and *Political Analysis*. She writes and distributes a weekly mentoring newsletter to academics called Mirya Holman's Aggressive Winning Scholars (#MHAWS).

Didi Kuo is senior research scholar and associate director for research at Stanford University's Center on Democracy, Development and the Rule of Law. She studies American and comparative politics, political parties, and democracy and capitalism. She runs the Program on American Democracy in Comparative Perspective and is a nonresident fellow in political reform at New America. Kuo is the author of *Clientelism, Capitalism, and Democracy: The Rise of Programmatic Politics in the United States and Britain* (Cambridge University Press, 2018).

David L. Leal is a professor of government at the University of Texas–Austin and a senior fellow at the Hoover Institution. His primary academic interest is Latino politics, and his work explores the political implications of demographic change in the United States. He teaches classes that include Latino politics, immigration politics, politics and religion, US Congress, and British politics. He served a three-year term (2019–22) on the Council of the American Political Science Association (APSA). He has also been an APSA Congressional Fellow, a Fulbright Distinguished Lecturer in Japan, and an associate member of Nuffield College at the University of Oxford. In 2013, he was named a Distinguished Alumni Scholar by Stanford University, where he received his undergraduate degree. He received his PhD in political science from Harvard University.

Victoria Ochoa is a graduate of the Harvard Kennedy School and the University of Pennsylvania Law School. Prior to attending law school, she worked at the US Department of Commerce and the US Senate. As an undergraduate at St. Edward's University (Austin, Texas), she was recognized nationally as a Harry S. Truman Scholar. She has published articles and opinion pieces in the *Washington Post*, *Houston Chronicle*, *Texas Tribune*, *Harvard Civil Rights–Civil Liberties Law Review* blog, *Columbia Human Rights Law Review*, and *Georgetown Immigration Law Journal*.

Miranda E. Sullivan is a PhD student in the Department of Government at the University of Texas–Austin. She studies American politics and public policy, focusing specifically on religion and politics, urban politics, immigration politics, and racial and ethnic politics.

Yiqian Alice Wang is a PhD candidate in political science at Stanford University and a JD candidate at Yale Law School. At Stanford, her research concerns US immigration law and the determinants of Mexico to US migration. Some of her current projects examine executive control over the US immigration courts, the dynamics of femicides and gender-based violence in Latin America, and the effects of guest worker policies on the labor market. She received BAs in philosophy and government from Smith College. She also holds an MA in political and legal theory from the University of Warwick, which she attended on a US–UK Fulbright scholarship.

Index

References to figures are indicated by an f.

ABAHO (Association of Bay Area Health Officials), 88–90
Abbott, Greg, 97, 103, 104–5, 111–12, 113–14, 115, 116f, 117, 119, 120, 121–22, 125, 126f, 127, 129–31, 129f, 132, 134, 135–40, 142, 197, 228–29, 247
abortion
  court evaluation of emergency orders restricting, 214–15
  Texas response to COVID-19 pandemic, 111–12
academic institutions, public health partnerships with, 86, 90–92
accountability, democratic governance and, 73, 264–69
ACLU of West Tennessee v. Chandler (1978), 226–27
Adler, Steve, 136, 140, 157
AIDS/HIV crisis, 91
airline travel, mandatory vaccinations for, 188, 189f
Alabama emergency powers, 39, 41, 47
Alaska emergency powers, 37, 40, 53
Aluttis, Christoph, 85
Amazon, 85–86
amending state laws and rules, 46–49
American exceptionalism, 24–29. *See also* federalism

American Legislative Exchange Council (ALEC), 76
American Samoa emergency powers, 39, 58
Angell, Sonia, 96n45
anticommandeering doctrine, 22–23, 25, 32n32
Aragón, Tomás, 89, 90, 91, 92
Arizona
  conflicts between governmental levels, 248
  emergency powers in, 34, 37, 47, 55–56
  eviction moratoriums in, 156
  reliance on state emergency powers, 228–29
  response to COVID-19 pandemic, 108–10, 109f
Arkansas
  conflicts between governmental levels, 248
  emergency powers in, 35, 37, 60–61
  intragovernmental challenges to emergency powers, 244
Armstrong, David A., II, 160
Association of Bay Area Health Officials (ABAHO), 88–90
attitudes on COVID-19 pandemic. *See* public opinion on COVID-19 pandemic

Augusta, Georgia, 157, 165
Austin, Texas, 133, 135–36, 142, 157

Bay Area of Northern California
  accountability of public officials, 265–66
  public health authority in, 71, 86–92
Bayley's Campground Inc. v. Mills (2020), 223
Beauvais, Sally, 134
Benjamin, Georges, 85
Biden, Joe, 252–53
big box stores, 258–59
bioterrorism, 78–79
Birdwell, Brian, 139
Black, Hugo, 20–21
border security policy, 228–29
Breed, London, 155
Brennan Center for Justice (New York University), xi, 35
Breyer, Stephen, 218, 220
broadcast employees, protections for, 55–56
Brown, Jerry, 277n54
bureaucrats. *See* democratic governance and emergency powers
business owners, constitutional challenges brought by, 221–24
business reopenings, public opinion on, 194, 195f

Cain, Bruce, viii
California
  accountability of public officials, 265–66
  Bay Area and public health capacity, 86–92
  clashes between science and politics, 263, 264
  county sheriffs refusing to enforce state orders, 250, 251
  court evaluation of emergency orders, 216, 219–20
  current status of public health, 79–80, 81f, 82f
  democratic governance and public health, 75–76
  determinants of public health capacity, 83–92
  dissatisfaction related to nature of restrictions, 259–62
  emergency powers in, viii, 37, 41–44
  eviction moratoriums, 156–57
  financing and COVID response, 80, 83, 83f
  history of public health in, 76–79
  local public health authority in, 74–75
  municipal policy action during pandemic, 154–55
  policy response to pandemic, 110, 110f
  public health after September 11, 2001, 78–79
  reorganization of public health authority, 76–78
  variation in public opinion on pandemic, 200–202
California Department of Public Health (CDPH), 76
California Emergency Services Act, 43–44
Calvary Chapel Dayton Valley v. Sisolak (2020), 216–17
caregiving responsibilities during pandemic, 163–64
"catchall" emergency clauses, 40–41
Center for Democracy, Development and the Rule of Law, xi
Challenge Seattle, 85–86
checkpoints, state authority to create, 53
Cheney, Liz, 113
childcare access during pandemic, 163–64

Cincinnatus, 8, 11
city governments. *See* local governments; municipal policy action during pandemic
civil unrest, court review of emergency responses to, 226–27
Civil War, 9, 12, 22, 23
Clemenceau, Georges, 271
Cody, Sara, 89, 91, 266, 269, 271, 273–74
Cold War, state-level reforms during, 34
Colfax, Grant, 90–91, 92
Colorado emergency powers, 60
Columbus Ale House v. Cuomo (2020), 222, 236n92
command of police and state military forces, 49–50
commandeering state officials, 22–23, 25, 32n32
Commonwealth of the Northern Mariana Islands (CNMI), 39, 48, 50, 53, 58
confiscation of private property, 50
Connecticut emergency powers, 37, 41, 58
consent of governed, ix–x. *See also* court evaluation of emergency orders; democratic governance and emergency powers; public opinion on COVID-19 pandemic
Constantine, Dow, 85
constitutional emergency powers, 3, 6–8, 11–13, 19–21
constitutional limitations on state emergency powers, 17
constitutional provisions for state emergency powers, 33–39, 42–44
constitutional rights. *See* fundamental rights infringement, court evaluation of
constitutional sheriff movement, 250

construction clauses, 40
contact tracing, 54–55
continuity of state government, constitutional provisions for, 35–37
controlling emergency powers, 19–22
Cook, Michael, 225
cooperative federalism, 18
county judges, and response to pandemic in Texas, 104
county public health departments (California)
  Bay Area case study, 88, 89–90
  current status, 80, 81f, 82f
  public health administration in California, 76, 77–78
county sheriffs refusing to enforce state orders, 249–52
court evaluation of emergency orders
  abortion claims, 111, 112, 214–15
  applying strict scrutiny to all uses of police powers, 227–30
  constitutional challenges brought by business owners, 221–24
  constitutional emergency powers, 13
  controlling emergency powers, 19–20, 21–22
  and democratic legitimacy, 267–68
  free exercise claims, 215–21
  general discussion, 230
  and legislative emergency powers, 15–16
  nonhealth emergencies, 224–27
  overview, ix, 207–9
  during pandemic, overview of, 212–14
  preemption, 133
  quarantine powers, 103
  state police powers overview, 209–12
  strict scrutiny, 210–12, 217–21, 223, 227–30
  in Texas, 137–38

COVID fatigue, 258
COVID-19 pandemic. *See also* California; court evaluation of emergency orders; municipal policy action during pandemic; public opinion on COVID-19 pandemic; Texas
  accountability of public officials during, 265–69
  American exceptionalism, 24–29
  Bay Area case study, 86–92
  Biden administration vaccine mandate, 252–53
  California, emergency declarations in, 42, 44
  California public health authority, 74–75, 80, 83, 83f
  clashes between science and politics, 262–64
  conflicts between governmental levels during, 247–48
  county sheriffs refusing to enforce state orders, 249–52
  death rates in, 27
  dissatisfaction related to nature of restrictions, 258–62
  emergency powers in, 3–5
  federalism and initial responses to, 152–54
  legislative action to limit emergency powers, 241–46
  legislative action to strengthen emergency powers, 246–47
  overview, vii–xi
  public health authority in, 71–76, 85–86
  representation problems for public officials, 269–74
  state emergency powers during, 61–62
  termination of emergency declarations in states, 41–42
cue taking, partisan, 196–97

Cuomo, Andrew, 113, 244, 246, 272, 273
curfews, 52, 225–27
Curley, Cali, 133–34

decentralized governmental structure, 26, 260–61
defense forces, command of state, 49–50
DeHart, Cameron, viii
Delaware emergency powers, 35, 47
delegation, consequences of, 73
democratic governance and emergency powers
  accountability, 73, 264–69
  clashes between science and politics, 262–64
  dissatisfaction related to nature of restrictions, 258–62
  overview, x, 75–76, 257, 264
  representation, 269–74
Democratic Party. *See also* partisanship
  American exceptionalism, 26, 29
  conflicts between state governmental levels, 247–48
  early public consensus on COVID-19, 179
  elite messaging on COVID restrictions, 196–97
  fragmentation of public opinion on COVID-19, 180–82, 180f, 181f, 182f, 183f, 184–85
  intragovernmental challenges to use of emergency powers, 243–46
  and municipal policy action during pandemic, 162
  state responses to pandemic, 110, 110f
  and Texas response to pandemic, 98–100, 130–31
Department of State Health Services (DSHS), Texas, 97, 104

DeSantis, Ron, 197, 247
dictatorship, as constitutional institution in Roman Republic, 7–8, 11
Dillon's Rule, 131–32
discretionary (prerogative) emergency power in executive, 6–7, 10–11
District of Columbia emergency powers, 46, 51, 52, 59. *See also* state emergency powers
Division of Emergency Management (Texas), 103
dualism, 20–22, 31n25
Ducey, Doug, 228–29
due process rights, 221–24

economy/economics
  impact of COVID on, 27, 151
  municipal policy action during pandemic, 155–57
  public opinion on threat of COVID-19, 184–85
  and representation, 270–71
  and Texas response to pandemic, 112–14, 123, 124f
educational settings, mandatory vaccinations in, 189–91, 191f
efficacy of COVID restrictions, 258–62
EIS (Epidemic Intelligence Service), 84
elected officials. *See* democratic governance and emergency powers
elite messaging on COVID restrictions, 196–97
emergency declarations
  constitutional provisions for declaring, 34
  court evaluation of emergency orders, 224–27
  legislative action centered on duration and extension of, 242–46
  statutory provisions for renewal of, 41
  statutory provisions for terminating, 41–42
  statutory provisions on grounds for, 39–41
  statutory provisions on officials with authority to make, 39
  Texas response to COVID-19 pandemic, 103
emergency legislation clauses in state constitutions, 37
emergency management (EM) agencies, state, 45–46, 58. *See also* state emergency powers
Emergency Power Limitation Act, 76
emergency powers. *See also* police powers; state emergency powers
  accountability and, 264–69
  American exceptionalism, 24–29
  clashes between science and politics, 262–64
  constitutional, 3, 6–8, 11–13, 19–21
  controlling, 19–22
  in COVID-19 pandemic, 3–5
  and democratic governance, overview, 75–76, 257, 264
  dissatisfaction related to nature of, 258–62
  federalism, 22–24
  legislative, 3, 5–6, 13–16, 20–22
  necessity-based, 3, 8–11, 19–20, 30n6
  overview, vii–xi
  representation and, 269–74
Emergency Powers of the Governor Act (Michigan), 243
emergency preparedness, state, 59–61
emergency spending, constitutional provisions authorizing, 37
Employment Division, Department of Human Resources of Oregon v. Smith (1990), 212
employment settings, mandatory vaccinations in, 189–91
enforcement of emergency orders, ix–x, 133–35

Epidemic Intelligence Service (EIS), 84
equal protection claims, court evaluation of, 210–11, 212–13, 221–24
Escott, Mark, 121
essential businesses, controversy related to, 258–59
evacuations, regulating, 51–53
eviction moratoriums
  by local governments, 156–57, 158, 159–60, 161f, 162–63, 165
  in Texas, 104–5
exception, notion of, 30n6
exceptionalism, American, 24–29. *See also* federalism
executive branches, state. *See also* state emergency powers
  delineation of authority to enforce emergency laws, 59
  emergency powers in, 45–46
executive emergency powers, federal, 13–16
Executive Order GA-08 (Texas), 104
Executive Order GA-14 (Texas), 106, 113–14
executive prerogative power, 6–7, 10–11
executive unilateralism, 29n1
expedited legislation clauses, in state constitutions, 37
expenditures on public health in California, 80, 81f, 82f

Facebook, 86
fairness of COVID restrictions, dissatisfaction related to, 258–62
Farris, Emily, viii
Fauci, Anthony, 262, 271–72
federal emergency powers. *See* emergency powers
federal government response to COVID-19 pandemic, 107–8, 108f, 119–20, 120f

federalism
  American exceptionalism, 28–29
  Biden administration vaccine mandate, 252–53
  cooperative, 18
  and initial responses to pandemic, 152–54
  and municipal policy action during pandemic, 165
  restrictions on emergency powers, 22–24
  Texas context, 98–100
Federman, Peter, 133–34
Ferejohn, John, 20, 30n6, 75
Fifth Amendment rights, 221–24
financial impact of COVID-19 pandemic, 123, 124f. *See also* economy/economics
financing for public health, 80, 83–84, 83f
firearms confiscation, limits on, 56–58
First Amendment protections
  challenges brought by business owners, 221–24
  free exercise claims, 211, 212, 215–21
  during nonhealth emergencies, 226–27
  restrictions on emergency powers, 55–56
  strict scrutiny review for, 210–11
first informer broadcasters, protections for, 55–56
first responders, liability immunity for, 60–61
fiscal emergency declarations, in California, 43
Florida
  ban on vaccine mandates, 248
  conflicts between governmental levels, 247
  court evaluation of emergency orders, 225–26

Florida (*continued*)
  emergency powers in, 37, 38, 39, 48
  response to COVID-19 pandemic, 108–10, 109f
4 Aces Enterprises, LLC v. Edwards (2020), 222, 236n92
Fourteenth Amendment rights, 210–11, 213, 221–24
Fourth Emergency Order (Texas Supreme Court), 104–5
France, constitution of, 11, 21
free exercise claims, court evaluation of, 211, 212, 215–21
Fremont, California, 156–57
fundamental rights infringement, court evaluation of
  abortion claims, 214–15
  constitutional challenges brought by business owners, 221–24
  and democratic legitimacy, 267–68
  free exercise claims, 215–21
  general discussion, 230
  nonhealth emergencies, 224–27
  overview, 207–9
  during pandemic, overview of, 212–14
  state police powers overview, 209–12
  strict scrutiny, 210–12, 217–21, 223, 227–30
funding for public health, 80, 83–84, 83f

gender differences in COVID attitudes, 197–200
Georgia
  ban on vaccine mandates, 248
  emergency powers in, 39, 61
  eviction moratoriums in, 157, 165
  response to COVID-19 pandemic, 108–10, 109f
Glendale, Arizona, 156
Goitein, Liza, ix

Google, 86
Gorsuch, Neil, 218–19, 220
government
  constitutional provisions for emergencies, 34–37
  transformation related to legislative emergency powers, 5–6
Government Health and Safety Code (California), 78–79
governors. *See also* intragovernmental challenges to use of emergency powers
  accountability of, 268–69
  California emergency declarations, 42–43
  command of police and state military forces, 49–50
  constitutional provisions for emergencies, 35
  preemption by, 132–33
  state emergency powers, 16–19, 31n24, 45–46
  statutory provisions for emergency proclamations, 39, 41
  suspending and amending state laws and rules, 46–49
  Texas response to COVID-19 pandemic, 102–3, 135–38
Grossman, Guy, 197
group gatherings, restrictions on, 193, 193f
Guam emergency powers, 50, 52, 58
gun confiscation, limits on, 56–58

H1N1 influenza pandemic, 88
Hamilton, Alexander, 9–10, 15–16, 31n25
Harrison, Nicky, 133–34
Hawaii emergency powers, 41, 57
health care reform, support for, 195–96
health impact of COVID-19 pandemic in Texas, 123, 124f

health officers, in California, 77–78. *See also* public health
Health Officers Association of California (HOAC), 78–79
Hellerstedt, John, 97, 104
Hickox v. Christie (2015), 103
Hidalgo, Lina, 104
Hinojosa, Gilberto, 114
hiring waivers during emergencies, 48
Hobbes, Thomas, 30n6
Holman, Mirya, viii
Home Building and Loan Association v. Blaisdell (1934), 224, 228
Hoover Institution, xi
Hopkins Hawley LLC v. Cuomo (2021), 222–23
House Bill 3 (Texas), 139–40
Hui, Iris, viii
Hurricane Andrew, 225–26
Hurricane Hugo, 226

Idaho emergency powers, 50
Illinois
  attempts to strengthen state powers in, 246–47
  emergency powers in, 37, 41, 48
  response to COVID-19 pandemic, 110, 110f
immigration policy, 228–29
immunizations. *See* vaccination
implementation of emergency orders, viii–x. *See also* California; intragovernmental challenges to use of emergency powers; municipal policy action during pandemic; public health; Texas
In re Abbott (2020), 213–14
Indiana
  ban on vaccine mandates, 248
  intragovernmental challenges to use of emergency powers, 245
intermediate-scrutiny review, 211

international travel, restrictions on, 192–93, 192f
intragovernmental challenges to use of emergency powers
  accountability of public officials, 268–69
  attempts to strengthen state powers, 246–47
  Biden administration vaccine mandate, 252–53
  conflicts between governmental levels, 247–48
  county sheriffs refusing to enforce state orders, 249–52
  duration and extension of emergency declarations, 242–46
  overview, ix–x, 241–42
  specific exceptions, 246
Iowa emergency powers, 41, 52

Jackson, Robert, 19–21, 31n25
Jacobson v. Massachusetts (1905), 17, 208, 212–14, 215, 218–23, 228
Jew Ho v. Williamson (1900), 210
Jones, Richard, 251
Jordan, Jim, 271
judicial review of state emergency powers. *See* court evaluation of emergency orders

Kagan, Elena, 218, 220
Kansas
  emergency powers in, 60
  intragovernmental challenges to use of emergency powers, 243, 244
Katz, Mitch, 88
Kavanaugh, Brett, 216, 217
Kelly, Chari, 137
Kentucky
  emergency powers in, 60
  intragovernmental challenges to use of emergency powers, 243

Klotman, Paul, 121
Korean conflict, 21
Korematsu v. United States (1944), 19–20, 21, 31n25, 210
Kuo, Didi, viii

labor disputes, 58
Lane Center for the Study of the American West (Stanford), viii, xi
laws, suspending and amending state, 46–49
lawsuits. *See* court evaluation of emergency orders
Leal, David, viii
legislative emergency powers, 3, 5–6, 13–16, 20–22
legislature, state. *See also* intragovernmental challenges to use of emergency powers
  authorization for state emergency powers, 17–18
  California, emergency declarations in, 42–43
  constitutional provisions for emergencies, 34–37
  statutory provisions for emergency proclamations, 39, 41
  Texas response to COVID-19 pandemic, 138–40
Lewis, Michael, 79
liability immunity for state and first responders, 60–61
"liberally construed" interpretation of EP statutes, 40
Liccardo, Sam, 261
Lincoln, Abraham, 9, 12, 30n14
Livingston, Lora, 136
local governments. *See also* municipal policy action during pandemic
  American exceptionalism, 25–26, 28–29
  economics and reopening, debate over, 113
  enforcement of emergency orders, 134
  initial response to pandemic, 104, 105–6
  nuances and difficulties of federalism, 153
  overview, viii
  preemption, 131–33
  public opinion after reopening, 125, 127, 128f, 129, 130, 130f
  public opinion changes, 142–43
  public opinion in early stages of pandemic, 115, 117, 118f, 119
  resistance to state orders, 135–38
local public health authority in California, 76, 77–78. *See also* public health
local school districts, COVID policies created by, 190
lockdown orders. *See* stay-at-home orders
Locke, John, 7, 8, 10
Lucas, Jack, 160

Machiavelli, Niccolò, 8
Madison, James, 5–6
Maine emergency powers, 37
mandatory vaccinations. *See* vaccination
Maryland emergency powers, 35, 37, 60
mask mandates
  in California, 92
  conflicts between governmental levels, 247–48
  county sheriffs refusing to enforce state orders, 251
  in Texas, 121, 122, 132, 133, 135–37
mask wearing
  partisan gap in, 180–81, 180f
  trends in during pandemic, 178–79
Massachusetts emergency powers, 49, 54
mayors. *See* municipal policy action during pandemic

McConaughey, Matthew, 100
medical procedures, emergency restrictions on, 51, 105, 111–12. *See also* abortion
medical research community, public health partnerships with, 90–91
Menotti v. City of Seattle (2005), 227
Michigan
  dissatisfaction related to nature of restrictions in, 260
  emergency powers in, 60
  intragovernmental challenges to use of emergency powers, 243
Microsoft, 85–86
military forces, command of state, 49–50
Minnesota emergency powers, 40, 49–50, 53, 63n14
Mississippi emergency powers, 41, 59
Missouri emergency powers, 37, 45–46
Montana
  ban on vaccine mandates, 248
  emergency powers in, 41, 52
Montesquieu, Charles de, 6
Mortenson, Julian Davis, 30n13
movement, regulating, 51–53
municipal policy action during pandemic
  data and methods, 157–59
  economic crises, 155–57
  federalism and initial responses, 152–53
  general discussion, 164–66
  other attempts at policy making, 163–64
  overview, 151–52
  public health actions, 154–55
  results, 159–60, 161f, 162–63

National Center for State Legislators (NCSL), 35–36
National Emergencies Act (NEA), 14–15, 31n17

national governments, responses to COVID by, 152–53. *See also* federalism
National Guard, 49–50
natural disasters, state emergency responses to, 225–26
Nebraska emergency powers, 37
necessity-based emergency powers, 3, 8–11, 19–20, 30n6
New Hampshire
  ban on vaccine mandates, 248
  emergency powers in, 39, 57–58
  intragovernmental challenges to use of emergency powers, 246
New Jersey emergency powers, 39, 60, 103
New Mexico emergency powers, 38
New York
  attempts to strengthen state powers in, 246
  emergency powers in, 53–54, 55
  intragovernmental challenges to use of emergency powers, 244
  public health authority in, 75
  response to COVID-19 pandemic, 110, 110f, 217–18
New York University Brennan Center for Justice, xi
Newsom, Gavin, 44, 74, 200–201, 250, 259–60
nonessential medical procedures, emergency restrictions on, 51, 105, 111–12. *See also* abortion
nonessential travel, restrictions on, 192–93, 192f
nonhealth emergencies, state police powers and, 224–27
North Carolina
  court evaluation of emergency orders, 226
  emergency powers in, 37, 39

North Dakota
  ban on vaccine mandates, 248
  emergency powers in, 58
Northern Mariana Islands emergency powers, 39, 48, 50, 53, 58

Occupational Safety and Health Administration (OSHA), 252–53
Ochoa, Victoria, ix
Ohio
  emergency powers in, 37, 41, 59
  intragovernmental challenges to use of emergency powers, 244, 246, 268
Oklahoma
  conflicts between governmental levels, 247–48
  emergency powers in, 39
  response to COVID-19 pandemic, 108–10, 109f
Oregon emergency powers, 37, 38, 39, 57
O'Rourke, Beto, 113
Oxford Government Response Index, 107, 108f, 120f

pandemic preparedness, 88. *See also* COVID-19 pandemic
partisanship
  business reopenings, restrictions on, 194, 195f
  early public consensus on COVID-19, 179
  factors driving, 196–97
  fragmentation of public opinion on COVID-19, 180–82, 180f, 181f, 182f, 183f, 184–85
  group gatherings, restrictions on, 193, 193f
  international and nonessential travel restrictions, 192–93, 192f
  intragovernmental challenges to use of emergency powers, 243–46
  mandatory vaccinations, 187–91, 187f, 189f, 191f
  and municipal policy action during COVID-19 pandemic, 162
  school reopenings, restrictions on, 194, 194f
  and state responses to COVID-19 pandemic, 108–10, 109f, 110f
  support for health care reform, 195–96
  in Texas, 98–100, 129–31, 141–43
  vaccine passports, 186–87
partnerships with stakeholders, role in public health authority, 84–86, 90–92
Pasquino, Pasquale, 20, 30n6
passports, vaccine, 185–87, 187f
Patrick, Dan, 112, 113, 114, 141
Pauper Act (California), 76
Paxton, Ken, 111, 132, 133, 135–36, 137, 142
penalties for violating state emergency laws, 59–60
Pennsylvania
  emergency powers in, 41, 51
  intragovernmental challenges to use of emergency powers, 244–45, 269
Pishko, Jessica, 252
Planned Parenthood of Southeastern Pennsylvania v. Casey (1992), 214
police forces, command of, 49–50
police powers
  applying strict scrutiny to all uses of, 227–30
  and COVID-19 emergency orders, 212–24
  federalism and, 153, 165
  and nonhealth emergencies, 224–27
  overview, 16–17, 207–12
  public health, 78–79
politicians, 75–76. *See also* democratic governance and emergency powers

politics. *See also* partisanship
  accountability and, 264–69
  clashes between science and, during pandemic, 262–64
  and designation of essential businesses, 259
  and early public consensus on COVID-19, 179
  explanation of American exceptionalism, 28–29
  fragmentation of public opinion on COVID-19, 180–82, 180f, 181f, 182f, 183f, 184–85
  and misuse of police powers, 228–29
  and municipal policy action during pandemic, 162
  prohibitions against emergency agencies intervening in, 58
  representation and, 269–74
  and state responses to pandemic, 108–10, 109f, 110f
  in Texas, 98–100, 137–38, 141–43
Posner, Eric, 29n1
Posse Comitatus Act, 25, 32n31
preemption, 99, 131–33
Premonition, The (Lewis), 79
prerogative (discretionary) emergency power in executive, 6–7, 10–11
press, protections for, 55–56
Preterm-Cleveland v. Attorney Gen. of Ohio (2020), 214–15
prices, regulating, 50–51
private property, confiscating, 50
process–reasonableness test for state emergency responses, 225–26
Proposition 3 (Texas), 107
protests, court review of emergency responses to, 226–27
public health. *See also* public opinion on COVID-19 pandemic
  American exceptionalism, 24–26
  Bay Area case study, 86–92
  clashes between science and politics, 262–64
  court evaluation of state police powers, 212–24
  current status in California, 79–80, 81f, 82f
  democratic governance and, 75–76
  determinants of capacity, 83–92
  effective communication regarding, 202–3
  financing and COVID response, 80, 83, 83f
  general discussion, 92–93
  history of in California, 76–79
  infrastructure in United States, 73, 85
  local authority in California, 74–75
  measures taken during pandemic, 4
  municipal policy action during pandemic, 154–55
  overview, 71–74
  reorganization of in California, 77–78
  after September 11, 2001, 78–79
  state emergency powers, 17, 53–55
  Texas response to pandemic, 101–7
public officials under democratic governance
  accountability, 264–69
  overview, 264
  representation, 264, 269–74
public opinion on COVID-19 pandemic
  business reopenings, 194, 195f
  dissatisfaction related to nature of restrictions, 258–62
  early public consensus, 176–79, 177f
  in early stages of pandemic, 114–15, 116f, 117, 118f, 119
  general discussion, 202–3
  group gatherings, 193, 193f
  health and economic impact, 123, 124f
  international and nonessential travel, 192–93, 192f

public opinion on COVID-19 pandemic (*continued*)
  mandatory vaccinations, 185–91, 189f, 191f
  overview, ix, 175–76, 257
  partisan and gender differences in COVID attitudes, 196–200
  from public consensus to fragmentation, 180–82, 183f, 184–85
  school reopenings, 194, 194f
  state-level variation in, 200–202
  support for health care reform, 195–96
  vaccine passports, 185–87, 187f
Puerto Rico emergency powers, 39, 50, 53, 54

quarantines, 53–54, 103

rational basis review, 211, 213, 218, 219, 222–23
rationing goods, 51
reasonableness test, for state emergency responses, 225–26
regime transformation, related to legislative emergency powers, 5–6
regional cooperation, 86, 88–90
regulating movement, transportation, and evacuations, 51–53
regulating prices, 50–51
religion, and Texas response to pandemic, 107. *See also* First Amendment protections
renewal of emergency proclamations, 41, 242–46
reopening stage, Texas
  economics and, 112–14
  overview, 119–23, 120f
representation, democratic governance and, 264, 269–74
Republican Party. *See also* partisanship
  American exceptionalism, 26, 29
  conflicts between state governmental levels, 247–48
  early public consensus on COVID-19, 179
  elite messaging on COVID restrictions, 196–97
  fragmentation of public opinion on COVID-19, 180–82, 180f, 181f, 182f, 183f, 184–85
  intragovernmental challenges to use of emergency powers, 243–46
  and municipal policy action during pandemic, 162
  state responses to pandemic, 108–10, 109f
  Texas context, 98–100, 131
restricting sales, 50–51
restrictions on state emergency powers, 55–58
Rhode Island emergency powers, 37, 41, 55
rights infringement. *See* fundamental rights infringement, court evaluation of
riots, court review of emergency responses to, 226–27
risk perception, gendered dynamics of, 197–99
roads, state emergency control over, 53
Roberts, John, 216, 220
Roman Catholic Diocese of Brooklyn v. Cuomo (2020), 217–19, 234n63
Roman Republic, 7–8, 11
Roosevelt, Franklin Delano, 21
rules, suspending and amending state, 46–49
Rutherford, George, 91–92

sales, restricting, 50–51
San Francisco Bay Area (California)
  accountability of public officials, 265–66
  public health authority in, 71, 86–92

San Francisco municipal policy (California), 155
San Mateo County (California), 261, 262
Santa Clara County (California), 261
Schmitt, Carl, 7, 8–9, 30n12
schools
  mask mandates in Texas, 135–37
  public opinion on COVID policies, 189–90
  reopenings, 194, 194f, 263–64
  science, clashes between politics and, 262–64
SDFs (state defense forces), command of, 49–50
Second Amendment protections, 56–58
Securing Access to Networks in Disasters Act, 56
Senate Bill 1025 (Texas), 139
Senate Bill 104 (SB 104, California), 78–79
Senate Bill 1360 (SB 1360, California), 76
September 11, 2001, public health authority after, 78–79
Sharfstein, Joshua, 85
shelter providers, liability immunity for, 61
shelter-in-place orders. *See* stay-at-home orders
sheriffs refusing to enforce state orders, 249–52
shutdown orders. *See* stay-at-home orders
Sides, John, 195–96
Skinner v. Oklahoma (1942), 210
small businesses, effect of pandemic on, 258–59
social distancing, partisan gap in, 180–81, 181f

Sotomayor, Sonia, 218, 220
South Bay United Pentecostal Church v. Newsom (2020), 216
South Bay United Pentecostal Church v. Newsom (2021), 219–20
South Carolina
  conflicts between governmental levels, 247–48
  county sheriffs refusing to enforce state orders, 252
  emergency powers in, 35, 38
South Dakota emergency powers, 39, 41
South Wind Women's Center LLC v. Stitt (2020), 214, 233n53
spending
  constitutional provisions authorizing emergency, 37
  on public health in California, 80, 81f, 82f
Stanford University, viii, xi, 260–61
state defense forces (SDFs), command of, 49–50
state emergency powers. *See also* California; court evaluation of emergency orders; intragovernmental challenges to use of emergency powers; police powers; public health; Texas
  American exceptionalism, 24–26, 28–29
  California case study, 42–44
  commanding police and state military forces, 49–50
  confiscating private property, 50
  constitutional provisions for, 33–39, 42–44
  during COVID-19 pandemic, 61–62, 154–55
  delineation of authority to enforce emergency laws, 59
  federalism restrictions on, 22–24

state emergency powers (*continued*)
  liability immunity for state and first responders, 60–61
  and municipal policy action during pandemic, 159–60, 161f, 165
  nonhealth, 224–27
  nuances and difficulties of federalism, 153
  overview, viii, 16–19, 33
  penalties for violating EP laws, 59–60
  preemption, 131–33
  regulating movement, transportation, and evacuations, 51–53
  restricting sales and regulating prices, 50–51
  restrictions on, 55–58
  in state executive branches, 45–46
  statutory provisions, 33–34, 39–45
  suspending and amending state laws and rules, 46–49
  vaccine passports, 186–87
state executive branches
  delineation of authority to enforce emergency laws, 59
  state emergency powers in, 45–46
state legislature. *See also* intragovernmental challenges to use of emergency powers
  authorization for state emergency powers, 17–18
  California, emergency declarations in, 42–43
  constitutional provisions for emergencies, 34–37
  statutory provisions for emergency proclamations, 39, 41
  Texas response to COVID-19 pandemic, 138–40
state of emergency declarations
  constitutional provisions for declaring, 34
  court evaluation of emergency orders, 224–27
  legislative action centered on duration and extension of, 242–46
  statutory provisions for renewal of, 41
  statutory provisions for terminating, 41–42
  statutory provisions on grounds for, 39–41
  statutory provisions on officials with authority to make, 39
  Texas response to COVID-19 pandemic, 103
statutory provisions for state emergency powers. *See also* intragovernmental challenges to use of emergency powers
  California case study, 42–44
  grounds for emergency declarations, 39–41
  officials empowered to declare state of emergency, 39
  overview, 33–34, 39, 44–45
  terminating emergency proclamations, 39–41
stay-at-home orders
  and accountability of public officials, 265–66
  Bay Area case study, 87, 89–90
  dissatisfaction related to nature of, 260–61
  first instances of, 71
  fragmentation of public opinion on COVID-19, 181–82, 182f
  municipal policy action during pandemic, 154–55, 158–60, 161f, 162–63, 165
  in Texas, 105–6
strict scrutiny of state exercise of police powers, 210–12, 217–21, 223, 227–30
Sullivan, Miranda, viii
Supreme Court. *See* court evaluation of emergency orders
suspending state laws and rules, 46–49

Takko, Dean, 36–37
Tandon v. Newsom (2021), 220
Tausanovitch, Chris, 195–96
Tennessee
  conflicts between governmental levels, 247–48
  court evaluation of emergency orders, 226–27
  emergency powers in, 56
  terminating emergency proclamations, 41–42
territorial emergency powers. *See* state emergency powers
Texas
  ban on vaccine mandates, 248
  conflicts between governmental levels, 247
  context of, 98–101
  emergency powers in, viii, 38–39, 41
  enforcement of emergency orders, 133–35
  eviction moratoriums in, 157
  general discussion, 140–43
  initial responses to pandemic, 103–7
  legislative response to pandemic emergency orders, 138–40
  local governments and preemption, 131–33
  local resistance to emergency orders, 135–38
  other state officials and policies, 111–14
  overview, 97–98
  public health context, 101–7, 102f
  public opinion after reopening, 125, 126f, 127, 128f, 129–31, 129f, 130f
  public opinion in early stages of pandemic, 114–15, 116f, 117, 118f, 119
  public opinion on health and economic impact, 123, 124f
  reliance on state emergency powers, 228–29
  reopening stage, 112–14, 119–23
  state–federal comparisons, 107–10, 108f, 109f, 110f
Texas Disaster Act, 103, 133, 137, 138
Texas Eviction Diversion Program, 105
Texas Health and Safety Code, 103
Texas Media and Society Survey, 123
Texas Politics Project, 130–31
Toyosaburo Korematsu v. United States (1944), 19–20, 21, 31n25
transportation, regulating, 51–53
travel
  mandatory vaccinations for, 188, 189f
  pandemic restrictions on, 192–93, 192f
  regulating, 51–53
Trickey, David, 16
Truman, Harry, 20–21
Trump, Donald, 24, 25, 26, 102, 112–13, 162, 197, 228–29

United States v. Carolene Products Co. (1938), 210
United States v. Chalk (1971), 226
University of California San Francisco (UCSF), 91–92
US territories, emergency powers in. *See* state emergency powers
US Virgin Islands (USVI), 50, 51, 226
Utah
  conflicts between governmental levels, 248
  emergency powers in, 39, 53, 56–57

vaccination
  Biden administration vaccine mandate, 252–53
  conflicts between governmental levels, 247, 248
  county sheriffs refusing to enforce state orders, 251–52
  court evaluation of state police powers, 212–14

vaccination (*continued*)
  effective public health communication regarding, 202–3
  fragmentation of public opinion on COVID-19, 182, 183f, 184
  gender differences in COVID attitudes, 199–200
  laws allowing for mandatory, 53–55
  public opinion on mandatory, 185–91, 187f, 189f, 191f
  state-level variation in public opinion on, 201
vaccine passports, 185–87, 187f
Vavreck, Lynn, 195–96
Vermeule, Adrian, 29n1
Vermont emergency powers, 39–40, 63n13
Villanueva, Alex, 251
Virginia emergency powers, 52–53
Vladeck, Stephen I., 229, 267

Wachter, Robert, 91–92
Walker, Lance, 223
Wang, Yiqian Alice, ix

war, permanent changes caused by, 5–6
Washington
  court evaluation of emergency orders, 227
  emergency powers in, 36–37
  eviction moratoriums in, 157
  response to COVID-19 pandemic, 110, 110f
Washington, George, 11
Weimar Constitution, 11, 21
Werdegar, David, 88
West Virginia emergency powers, 39, 41, 59
Whitmer, Gretchen, 243
Wiley, Lindsay F., 229, 267
Wisconsin emergency powers, 38, 54
Wisconsin v. Yoder (1972), 211–12
work settings, mandatory vaccinations in, 189–91
Wyoming emergency powers, 58

Youngstown Sheet & Tube Co. v. Sawyer (1952), 20–21